IP TELEPHONY

The Integration of Robust VoIP Services

ISBN 0-13-014118-6

90000

9 780130 141187

IP TELEPHONY

The Integration of Robust VoIP Services

Bill Douskalis

Prentice Hall PTR
Upper Saddle River, NJ 07458
www.phptr.com

Editorial/production supervision: *Patti Guerrieri*
Acquisitions editor: *Jill Pisoni*
Marketing manager: *Lisa Konzelmann*
Manufacturing manager: *Maura Goldstaub*
Editorial assistant: *Linda Ramagnano*
Cover design director: *Jerry Votta*
Cover designer: *Talar Agasyan*

Prentice Hall books are widely used by corporations and government agencies
for training, marketing, and resale.

The publisher offers discounts on this book when ordered in bulk quantities.
For more information, contact: Corporate Sales Department, Phone: 800-382-3419;
Fax: 201-236-7141; E-mail: corpsales@prenhall.com; or write: Prentice Hall PTR,
Corp. Sales Dept., One Lake Street, Upper Saddle River, NJ 07458.

Printed in the United States of America

10 9 8 7 6 5 4 3

ISBN   0-13-014118-6

Prentice-Hall International (UK) Limited, *London*
Prentice-Hall of Australia Pty. Limited, *Sydney*
Prentice-Hall Canada Inc., *Toronto*
Prentice-Hall Hispanoamericana, S.A., *Mexico*
Prentice-Hall of India Private Limited, *New Delhi*
Prentice-Hall of Japan, Inc., *Tokyo*
Pearson Education Asia Pte. Ltd.
Editora Prentice-Hall do Brasil, Ltda., *Rio de Janeiro*

Contents

Foreword

The impact of continuing advances in communications technology on our ability to exchange information in new ways, places us at the threshold of a new era. The promise of ubiquitous high-speed networks carrying voice, data, and multimedia services is happening today. *IP Telephony: The Integration of Robust VoIP Services* moves beyond the broad overviews and protocol fundamentals of Voice over IP (VoIP). This text is the culmination of many months of effort in this very fast moving and technically complex market. The result is a text that simplifies the technical complexity of the VoIP protocols and their interaction, and builds upon major industry efforts in the areas of MGCP, SIP and H.323. It takes the next steps by addressing the impact of voice quality in the presence of network impairments and addressing how other voiceband applications, such as fax, will operate in IP telephony networks (FoIP). Its contribution will be as a valuable tool for understanding how robust VoIP services can be integrated into today's networks and as a working reference for engineers, consultants, and network professionals working in this field.

The book has been divided into an Introduction and six chapters. It also contains a CD-ROM that includes two user interfaces: one for VoIP applications, and one for FoIP applications and additional information pertinent to IP telephony. The introduction is a short overview of the current industry structure, the direction it is headed and how the different chapters in the book fit into the overall picture. Chapters 1 and 2 introduce the new VoIP protocols and provide pertinent details regarding the actual operation of these protocols, their parameters, signaling, and call flow diagrams. Chapter 3 is a short overview of the SS7 signaling system, major parts of which are expected to migrate to IP telephony networks. Chapter 4 breaks new ground in the all-important area of delivering quality voice service in VoIP networks. Chapter 5 continues the investigation into voice quality and demonstrates the impact of voice quality in the presence of transcoding and network impairments. Chapter 6 moves the discussion of IP Telephony into the realm of other voiceband applications, such as delivering FoIP using the T.37 and T.38 protocols.

HP Agilent Technologies is the proud sponsor of this book and its author Bill Douskalis. Bill is an industry consultant to a number of companies implementing IP telephony and has worked with Hewlett-Packard in the past on projects in the communications area. Bill's background in both telephony (Bell Labs, Sprint) and data communications (equipment design), and his experience as a practicing network design engineer bring a wealth of knowledge and real-world perspectives to this book. HP Agilent Technologies' goal with this book is to augment the practical knowledge available to those working in new technology areas such as IP Telephony and to enable the realization of those new technologies for the benefit of all.

Mark Klingensmith
HP Agilent Technologies

Introduction

In the last five years of the twentieth century, we have seen developments in the telephone network which will affect our lives well into the new millennium. A continuing and massive effort by the industry is bringing closer the day when integrated services and multimedia will finally come to our homes—on demand and at affordable prices. The Plain Old Telephone Service, POTS as it has been known for most of the twentieth century, is giving way to modernization, service integration, and convergence of two fundamentally different types of technologics: voice and data.

There is nothing wrong with the quality of the Public Switched Telephone Network, the PSTN as we have known it for so many years, either in the delivered speech quality or in its reliability. On the contrary, it is the model of robustness and security, and those of us who know its intricate details are amazed by how something this large and this complex can function so reliably and so well. But the quality of a telephone conversation seems to have given way to other, higher priorities and is no longer the only driving factor for modernizing the network. Changing needs in both the business and residential market segments require new telephony features and capabilities that are neither simple nor economical for service providers to create on top of the PSTN infrastructure. This contrasts the current fact of life of the telephone companies, which are approaching the point of not being able to produce a single new feature in their present networks without substantial expenditures and delays. Service and feature creation on standard Class 5 service platforms became simply an intractable and very expensive proposition.

So, when the requirements of the market aligned with the needs of the service providers, it was only a matter of a short time before it became obvious the PSTN had to be transformed and modernized, not in an evolutionary manner but in a revolutionary manner. But is the new PSTN that is coming our way going to be better? And who defines what better is? And who will pay for all this modernization? There are both simple and complex answers for these three questions.

In the mid-1990s when I started consulting outside my immediate home base, it became necessary to communicate electronically with my customers. ISDN BRI 128Kbps service did the trick to provide sufficient data bandwidth for web access and receiving and sending 10 Mb+ email attachments in moderate time, but ISDN service never became a commodity telephony product. In fact, part of the reason we are witnessing the modernization of the PSTN is because service providers cannot offer us enough bandwidth at a reasonable price, because it costs them too much money to add and upgrade existing network equipment. And even after they do it, we still do not have benefit of service integration and multimedia capability because 128 Kbps is simply not enough bandwidth to converge voice, video, and data services. The world's brightest minds have pursued a feasible and economical solution, and in the last couple of years major decisions have been made to steer the network revolution in specific directions.

Many papers have been written in the past few years about the need to bring integrated telephone services to the customer premise, and they are all informative but somehow the big picture has not been completely described. Part of the reason is that things are changing very rapidly—even as this book is being written. Another reason is one's perspective of what integrated telephone services will be, which may not always encompass all aspects of the new public network. It is not easy to develop a complete perspective of the public network details without getting intimately familiar with telecommunications technology, but I believe an effort to present the high level big picture is worthwhile even in simplified form. So, let's take a look at a concise view of what the PSTN is today, what is changing in the new world, and what is staying; how the changes are being approached and the reasons why the reference points have been selected for change. It would take hundreds of pages or more to go into every detail of the PSTN architecture, but I hope a simplified view will make it easier for the reader to understand the big picture.

WHY DOES THE PSTN NEED TO CHANGE?

The PSTN is the collection of all the switching and networking equipment that belongs to the carriers which are involved in providing telephone service.

When we talk about the PSTN, we mean primarily the wireline telephone network and its access points to wireless networks, such as cellular, PCS, and satellite communications. Subscriber access to the PSTN wireline network is through large voice switches, which are located in a telephone company central office, and bring us basic telephone service through ordinary analog telephones or digital PBX systems. Access can be either through wireline telephones, or via a wireless network.

Voice from the telephone set in our homes to the central office exists either in analog form for basic service or in digital form if access to the carrier is via a PBX. However, once it reaches the central office, voice exists in digital form on the PSTN—on time division multiplexed channels of 64 Kbps each, which carry pulse code modulated voice samples. There is never any doubt as to the kind of speech quality we will experience when we make a call on the TDM network, and the quality of service for a voice call has never been a negotiable parameter. However, delivering this quality comes at a huge cost to the service providers who need to tie up network resources for the duration of an entire call, regardless of the actual bandwidth utilized by the conferring parties at any instant. Even simple traffic analysis using the fundamental Erlang models shows a steep linear dependence of network resources to the user population served by the network. Furthermore, the enormous appetite for web access in the last few years has caused an even bigger problem in the TDM network—network resources, which are always voice-grade TDM circuits, are tied up while we browse the web at our leisure. Clearly this is an uneconomical proposition for the telephone companies who find themselves unable to enhance their networks and provide additional services in the current public network infrastructure. The culprit has been widely recognized as the lack of integration between voice and data services and the low bandwidth of the analog links in the "last mile."

How does one go about fixing this problem? It isn't easy and it is also very expensive. Since the mid-1980s it has been viewed as necessary to replace the TDM public network with a universal and ubiquitous packet-based alternative with nodes and links whose bandwidth can be managed in a dynamic manner all the way to the edge and onto the customer premise. Part of this promise seemed to be fulfilled with the ATM technology, which is still a major key for revamping the backbone such that application convergence can be realized. But while ATM technologists spent years developing accurate and broad standards to support the new age of the public network, the Internet experienced explosive growth and brought us a taste of what convergence and integration would be like, if we could only merge technologies and get enough bandwidth to the premise. The Internet Protocol, our beloved IP, is now the king of network protocols, up to which virtually all applications seem to looking to become part of the new convergent network. The first two are voice telephony and data applications. Still, simple convergence of a voice telephone call with a data application that requires bandwidth management has proven to be a non-trivial task. The requirements are often conflicting and the proprietary early implementations of convergent networks must eventually become interoperable in the public network to gain wide consumer acceptance. At the same time, each provider is trying to get a jump on the market. These issues have been at the heart of the problem and work continues at a frantic pace.

A simple call between two parties with analog phones is not simple, even with the current scheme of things in the public network. First and foremost is the fact that there are really two "clouds" in the PSTN: the one that carries signaling and the one for voiceband transport, as shown in Figure I.1. Part of the problem with convergence in the current infrastructure is that signaling at the local access for basic service is hardware-based and tailored for voice telephony, with some fundamental considerations for point-to-point video over ISDN circuits, for those who can afford it. This is a severe limitation and a good reason to pursue change. The second aspect is the difficulty for bringing interactive multimedia applications, such as distance learning, to the home. Both the signaling and the lack of sufficient bandwidth are severe limitations. On-demand entertainment and shopping convenience are also driving factors for the pursuit of network modernization. Affordable full-color, full-motion video conferencing with whiteboard capability may not be far away in the new telephone services. All these new capabilities may have the side effect of rendering us to couch potatoes, but they do have serious benefits by making possible the exchange of information in a manner and convenience we have never experienced before.

WHAT IS CHANGING IN THE PUBLIC NETWORK AND HOW?

If we start by assuming the access bandwidth issue will be resolved somehow, the remaining technical issues form a mountain of problems in their own right. Starting with the residential customer premise, signaling and media transport must be re-engineered in their entirety to facilitate convergence. The analog local loop will be a thing of the past and voice will exist in digital form end-to-end.

The packet technology of the new infrastructure is being designed on IP-based protocols and the new connectivity will be provided over various link layers, such as ATM. A single signaling technology has not been determined yet, but three front runners—MGCP, SIP, and H.323—have set the pace in all new equipment and service designs. This means we are starting out immediately with signaling incompatibilities at the packet layer among carriers, and

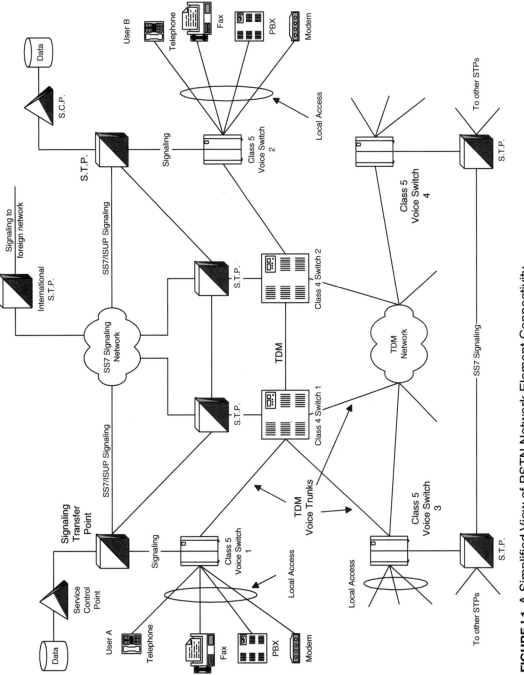

FIGURE I.1 A Simplified View of PSTN Network Element Connectivity

if we can't signal, we can't make a call. This potential impasse will be avoided by the natural inertia associated with rolling out new telephone services. Since it takes enormous expense and effort to offer packet-based telephony, the first step for the service providers is to offer it in pieces. The first piece, which has been in the works for the last couple of years, offers integration of service up to the central office. This is now a re-engineered Class 5 system that offers most of the popular telephony features of the TDM network, but over IP-based technology. When this step is complete, we will be pretty much where we are now, from the perspective of telephone service features perceived by the subscriber; but now the horizon is cleared for the providers to start adding value to the basic telephone service.

Media transport will be packet based and there appears to be no controversy that the Real Time Protocol (RTP) is the method of choice for VoIP service, regardless of the signaling protocol used to set up calls. But there is a new headache coming up, which the PSTN does not have. In the effort to converge applications and manage bandwidth more efficiently, compressed voice telephony will start making inroads in residential service. This may have as yet unseen ramifications in the wider market because objective measurements on delivered voice quality only recently became feasible. In fact, measurement of voice quality is one of the major topics of this book. This issue inevitably leads to the next discussion of quality of service classes. There is a lot of work to be done in the next few years in the area of QoS in the converged network, and only time and actual data will tell us if assumptions and projections we have made about the design of the new public network are correct.

The real problem begins once we leave the Class 5 domain and start getting into the backbone network. In the PSTN, all carriers are interoperable through SS7 signaling and PCM voice encoding. Plain and simple. Replacing the core PSTN, however, with an untested and non-uniform packet network may be a bit too much of an undertaking, and this is recognized by both the service providers and equipment vendors. So, the PSTN is expected to survive for some time, and the new packet-based Class 5 domains will become gateways to the PSTN for voice telephony. This means packet-based-to-SS7 signaling interworking and media transcodings will be a necessary fact of life. This may come at the cost of some quality degradation, but will have the immediate benefit of interoperability between dissimilar packet-based VoIP technologies through the TDM network. After all, what good is any new technology if we can't make the same telephone calls we always could?

Service integration even with the PSTN in the middle, however, will still be a powerful offering. It's a matter of the new Class 5 domains also becoming gateways to the data networks and the Internet. There they will serve as funnels and aggregators, neither of which is pretty as an ultimate solution, but it will be effective in delivering the promise of convergence as a starting step. The first things we will notice are changes in the ISP dial-up paradigm, with faster and ubiquitous service access, higher mobility of our service profiles, and more fixed and mobile telephones with a richer feature set.

All this means is that the new packet-based Class 5 domains will treat everything as data—packet data—but some data packets will be more equal than others. Indeed, the continuing presence of the PSTN in the backbone may mitigate the potential problems of convergence into a single network, because for some time to come we will not have to decide on how to treat the different priorities of data through single routing points. As we learn about emerging patterns in service usage in the new network, whatever decisions are made to place a piece of the PSTN into a single IP-based backbone will be a more educated guess at the time.

There are other major issues associated with this modernization process. The first one deals with security. The PSTN is extremely secure because the signaling network is closed to the outside world. The same cannot be said of IP-based networks, but the lessons learned in the last few years have raised the consciousness level in the area of security; and protocols like IPsec are expected to play a major role. Even so, the potential of signaling and media traversing the same links as the modus operandi of the new network is bound to be met with some skepticism from many of those who put the present PSTN together.

The second potential issue deals with continuing support for applications that are working just fine in the present TDM network. The biggest one is facsimile. Facsimile represents 30–40% of corporate phone bills and is a relatively large revenue stream for the telephone companies. The desire of the business users is to lower the cost of sending a fax, while as a minimum maintaining the status quo of the current feature set and quality of the overall user experience. This business driver has already resulted in more than one method to bring IP-based fax to the customer premise for users with varying needs and budgets.

Another potential issue is that there are numerous federal regulations that govern both POTS service and the carriers. It is hard to believe there will be no changes to the regulations, but at this time it is too soon to tell the degree to which the consumers and the service providers will be affected.

Finally, let's not forget the international telephone networks with which we have to interwork at their access points to the PSTN. It will be some time before the public networks around the world become packet based, and this will mandate continuing international interworking as the new public network is modernized.

Figure I.2 shows where we are headed with telephone services as part of a convergent network, regardless of what type of carrier brings it to our premise. The short term paradigm will consist of packet-based networks connecting to the PSTN for ubiquitous telephone service. Calls between subscribers of the same carrier can be routed over either their own piece of the PSTN or their packet infrastructure without touching the PSTN. The long-term view and desire is for one packet network to connect all carriers and all services in a compatible manner, but based on the current state of the art this reality is still a few years ahead of us. But it will indeed be a reality some day.

ARE THERE TECHNICAL PROBLEMS IN THE NEW PUBLIC NETWORK?

In order for VoIP to succeed as the forerunner to the convergent network, it is imperative for the new services to preserve the user experience of the simple two-party POTS telephone call. But it has long been argued that any packet-based technology will introduce delay in the voice stream, which can at times be perceived by the user during the conversation and yield unsatisfactory results. VoIP technology in the public network must overcome this potential problem and bring delays down to non-perceivable levels. Another factor is the voice quality delivered by VoIP in conjunction with the newest voice compression technologies. If we combine the potential delay issue with inevitable reduction in quality from voice compression, the user experience may suffer as a result. Voice quality can now be measured in an objective manner, and the gap can be bridged through the availability of more data, information, and knowledge gained from actual experience.

Finally, telephone service is also measured by the degree of robustness of the provider's network. Service availability is also a parameter regulated by the FCC. The PSTN is a "five nines" network, operating with 99.999% specified availability, and in reality even more. A reduction to "four nines" or "three nines" will mean more frequent outages and consumer dissatisfaction. This is one more reason to proceed slowly into the core network and ensure all aspects of quality are met before a piece of the PSTN is renovated.

ECONOMIC FACTORS—WHAT'S IN IT FOR ALL THE PARTIES?

There is obviously money at the end of the rainbow to justify the enormous expenditures in equipment and labor to revamp the public network. When voice over IP first appeared on the Internet, it was exciting for the public at large for its potential of making long distance phone calls for free. There are

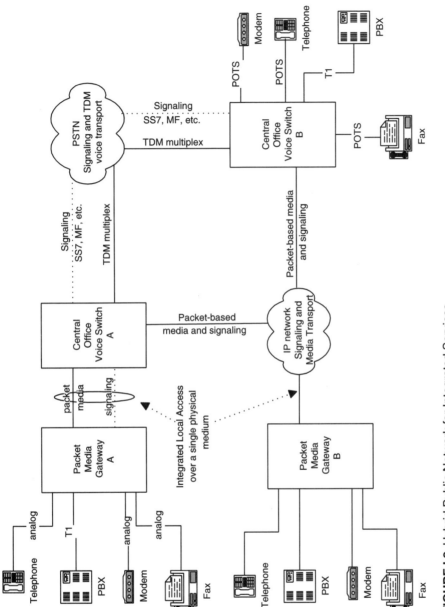

FIGURE I.2 Hybrid Public Network for Integrated Services

still people who associate VoIP with free telephone service over the data networks, but the new services will not be free and some people will be disappointed to find out there is a bill for these new voice services. So, who will pay for all this renovation? The consumer is a good answer. We will indeed get the benefits of a converged network with the promise of the information superhighway at highway speeds but hopefully at an affordable price. The service providers will get the benefit of a single, unified multiservice network some day with favorable scalability to ensure their continuing economic survivability. And the overall benefit will be greater availability and flow of information, very convenient and secure electronic commerce, simplified distance learning, and other uses and applications we have not yet imagined.

WHAT THE BOOK COVERS

This is a technical book. We will not discuss business or social issues resulting from the modernization of the public network, but we will concentrate on some of the major technical aspects of the new VoIP services for the purpose of bringing to light relevant issues and potential solutions. In the first three chapters, we will be looking at the new signaling protocols in the new public network and the enterprise and cover the details of transporting media across similar and dissimilar network domains. We will visit the SS7 signaling protocol of the PSTN in a high-level overview but with enough detail to make the point as to where changes may be coming with integrated VoIP signaling; and we look at call flows in homogeneous and heterogeneous signaling topologies per the definitions given in the text. The reader is expected to have basic familiarity with the IP protocol as well as TCP and UDP, but intimate bit-level familiarity is not necessary to understand the concepts. Throughout the text we show several IP signaling packets, captured live with the help of the Hewlett-Packard Agilent Technologies Internet Advisor.

In Chapter 4 we cover the subject of perceptual voice coding, voice quality measurement techniques, and discuss in detail the Perceptual Speech Quality Measurement (PSQM) algorithm, as implemented in the Hewlett-Packard Agilent Technologies Telegra® Voice Quality Tester (VQT). Chapter 4 also discusses network parameters which relate to voice quality and affect the overall user experience, such as echo. In Chapter 5 we move to the lab where we set up a small reference network to take speech quality measurements and discuss the issues of delay and clarity in proper context. This is the first time we see network impairments and voice compression included in the results of objective speech quality measurement. Finally, in Chapter 6 we discuss facsimile support in IP networks and close the text with a detailed discussion of V.34 fax, which seems to be the final frontier in facsimile using the analog facilities of the PSTN.

ACKNOWLEDGMENTS

This book would not have been possible without the support of Hewlett-Packard and Agilent Technologies and especially the hard-working individuals who made sure I wrote what I meant and meant what I wrote every step of the way. From the beginning, Bill Mortimer and John Morrish of HP/Agilent believed in and supported the project. I am also very thankful to Mark Klingensmith for launching this project and his continuing support and hard work in seeing it through to completion. Mike Gray, founder and President of Telegra (now HP-Telegra), gave me valuable guidance in the facsimile area for which I am very thankful. Stefan Pracht provided valuable insight in several areas through his contribution, and the time spent by Paul Denisowski, Tom Doumas, Gregan Crawford, and Richard Jobson reviewing the book only made the text better—many thanks. My special thanks also go to Sandy Ritchie, Reda Habib, Janet Martino, Patti Guerrieri, Truly Donovan, and Jill Pisoni for their work on this project.

Bill Douskalis
October 31, 1999

CHAPTER 1

Protocols for Voice Over IP and Interactive Applications

The communications industry has spent considerable effort in defining a set of new signaling and media transport mechanisms that can deliver voice and voiceband telephony with the hope of matching the quality of the PSTN. This effort has concentrated in two major areas:

1. Development of sophisticated signaling mechanisms to support all the call features of plain telephony service, with support for the next generation of interactive multimedia services.

2. Development of transport mechanisms for delivery of the media streams with the highest quality possible.

In this first chapter we look at the dominant signaling protocols used in IP-based telephony, with perspectives and comparisons to the degree data is known. The media transport mechanism for IP network is the Real-time Transport Protocol (RTP, RFC 1889), with the Real-time Transport Control Protocol (RTCP) providing QoS information to the participants in the call. Signaling for call setup is very challenging because of its inherent complexity, stemming from the need to support the plethora of telephony features of Plain Old Telephone Service (POTS) and additional value-added services. POTS service may be old, but it is anything but plain and simple to duplicate with a new technology. Support for the consumer CLASS[1] feature set is proving to be a big task for VoIP service offerings, and without this support VoIP will lag in market acceptance. When one introduces integrated real-time multimedia in the picture, it is not hard to see the magnitude of the problem.

In the area of signaling and call processing, the approaches and proposals that have found the most acceptance in the standards groups are H.323 from the ITU, the Session Initiation Protocol (SIP, RFC 2543) and a composite protocol proposal that we will refer to as S/MGCP in this text. SIP and MGCP are RFC-draft standards in the IETF. SGCP was the original proposal, but was abandoned in favor of combining the merits of the proposals of IPDC and its own. The resulting proposal is MGCP. We will discuss what all these terms mean as we go along in this chapter. This author has seen many times before, that as feedback of the merits of a particular design approach starts trickling back, new enhancements to the approach are proposed, some of which are radical departures from what has been built and installed in the market. The intent is to arrive at as flawless a solution for controlling VoIP networks as possible, but market forces eventually take over and the products with the largest market acceptance tend to dominate, regardless of the embedded elegance in their solution offering.

Other IP-based protocols have found homes under the auspices of the signaling protocols. Some of these auxiliary protocols augment the services of the basic signaling mechanisms by providing means for offering predictable QoS, as is the case with RSVP. The Session Description Protocol (SDP, RFC 2327) is another assist mechanism, and offers the ability to the basic signaling protocol to describe call session parameters. It is expected that as the service providers begin to look seriously at offering interactive multimedia services and the VoIP technology matures, VoIP call control will consist of a suite of many IP-based protocols to complement the basic signaling functions.

Products using all three dominant signaling methods have seen early acceptance, based the vendors' faith that their standard of choice will dominate the other proposals and standards in IP-based signaling implementations. The standards for point-to-point and conference-style calls are sometimes confusing, even for those experienced in the art. It is hard to determine the level of acceptance of a particular solution from reading RFCs and specifications. The stakes are high for those proposing and implementing solutions and, consistent with the norm in the industry, some of the proposals

---

1.   CLASS stands for Custom Local Area Signaling Services, such as Caller ID, Distinctive Ringing, and others.

in VoIP signaling carry a definite slant toward the long-term views of the their advocates.

The advent of IP telephony has brought us a plethora of new terms and acronyms, as is usually the case with any new technology. It is not easy to remember all the acronyms, and the meaning and perspective of each new term, if you do not work with the technology on a regular basis. So, we start with a basic protocol stack diagram to show the relative position of each standard in the IP protocol suite, and take it from there. We will not discuss the details of IP, TCP, UDP, and general link and network layer protocols in this book, as such discussions can consume entire books on their own. The reader can follow our discussion even with limited knowledge of these protocols. Those with expertise in the field usually have very good references for those protocols, if questions arise from our discussion of the application layer signaling protocols.

Figure 1.1 is a simplified road map and reference guide to the pertinent IP-based transport protocols that find use in IP based telephony.

We address H.323, SIP, S/MGCP, RSVP, RTP, and RTCP in the context of call flows and show captured packets from real-time traces. Most of the protocols in the new signaling suite are designed to co-exist with all the other network layer protocols in the same hosts or router. However, as we will see throughout this text, there are implementation limitations that may cause segmentation of media streams in order to achieve specific operating performance points for each offered telephone service. Performance issues range from simple server capacity to reliability of service and number and type of features that can be offered to the user. Performance and other limitations will be examined in case studies of heterogeneous call processing in the reference topology of this text.

In our treatment of the subject of IP based telephony we will run into some key terms and concepts many times. The most fundamental definitions we need to proceed with the issues of this chapter are the *media gateway, media gateway controller, switch, router* and the PSTN.

A *media gateway* (MG) is characterized by a collection of endpoints and connections. The MG is a box of various morphologies depending on the number of users, trunks and services it supports. The MG is the device that may be installed on the customer premise to attach the POTS telephones, data network, and other multimedia connections available through your favorite carrier. It is also possible for media gateways to be installed in the points of presence (POPs) of the telephone companies, although this would limit the types of integrated services that can be brought to the customer premise.

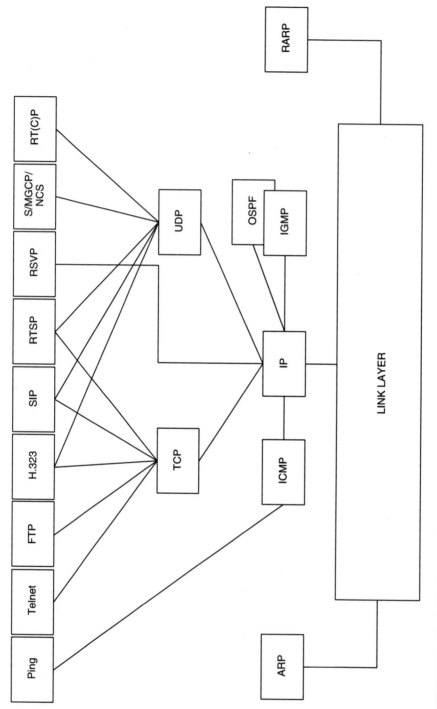

FIGURE 1.1 Partial IP Protocol Stack

4

An *endpoint* is defined as a point of entry and exit of media flows.[2] In simple terms, an endpoint is the collection of software and hardware inside the MG that can be accessed via signaling by the central office so that your telephone call can be completed. These points of entry and exit can be physical or virtual. Examples of a physical endpoint include an RTP port, a DS0 on an T1 trunk interface, an interface on the MG that terminates a POTS line, an ATM virtual channel, etc. Examples of a virtual endpoint include an audio source or an audio server.

A media gateway that provides termination for residential POTS lines to residential subscribers is also referred to as a *residential gateway*. Other names exist to differentiate capabilities of MGs, but we will use this definitions throughout the text, without loss of generality for scaled applications, such as those in business environments.

A *connection* is an association of endpoints on different MGs across a network, or a single MG, for the purpose of transferring data between these endpoints. In simple terms, a connection is what allows you to hear the other party on a point-to-point call. Connections can be point-to-point or multipoint. This means that conference calls are possible with VoIP technology in much simpler terms than over the PSTN. In this text we will concentrate on dynamically created connections via signaling control, with examples from the three main contending protocols. There are also limited cases of permanent connections between special-purpose endpoints but their static nature does not present the designer with exciting problems in call establishment and control.

A *call* is a logical association of connections between two or more endpoints. A point-to-point call contains a single connection between two endpoints. An active three-way call contains two connections among three endpoints. Connections within a call can be active or inactive, that is, if the connection is inactive, it is established between the endpoints but no media is played to the physical or virtual endpoint, even though media streams may be flowing between the endpoints. The state of a connection at each endpoint is independently controlled by the signaling protocol.

The purpose of the signaling protocol is to create and manage connections between endpoints, as well as create and manage calls. The signaling protocol runs inside the media gateway controller (MGC) and the MG. The current suite of VoIP signaling protocols is asymmetric. This means that different portions of the signaling protocol run in the MG and different portions in the MGC servers. This is similar to the concepts of client-server technology.

---

2.   From *MEGACO protocol architecture and requirements*, Nancy Greene and Michael Ramalho, authors.

Some signaling protocols have embedded robustness to acquire and interpret physical status from the MG, the connections, and the calls that have been established. Most early signaling protocols were adequately described via state machines, for example, the ITU-T Q.931 protocol. The new generation of IETF protocols for VoIP signaling have defined stateless signaling protocols, and the ITU is moving in the same direction with MEGACO. Text-based protocols simplify the protocol stack itself and parts of the implementation, but run head-on into other system-related problems, which must be picked up and solved through other methods. Some of these issues we see unfolding as we enter the protocol descriptions.

A *media gateway controller* (MGC) is a big server that supports all the users and their subscribed telephony features. MGCs signal to endpoints inside the MGs, which correspond to devices attached to them, for example, a telephone set, a fax machine, or a LAN router. MGCs have acquired more specific names depending on the specifics of the technology. For example, the MGC in H.323 networks is pretty much the Gatekeeper, whose functionality we will discuss later in this chapter, and may contain the functionality of a Gateway. The MGC in public network telephony resides in your carrier's central office and replaces the telephony features of the Class 5 local switch.

We will use Figure 1.2 as a reference guide in our discussions of VoIP signaling. Similar views of this diagram have appeared in industry standards groups, and we will present adaptations and modifications as the need arises to make the points. The discussions in this text will place the demarcation Reference Point A on the customer premise, together with the media gateway. Reference Point B is a high-speed access for residential and business service and can be copper-based (ADSL, T1, cable, etc.) or fiber-optic, such as SONET, or fiber T3. The industry is embracing ADSL and Cable access for residential and small office applications, whereas the higher rates are mostly offered over fiber and are targeted for businesses.

The element labeled *Switch/Router Concentrator* may or may not be a real device, or it may be a collection of devices. For enterprise signaling it may be the local LAN or a number of actual LAN segments separating the MGs and the MGC. Switches and routers will be present in geographically distributed enterprise LANs and central offices of carriers offering VoIP service. In all the examples we will see in VoIP transport, the media is transported over RTP, often with the help of lower-level protocols.

For telephony support across the PSTN, the presence of a PSTN gateway is mandatory somewhere in the network where it can be signaled to by the MGC. This device is usually found in the CO, although a PSTN gateway might not be co-located with the MGC.

We are ready to begin our discussion of VoIP signaling with a look at the basic requirements, and proceed to look at the signaling protocols.

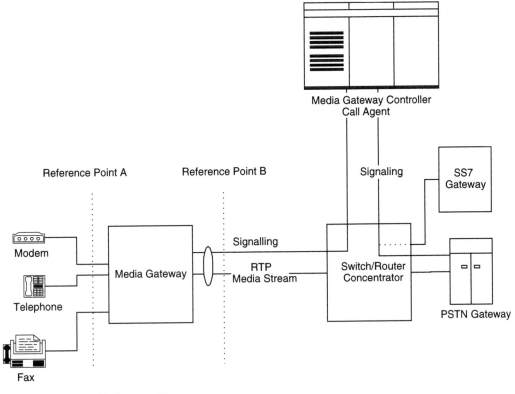

FIGURE 1.2 VoIP Reference Diagram

1.1 IP TELEPHONY FUNDAMENTALS

We begin by offering definitions and fundamentals of signaling and call control of voice and voiceband telephony over an IP network. There is a distinction between plain voice and voiceband telephony over IP, such as fax and modem support. The VoIP signaling protocols we visit in this text define methods to accommodate the requirements of both types of telephony applications, in various degrees and with differing complexities.

We start with the S/MGCP protocol by looking at the fundamental constructs, message formats, and packet definitions, with a brief overview of usage in controlling a connection. We then visit the H.323 protocol of the ITU-T, and end with the Session Initiation Protocol. S/MGCP and SIP are from a school of thought that has promoted text-based protocols. One of the best attributes of text protocols is that they remove machine dependencies across platforms. There is no such thing anymore as worrying about big-endian vs. little endian notation. Developing and debugging protocol software is also much simpler and less expensive. SGCP is no longer being pursued, but MGCP has been adopted to a large degree by cable telephony and is a major part of the NCS specification. H.323 for VoIP control on the other hand is a set of binary protocols. The merits of both types of protocols will be discussed and compared as we go along.

At the time this text went to print, a cooperative effort was in the works between the IETF and ITU to arrive at a common signaling protocol for VoIP and thus combine forces to arrive at a more universal way to implement the next generation VoIP networks. The signs are that the IETF and the ITU will adopt a single call control and signaling standard for voice and voiceband telephony over IP. This is the agenda of the MEGACO working group in the IETF and the H.GCP group in the ITU.

Our primary focus in this chapter is on call control but the choice of protocol to carry the media traffic is also important and requires major decisions regarding ease of use, robustness, and reliability of the end-to-end connection. In Chapter 2 we discuss fundamentals of the RTP/RTCP protocol for transport of the media channel and other issues relating to media transport over IP. But before we begin the protocol discussions, it is necessary to take a quick look at some common and not-so-common terminology we will be using throughout this text, for reader familiarity. The reader should keep in mind that this text is not a substitute for the specifications of the protocols being presented. Our objective is to review the protocol fundamentals, in the context of real examples, and assist in a general understanding of the procedures involved in call control. The corresponding specifications must be used if product development is being contemplated.

1.1.1 Acronyms and Abbreviations

A lot of acronyms and abbreviations in VoIP come from the legacy of PSTN and from other technologies such as ATM. We combine all of the major terms in Table 1.1, some of which we will need in the discussions in this text, with a brief explanation of the meaning of each term. Many more terms will be encountered as we visit each protocol, and they will be explained in their proper context at that time.

1.1.2 Signaling and Signaling Protocols

The term "signaling" is not self-explanatory in VoIP telephony and clarifications are always necessary, depending on the application. The typical way to make calls on the PSTN is to dial digits on the Keypad. If the call is going to be successfully completed, we will hear a ringing tone until the party we are

TABLE 1.1 Useful Acronyms and Abbreviations

ABBREVIATION	MEANING
AAL2	**Asynchronous** Transfer Mode (ATM) **Adaptation Layer 2**. Used for efficient transport of voice and real-time streams across an ATM backbone with lower latency than pure IP transport.
ANI	**Automatic Number Identification**, for example, Caller ID.
CAS	**Channel Associated Signaling**, or in-band signaling. This type of signaling is performed over the same circuit that carries the voice data The term is general but is used extensively on the PSTN. Examples of CAS signaling are POTS (Plain Old Telephone Service), MF signaling (below) and a/b/c/d robbed-bit signaling in T1 facilities.
CCS	**Common Channel Signaling**. This is the alternative signaling method to CAS, and is performed over a different circuit than the one that carries the voice data. It is referred to as out-of-band signaling. There are two main categories of CSS: *Associated* CCS signaling is performed over the same physical facility that carries the voice circuit, but over a different circuit. An example is PRI signaling for ISDN. *Non-associated* CCS signaling is performed over an entirely different facility, or even network. An example is Signaling System 7 (SS7).
Gatekeeper (GK)	Used in the context of the H.323 protocol, but is used in other protocols as well. It is similar in concept to the generic Media Gateway Controller that we saw earlier. The Gatekeeper is considered the brains of an H.323 signaling topology, but it is also not required in the network, per the specification.
H.323	This is the ITU-T recommendation for packet-based multimedia communication. It uses protocol H.225.0 for registration, admission, status, call signaling, and control. It also uses protocol H.245 for media description and control, terminal capability exchange, and general control of the logical channel carrying the media stream(s). Other protocols make up the complete H.323 specification, and we will present a protocol stack for H.323 signaling and media transport.
H.GCP (also H.248)	The ITU-T protocol proposal, which is intended to merge and unify the IETF and ITU signaling standards as the MEGACO protocol.
ISUP	**ISDN User Part** of the SS7 signaling network. The upper layer packet-switched protocol used by the SS7 signaling network, it is responsible for setting up telephone calls in the PSTN, and user features such as Caller ID, Call Forwarding, etc. For link-by-link signaling in call setup and teardown it is a 4th layer protocol interfacing directly with MTP. For non-facility-associated end-to-end signaling, it interfaces with SCCP and is a peer of TCAP.

TABLE 1.1 Useful Acronyms and Abbreviations (Continued)

MCU	A **Multipoint Control Unit** is an element of an H.323 network. It provides multipoint conference support for three or more terminals. It also provides resource management and codec negotiation between the participating endpoints.
MEGACO	The IETF **ME**dia **GA**teway **CO**ntrol protocol. This is the on-going effort in the IETF/ITU-T working groups to arrive at a common signaling protocol for all future IP-based telephony implementations.
MF	**MultiFrequency** Signaling. A common type of in-band CAS signaling using a pair of frequencies to synthesize digits 0 through 9, and the control codes KP (start of digit pulsing) and ST (end of digit pulsing). It is used on the PSTN, and its use is expected to last for a long time because it is still being used for signaling and call setup to emergency services (e.g., 911 calls[*]).
MGCP	The **Media Gateway Control Protocol**, which is based primarily on SGCP with elements of IPDC. The composite S/MGCP protocol will be discussed in the next section.
MTP	**Message Transfer Part** of the SS7 protocol stack. It provides for error-controlled and flow-control transfer of information generated by the upper protocols in the SS7 hierarchy, as well as information generated within the MTP layers and the management layer of the network. MTP has three layers: MTP1 is the physical layer, or signaling data link (SDL). MTP2 is the link layer part, or signaling link (SL). MTP3 is the equivalent to the network layer and interfaces to the upper layers in the SS7 protocol stack, such as ISUP, TUP, and SCCP. It also provides for message routing and rerouting in the network.
NCS	**NCS** is the PacketCable™ **N**etwork-based **C**all **S**ignaling protocol standard, and is based on MGCP. Its full specification can be found in document number Pkt-SP-EC-MGCP-I01-990312.
PSTN	**Public Switched Telephone Network**. This is the current North American and international wireline telephone network, which offers TDM connections and SS7 signaling for call setup.
RTP/RTCP	RTP is the **Real-time Transport Protocol**, and RTCP is its companion **Real-time Transport Control Protocol**. Media streams are packetized according to a predefined format and placed in RTP packets. RTP provides delivery monitoring of its payload types through sequencing and timestamping. RTCP offers an insight on the performance and behavior of the media stream, such as media stream jitter. Both protocols are discussed in the Chapter 2.

TABLE 1.1 Useful Acronyms and Abbreviations (Continued)

SCCP	**Signaling Connection Control Part** of the SS7 protocol stack. This is a 4th layer protocol, which supports end-to-end signaling not associated with trunks or circuits in the PSTN.
SCN	**Switched Circuit Network**. Used synonymously with PSTN.
SDP	**Session Description Protocol**. Used mostly by the IETF signaling protocols in a passive manner as payload in signaling packets for MGCs and MGs to exchange session description and capabilities information. SDP syntax is used in call establishment in SGCP, MGCP, and SIP. H.323 uses a different mechanism altogether.
SGCP	**Simple Gateway Control Protocol**. An ASCII string-based signaling protocol, which is also stateless in nature. SGCP laid the foundation for MGCP and the PacketCable version of MGCP defined in the NCS protocol specification.
SIP	**Session Initiation Protocol**. A text-based, IP-based protocol used for initiating a unicast or for multicast session initiation and control. SIP is discussed in Chapter 2.
SS7	**Signaling System 7**. This is the set of protocols used for call setup, teardown, and maintenance in the PSTN. SS7 is one of the topics of this text.
TCAP	**Transaction Capabilities Application Part** of the SS7 network. A peer protocol to ISUP in the SS7 protocol hierarchy for end-to-end signaling not associated with call setup or specific trunks in the PSTN network. Some of its main uses are toll-free 800 number translation for routing cross the network, local number portability (LNP), and support for mobile subscriber (MS) features in the cellular network, such as roaming.
TDM	**Time Division Multiplex**. The PSTN uses TDM facilities to transport voice-telephony. TDM circuits between the central offices of carriers are set up at call initiation and normally occupy a DS-0 timeslot in the digital hierarchy (64 Kbps).
TIPHON	**Telecommunications and Internet Protocol Harmonization Over Networks**. This international multi-vendor project seeks to define a set of requirements for service interoperability, reference configurations, interfaces and functional models. It also has as an objective to define call control signaling, protocols, and media flows.
VoIP	Voice over IP.

* Access to emergency services via SS7 is also possible, but MF is the dominant signaling method.

trying to reach answers the phone. There are multiple and complex levels of signaling that must take place in order to accomplish this simple result, and the complexities escalate when we allow VoIP users in packet networks to communicate with POTS subscribers. Regardless of the VoIP signaling technology used, the MG must be set up with sufficient parameters to allow proper media encoding and the use of typical telephony features, such as call forwarding, etc. The intelligent entity serving a subscriber inside the media gateway is called an *endpoint*. Once the parties agree on how to communicate, and communication is established with signaling, the *media stream—* the packetized voice conversation—will flow between the two entities on a virtual circuit, which may be either purely logical or contain physical segments if the call spans hops on the PSTN. Signaling is an independent set of actions to the media flow; it controls the type of media used in a call. Signaling does not necessarily stop when the call is set up, until one or more participants in a call departs. Signaling can occur while a call is active, for example to modify session parameters, and can be concurrent with the media flow.

We believe the best way to describe the signaling methods in a VoIP network is through example uses of the fundamental operations of the protocols. These examples are shown in the form of signaling call flows between endpoints, with emphasis on interworking across network segments of different signaling technologies.

The notation in the call flows presented in this text shows signaling paths between entities as dotted lines. Media paths are shown as solid lines. Sometimes signaling and media paths between two entities are shown traversing different pieces of equipment. This in fact may be the case, and is the case with SS7 signaling. The actual details of engineering media transport in packet networks is the subject of intense analysis in network design. The fundamental complexity is the delivery of predictable QoS in packet voice telephony. We will see issues associated with the setting up of paths between endpoints in Chapter 2.

1.1.3 Models for VoIP Telephony

We will take a leap forward and tackle VoIP services in wide area networks. VoIP in the enterprise LAN will be discussed in the context of call establishment across dissimilar networks, as it is a sub-case of the bigger problem of providing VoIP services with basic telephony features.

The first order of business in providing IP-based integrated services in the public network is to ensure that users of POTS service can be accessed by users of the packet-based networks, and vice versa. The PSTN uses packet-based signaling for call and resource control, Signaling System 7 (SS7) in North America, but it is completely unrelated to the new IP-based signaling standards and proposed standards. This creates the immediate problem of mapping of functionality between signaling technologies, and then of media transport across dissimilar and non-homogeneous networks.

Figure 1.3 is the highest level of conceptualizing the interaction of an IP-based signaling service network with the elements of the PSTN. The figure shows the central office in the central role of serving POTS and VoIP customers. Calls between subscribers of the two technologies can be completed across the IP network, or through a hop on the PSTN, with procedures we will be discussing later in the book. VoIP users communicate with the PSTN network through call control procedures, which invoke standard PSTN signaling for call control on the PSTN side. Interaction and message mapping between the various IP-based protocols and the PSTN is also a topic we discuss later.

The signaling procedures to complete a simple telephone call between users in different technologies are very complex and not yet quite worked out in the industry. The COs, for example, could belong to different carriers. Making a VoIP-to-VoIP call across the IP network between carriers is not yet there. When VoIP services roll out, PSTN hops will be the norm for calls originating and terminating on different carriers. In fact, the case is that the existence of three contending IP-based signaling protocols has substantially complicated the architecture at the next level of detail.

The industry has adopted H.323 as the umbrella protocol for IP-based telephony across LANs that do not necessarily employ quality of service (QoS) controls. For H.323 users to interact with the PSTN, however, it is very important to address the QoS issue, as well streamlining the message exchange between entities for efficient call control. These two and other reasons have been the drivers for the search for other IP-based signaling architectures and approaches, and the result is the inevitable integration of all the approaches that are enjoying successful implementations and deployments. Let's look at an overview of the protocols we cover in this text.

The integration of the SS7 signaling protocol with the major IP-based signaling methods is shown in Figure 1.4. In later chapters, this book addresses the major signaling attributes of the specifications and their interaction with the objective to present the issues and approaches for "putting it all together" at a conceptual and architectural level.

Figure 1.4 shows three stacks: one for the SS7 network (on the left), one for S/MGCP-based signaling, and the H.323 umbrella specification. The key to successful system integration of multiple signaling technologies is in accurately and thoroughly designing the interface layer in the architecture where their presence becomes transparent to the higher layers. Top-down design in this area can ensure the design of the service layer for telephony application is not dependent on the signaling protocols, and can thus exist in any scaled incarnation of the service platform.

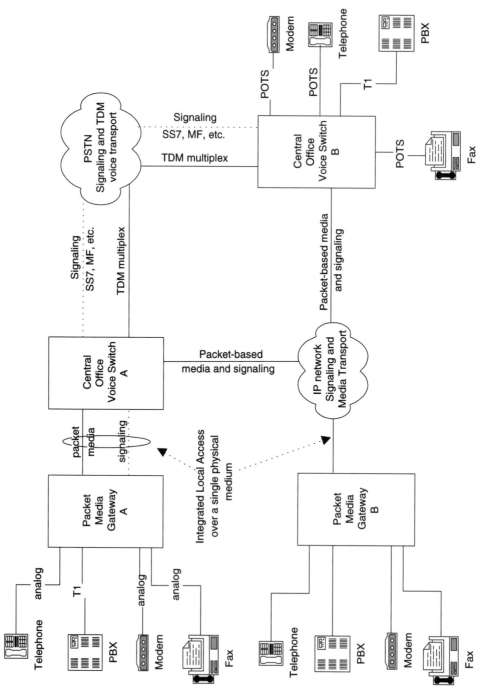

FIGURE 1.3 PSTN-to-IP Network Architecture

Application Call Control and Resource Management

	Audio/Video Applications	H.323 Terminal Control and Management			Data Applications
MGCP SIP Integrated Service	G.nnn H.261 H.263				T.124
			H.245 Logical Channel Signaling		T.125
	RTCP	H.225.0 Terminal to GK Signaling (RAS)	H.225.0 Call Signaling		
	RTP				
UDP	UDP		TCP		T.123
IP	IP Layer				
	Link & Physical Layers for IP transport				

AIN API	TCAP
ISDN User Part (ISUP)	SCCP Signaling Connection Control Part
MTP3 - SS7 Network Layer	
MTP2 - SS7 Link Layer	
MTP1 - SS7 Physical Layer	

FIGURE 1.4 PSTN/IP Service Integration Architecture With IP Signaling

The SS7 signaling stack has a similar structure to the OSI protocol stack. SS7 is an out-of-band, non-associated signaling network, which we review in Chapter 3. MTP and the complete SCCP layer (or a major portions of SCCP) are implemented inside signaling transfer points (STP). The lowest layer is MTP1 (message transfer part 1), and corresponds to the physical layer of the OSI architecture. Signaling in SS7 runs mostly over 64-Kbps digital circuits, DS0 channels, or T1 facilities.

MTP2 is the signaling link (SL) layer, and its responsibilities include error control, recovery, and the prevention of out-of-sequence signaling messages. The MTP2 operates in protocol message units known as MSUs (message signaling units), which include the message part from MTP3 (the network layer), and information generated by MTP2.

The specification of SS7 calls for a very low probability for undetectable errors in MTP2 messages, that is, $P_{u\_error} < 10^{-10}$. The bit error rate on digital links is often higher than this maximum, which in turn calls for rigorous error control in a manner that precludes out-of-sequence messages in the signaling network. Excellent detailed description of the SS7 signaling network can be found in the references.

MTP3 is the network layer of SS7 and the interface to the higher layer protocols. The upper layer protocols we discuss are the switching connection control part (SCCP), ISDN user part (ISUP), and the transaction capabilities application part (TCAP). MTP3 receives the messages from the higher layers and forms an MTP3 message for handling by MTP2 and MTP1. Similarly, in the other direction, messages received by the lower layers in the STP are demultiplexed and delivered to the proper users via MTP3. The MTP3 layer is also responsible for routing signaling messages, and as such it contains functionality commonly found in router implementations. In the following discussions we classify the types of signaling into end-to-end signaling not associated with trunks and call setup, and signaling methods for the management of trunks and circuits in the process of controlling telephone calls.

The signaling connection control part provides end-to-end signaling in the SS7 network. It offers services to the transaction capabilities control part, which in turn offers intelligent network functionality to telephone subscribers, such as 800-number translation into routable numbers, local number portability (LNP), and other telephony features.

ISUP is the protocol defined for control of the circuit-switched network in North America. In summary, it supports bearer services for analog and digital telephony; it can transfer Q.931 information for support of ISDN users end-to-end and offers direct signaling services to analog POTS customers. We focus on examples using mixed network telephony with IP-based and ISUP signaling interworking.

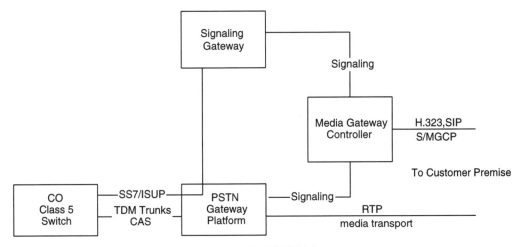

FIGURE 1.5 Composite Reference Model for VoIP/PSTN Access

Detailed and refined models for VoIP telephony address trunking gateways, SS7/ISUP signaling gateways, CAS/MF gateways, ISDN signaling gateways and ATM gateways. A composite such reference model is shown in Figure 1.5. In the discussions that follow in the sections of this chapter we map signaling protocols to reference models and treat their operation and behavior through examples in call establishment, maintenance and tear-down.

The model consists of a CO switch, which is connected to a PSTN gateway through trunks and signaling links. Signaling between the PSTN gateway and the CO is via SS7 or CAS. The signaling gateway handles out-of-band signaling, although this functionality can be included in the PSTN gateway. The signaling performed among the PSTN gateway, the media gateway controller and the signaling gateway can be standard based, but in all likelihood it will be proprietary to optimize the performance of the features offered by the platform.

> The signaling gateway and MGC may be implemented either on a single centralized computing platform, or as part of a distributed system.

Signaling and media to the customer premise are carried over a number of physical layer technologies. In residential deployments, the majority will be cable-based or ADSL. For business applications, T1, T3, and high-bandwidth fiber are the predominant technologies.

We are now ready to look at the specific signaling protocols in VoIP telephony, starting with S/MGCP.

1.2 SGCP, MGCP AND NCS—OVERVIEWS

SGCP[3] is the original Simple Gateway Control Protocol, and was submitted to the IETF as a draft in 1998. The proposal defined a text-based protocol for controlling VoIP media gateways from external call control elements, such as media gateway controllers. SGCP assumes a call control architecture where the call-control "intelligence" is outside the media gateways and handled by external call-control elements. In other words, calls are established and controlled by a media gateway controller (MGC), which is external and can be geographically separated from the MG. A key attribute to SGCP is that it is designed as an internal protocol within a distributed system that appears to the outside as a single VoIP gateway. This means that to the outside world, for example, an entity wishing to establish a call with a MG device controlled by the MGC, the entity perceives a single VoIP system. SGCP and MCGP support the same basic call model, but leave quite a few details up to interpretation in the development process.

In this discussion we refer to S/MGCP and the NCS PacketCable™ standard, and indicate deviations from the other two protocols. NCS is based on MGCP.

SGCP and MGCP are stateless protocols, and this concept is at the heart of the design philosophy. The term *stateless* means the protocol does not require a state machine to describe a sequence of transactions between two signaling entities and keeps no memory of previous transactions between the MGC and the media gateway. This should not be confused with the call state. The *call state* is kept in the media gateway controller. The basic call flows between the MGC and media gateway are in their basic construction state machines, so the burden of state management has been shifted from one part to another in the system design.

Protocol Fundamentals

We will tailor the protocol discussion to our reference models presented earlier in this chapter for simplicity of explanation of the basic concepts and mechanisms. The definitive authority for the protocol specifications are the corresponding IETF draft documents, which the reader is advised to read if an implementation is being contemplated. At the time of writing this text,

---

3.   Mauricio Arango, Christian Huitema, Version 1.1.

MGCP is in draft status and NCS is an independent standard for the cable industry.

MGCP Relationship to the IP Protocol Stack: MGCP is an Application on Top of UDP.

MGCP performs its functions in sequences of commands and mandatory acknowledgments. The MGC is responsible for sending MGCP commands to the endpoints and receives an acknowledgment (ACK) for each command. The commands and responses are ASCII-encoded strings. Commands contain a requested *verb* (action to be performed by the recipient endpoint) and additional parameters. There are eight commands in the MGCP vocabulary, as shown in Table 1.2.

The notation column indicates which signaling protocol supports the respective command.

TABLE 1.2 S/MGCP Verbs

VERB	CODE	DIRECTION	NOTES
CreateConnection	CRCX	MGC - > MG	S/MGCP/NCS
ModifyConnection	MDCX	MGC - > MG	S/MGCP/NCS
DeleteConnection	DLCX	MGC - > MG or MG -> MGC	S/MGCP/NCS
NotificationRequest	RQNT	MGC - > MG	S/MGCP/NCS
Notify	NTFY	MG - >MGC	S/MGCP/NCS
AuditEndpoint	AUEP	MGC - > MG	MGCP/NCS
AuditConnection	AUCX	MGC - > MG	MGCP/NCS
ReStartInProgress	RSIP	MG -> MGC	MGCP/NCS

All MGCP commands have a header, and may contain other parameters such as a session descriptor. A *session descriptor* is a set of parameters that sets up an endpoint to produce and recognize the proper media formats. Its encoding is per the rules of the session description protocol, which we discuss briefly in the next section.

Responses consist of a header and maybe additional parameters. Some responses may also include a session descriptor, as in the process of negotiating parameters for setting up a call. The usage of session descriptors is best seen in our simple call flow at the end of this section, and in Chapter 2. Headers and session descriptors are separated by a carriage return and linefeed character, or single linefeed character. There must be an empty line between a header and a session descriptor.

MGCP requires correlation of commands and responses and uses a *TransactionIdentifier* to accommodate this requirement. The Transaction-Identifier is encoded as part of the command header and appears in the response header. It takes values in the range between 1 and 999999999.

The command header may also include parameter lines (Table 1.3). The command line in the command header consists of the name of the verb, the TransactionIdentifier, the name of the endpoint(s) that should execute the command and the protocol version.

TABLE 1.3 Parameters for S/MGCP Commands

PARAMETER NAME	CODE	PARAMETER VALUE	NOTES
CallID	C	Hexadecimal string, of at most 32 characters long. The value is sent by the MGC to the MG endpoint and identifies the call, which may involve one or more local connections.	
ConnectionID	I	This value is selected by the MG endpoint as the result of a CRCX command.	
NotifiedEntity	N	An identifier in RFC821 formats, as in MGC@ca.anynet.com:5625 *or* Joe@[128.23.0.4]. *If the actual IP address is used, it must be enclosed in brackets.* The entity specified is supposed to receive all notifications for requested events. If this parameter is omitted, the endpoint sends its observed events to the last entity to have sent it a valid command.	
RequestIdentifier	X	This parameter is selected by the MGC and sent to the MG whenever an event notification is requested. The MG replies with the same parameter value when the requested event is observed and a NTFY is sent to the MFC.	

TABLE 1.3 Parameters for S/MGCP Commands (Continued)

PARAMETER NAME	CODE	PARAMETER VALUE	NOTES
LocalConnection Options	L	This structure characterizes the encoding method for the media stream, packetization period, bandwidth to be used, the type of service and the use of echo cancellation. It is sent by the MGC to the endpoint, usually in a CRCX command.	
ConnectionMode	M	Defines the communication channel as fdx, hdx (send or receive only), loopback, inactive, continuity check, or data. Sent by the MGC to the endpoint.	
RequestedEvents	R	The MGC sends one or more even codes to the looked-for by the MG endpoint with this parameter. Events include On-Hook, Off-Hook, Digits Collected, etc. Events can be requested to be sent immediately, quarantined for later transmission, or accumulated.	
SignalRequests	S	This parameter is sent by the MGC to the MG endpoint to request playout of a signal, such as dial tone.	
DigitMap	D	The digit map is sent by the MGC to the MG endpoint to facilitate valid digit string collection according to a numbering plan. It is done so that preliminary digit analysis can be done before a string is passed to the MGC for further analysis. Strings that do not match the current plan are not transmitted by the MG.	
ObservedEvents	O	This is sent by the MG to the MGC when one or more requested even have been observed by the endpoint.	
Connection Parameters	P	These are general statistics about the performance of the connection. They are sent by the endpoint when a connection is deleted.	
SpecifiedEnd PointID	Z	An identifier in RFC821 format, as in EndPoint@hub1.anynet.com:5625, [128.32.0.4]	
RequestedInfo	F	See description in Table 1.8.	
Quarantine Handling	Q	Requested Events can occur immediately after a previously detected event caused a NTFY to be generated, and before the ACK was received by the MGC. This is known as the "notification state." The keyword "process" requests that quarantined observed events be stored and the keyword "discard" requests they be discarded by the endpoint.	

TABLE 1.3 Parameters for S/MGCP Commands (Continued)

PARAMETER NAME	CODE	PARAMETER VALUE	NOTES
DetectEvents	T	This list of requested events is the minimum that must be detected by the MG endpoint while in the "notification" state. It is sent by the MGC to the endpoint.	
EventStates	ES	This is a list of endpoint states that can be audited and must be returned to the MGC in response to an AuditEndpoint command. For example, ES: hu-- the phone is off-hook.	
RestartMethod	RM	Supported methods are "graceful," "forced," "restart," or "disconnected." It is sent by the MG to indicate an endpoint is being taken out of service or being placed back in service.	
RestartDelay	RD	Sent by the MG when a RestartInProgess is sent for an endpoint. It specifies the number of seconds after which the endpoint will perform the RestartMethod, except for "forced," which is immediate. If it is missing, the delay is zero.	
Capabilities	A	The capabilities of the endpoint may be requested by the MGC via an AuditEndpoint command. Capabilities are the compression algorithm (list of supported codecs), packetization period (range), bandwidth (range), echo cancellation, silence suppression, connection modes, the type of service, and event package. An event package is a bundling of signals and events supported by a specific endpoint type, for example an analog phone.	

MGCP Parameters

Endpoint names are encoded per RFC821, for example, mailto:aaln/ 1@ncs2.whatever.net., or aaln/1@[128.32.0.6]. Our example means *line 1 in embedded client ncs2 in the "whatever" domain, or network*. If IP addresses are used, they must be enclosed in brackets.

Table 1.4 gives the association between parameter lines and the MGCP commands. "M" is mandatory, "-" is forbidden, "O" is optional. If a command is sent with inappropriate associations, a protocol error is indicated in the response code, per the encodings of the error table, and the command is not executed by the endpoint.

TABLE 1.4 Association of S/MGCP Parameters and Commands

NAME	CRCX	MDCX	DLCX	RQNT	NTFY	AUEP	AUEX	RSIP
CallID	M	M	O	-	-	-	-	-
ConnectionID	-	M	O	-	-	-	M	-
RequestIdentifier	O	O	O	M	M	-	-	-
LocalConnectionOptions	M	O	-	-	-	-	-	-
ConnectionMode	M	O	-	-	-	-	-	-
RequestedEvents	O	O	O	O*	-	-	-	-
SignalRequests	O	O	O	O**	-	-	-	-
NotifiedEntity	O	O	O	O	O	-	-	-
ReasonCode	-	-	O	-	-	-	-	-
DigitMap	O	O	O	O	-	-	-	-
ObservedEvents	-	-	-	-	M	-	-	-
ConnectionParameters	-	-	O	-	-	-	-	-
SpecificEndPointID	-	-	-	-	-	-	-	-
RequestedInfo	-	-	-	-	-	O	O	-
QuarantineHandling	O	O	O	O	-	-	-	-
DetectEvents	O	O	O	O	-	-	-	-
EventStates	-	-	-	-	-	-	-	-
RestartMethod	-	-	-	-	-	-	-	M
RestartDelay	-	-	-	-	-	-	-	O
Capabilities	-	-	-	-	-	-	-	-

   *   If absent the list will be considered empty, and no events are being requested

   **   If absent the list will be considered empty, and no signals are being requested

Connection Parameter Types

Connection parameters, as shown in Table 1.5, are values that represent the performance of a connection. These values are sent by the MG upstream to the MGC when the connection is deleted via a DLCX command, and they flow upstream from the MG to the MGC in the body of the ACK response.

TABLE 1.5 Connection Parameter Types

CONNECTION PARAMETER NAME	CODE	CONNECTION PARAMETER VALUE	NOTES
Packets Sent	PS	The total number of packets sent in the duration of the connection	
Octets Sent	OS	The total number of octets sent in the duration of the connection	
Packets Received	PR	The total number of packets received in the duration of the connection	
Octets Received	OR	The total number of octets received in the duration of the connection	
Packets Lost	PL	The total number of packets lost in the duration of the connection, as indicated by gaps in the sequence numbers	
Jitter	JI	An integer expressing the average packet inter-arrival jitter	
Latency	LA	Average Latency, in milliseconds, in integer format	

Supported Connection Modes

The MGCP protocol allows for a variety of connection modes, as shown in Table 1.6. A connection mode can be changed to any other mode via the MDCX command and appropriate parameters, which may include a new session description. It is permitted for a MG endpoint not to support certain connection modes. In such cases, the appropriate error code is returned in the response to a CRCX or MDCX, if a non-supported mode is requested. Loopback and continuity test mode are diagnostic connection modes, but may be invoked by an MGC when the corresponding features of SS7 are mapped to an IP voice network, such as a request for continuity testing between exchanges. This would be applicable for networks utilizing PSTN gateways.

The RequestedEvents parameter in the command header includes the list of events to be looked for by the MG. Table 1.7 lists the method of notification by the MG when events occur. All the requested events in a command cause notifications per the single qualifier in the header when they occur.

TABLE 1.6 Connection Modes for S/MGCP/NCS

MODE	MEANING	NOTES
M:sendonly	The gateway should only send packets on this connection.	S/MGCP
M:reconly	The gateway should only receive packets on this connection.	S/MGCP
M:sendrcv	The gateway should both send and receive packets on this connection.	S/MGCP
M:confrnce	The gateway should both send and receive packets on this connection, according to conference mode.	NCS
M:inactive	The gateway should neither send nor receive packets on this connection.	S/MGCP
M:netwloop	The endpoint should be placed in network loopback mode.	S/MGCP
M:netwtest	The endpoint should be placed in network continuity test mode.	S/MGCP

TABLE 1.7 RequestedEvents Qualification

ACTION	CODE
Notify immediately	N
Accumulate	A
Accumulate according to digit map	D
Ignore	I
Keep Signal(s) Active	K
Embedded NotificationRequest	E

The RequestedInfo parameters of Table 1.8 allow the MGC to obtain information of the current state of the MG endpoint, such as the NotifiedEntity, RequestedEvents, DigitMap, etc. The two codes allow inquiry of the local and remote connection descriptors.

TABLE 1.8 RequestedInfo Parameters

REQUESTEDINFO PARAMETER	CODE
LocalConnectionDescriptor	LC
RemoteConnectionDescriptor	RC

Digit Maps

Digit Maps are ASCII text strings, which must be loaded in the MG in order to make efficient use of messaging with the MGC during digit collection. The purpose of a digit map is to allow the endpoint to make a decision whether a valid digit sequence is being dialed, before messages are exchanged with the MGC. In POTS service, the switch in the local exchange analyzes each digit as it is dialed on the keypad by the subscriber, and when a valid dialed sequence is detected, call processing begins. However, in an IP-based signaling environment the number of messages exchanged between the MGC and the MG can be significant. As we see later in the book, there are several messages required in order to commence call processing after digits have been entered, analyzed, and a decision has been made by the MG that the user has dialed a valid string.

The following is an example of a digit map. T signifies digit timeout is enabled.

D:([2-9]xxxxxx | 703xxxxxxx | *xx | 101xxxx | [01][2-9]xxxxxxxxx | 0T | 00 | [4679]11 | 01x.[T#])

The example matches in the above digit map are for North America Systems. Example syntax for a digit map is as follows:

- [2-9]xxxxxx—a normal 7-digit number for a local call
- 703xxxxxxx—a 10-digit local number
- *xx—a request for a feature (e.g. ,*72 for enabling call forwarding)
- 101xxxx—casual calling, selects the carrier of your choice
- [01][2-9]xxxxxxxxx—long distance call (direct dial or calling card)
- 0T—call to the operator
- 00—call to the long distance operator
- [4679]11—for 411, 611, 711 or 911 call (for North America systems)

If the MGC had to do digit analysis at this level for each of the (potentially) thousands of endpoints it serves, it is easy to see that there could be a dual problem. First, the number of messages could overwhelm a narrowband link between the MGC and MG, thus affecting the number of endpoints that can be served by a MG. Second, the computational requirements inside the MGC would make it uneconomical to support an acceptable size population with a single platform.

Responses with Error Codes

S/MGCP define the use of error codes to be returned to the MGC when failure conditions exist in or around the media gateway. Only one error code is reported per transaction, and there is ambiguity in the specification for selecting the code to send to the MGC in case multiple conditions exist. In other words, there is no error precedence defined in the specification. It is advisable for the service provider to employ other means of obtaining accurate information about the health of a media gateway of a specific endpoint served by the MG.

Table 1.9 is a list of response codes that can be returned by endpoints.

TABLE 1.9 MGCP Error Codes

CODE	MEANING
200	The requested transaction was executed normally
250	Connections were deleted
400	Transient error – transaction not executed
401	Phone is already off-hook
402	Phone is already on-hook
500	Endpoint unknown
501	Endpoint not ready
510	Protocol error
511	Command contained unrecognized extension
512	Gateway not equipped to detect one of the requested signals
513	Gateway not equipped to generate one of the requested signals
514	Gateway could not send the specified announcement
515	Incorrect connection ID
516	Unknown call ID
517	Unsupported or invalid mode
518	Unsupported or unknown package
519	Endpoint does not have a digit map
520	Endpoint is restarting
521	Endpoint redirected to another MGC
522	No such event or signal
523	Unknown action or illegal combination of actions
524	Internal inconsistency in LocalConnectionOptions

TABLE 1.9 MGCP Error Codes (Continued)

CODE	MEANING
525	Unknown extension in LocalConnectionOptions
526	Insufficient bandwidth
527	Missing RemoteConnectionDescriptor
528	Incompatible protocol version

It is apparent from the list that there can be ambiguity in the selection of a code when multiple errors are present in the MG or its environment. The defined codes also do not seem to support internal hardware faults yet, although work is in progress to accommodate internal failure reporting. The main focus of the error codes seems to be to protect against protocol, configuration, and box capability errors. It is impossible to implement meaningful diagnosability based on information supplied in these error codes, and the issue of system robustness was not preeminent in the early stages of the protocol. The question of robustness, redundancy, and diagnosability has been left as an implementation detail, and other methods need to be implemented to obtain diagnostic information from media gateways and endpoints. SNMP is one such possible means, and it is certainly bound to find a home in VoIP media gateway design.

Reason codes, as shown in Table 1.10, are generated by endpoints when they take a unilateral action to delete one or more connections. An example of the kind of ambiguity that may occur in cases of endpoint malfunction is the following scenario. An endpoint receives a CRCX command that is parsed properly and an ACK is returned promptly. The MGC goes on about its business, thinking the command has been executed, and attempts to connect the remote endpoint in the call. After attempting to perform the connection, the MG discovers it is malfunctioning. It then returns a DLCX command to the MGC with code 900. This causes the MGC to start teardown procedures and cleanup of the call, which was only partially set up.

A possible implementation to avoid the runaround of the above example is to keep the current state of the endpoint available when a command is received and reject it based on a priori knowledge of whether it can be completed. This would speed up return of an ACK or NAK with error code and avoid unnecessary actions by the MGC. When we consider that some of these calls will be across the country some day, it is important to note that speed of execution of the call setup transactions is of the utmost importance to give the user the look and feel of primary line telephone service.

TABLE 1.10 MGCP Reason Codes for Gateway-
Generated DLCX Commands

CODE	MEANING
900	Endpoint malfunctioning
901	Endpoint taken out of service
902	Loss of lower layer connectivity

Additional Error Codes in the Works

The industry and the standards groups are working to augment the current set of error codes to account for other devices with specific error reporting needs. One such device, which is not explicitly addressed by MGCP, is the common PBX. There are four main varieties of PBX types: Wink Start, Immediate Start, Ground Start and Loop Start. Signaling is also performed either in a CAS manner via robbed bit A/B signaling (the older method) or via PRI Q.931 signaling. New error codes will offer specific reporting for PBX trunk failures, and possibly a closer look into gateway internal failure reasons.

One very serious issue designers will face in the first deployments of SGCP-based text protocols is robustness and reliability of call setup and call maintenance. S/MGCP itself is a stateless protocol, which means every protocol handshake between two endpoints is autonomous and does not depend on a previous or subsequent handshake. When we examine the call flows for S/MGCP later, we will insert failures to see what possible actions can be considered at each step of the call setup process.

A Few Words About the NotifiedEntity Parameter

The NotifiedEntity parameter can be passed with a NTFY command from the Media Gateway Controller to the MG. Implementations of MGCs may be multiprocessor systems, with multiple IP addresses. The MGC controlling the call setup may not be the processor handling notifications for requested events. The reasons may be reliability, load balancing, or simply a scalability consideration in the MGC design.

S/MGCP Signaling Reference Diagram

Figure 1.6 is a simple topology, which shows a single MGC with connectivity to two MGs, and their respective endpoints. A routing network between the MGC and the MGs may exist in various degrees of sophistication and complexity, and construction of this network is beyond the scope of this text. The call flows in Chapter 3 include a basic call between two users served by a single MGC, and more complex interworking flows with other signaling protocols.

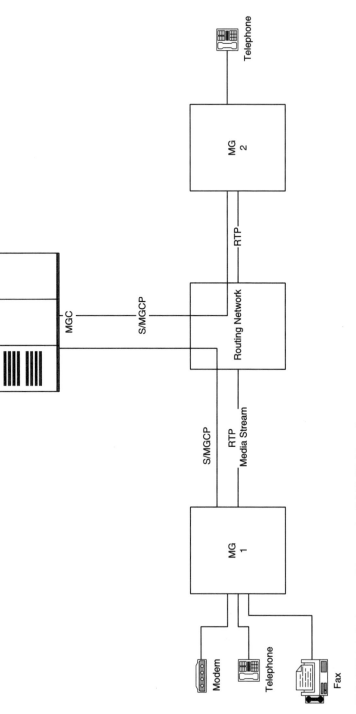

FIGURE 1.6 Reference Diagram for S/MGCP Signaling

Usage of SDP for Describing Sessions

In order to complete a call, the MGC needs to provision the endpoints with the description of connection parameters such as IP addresses, UDP port, and a description of the media format, packetization method, etc. These session descriptions are included in the body of the CRCX and MDCX commands and their syntax follows the conventions of the Session Description Protocol (RFC 2327).

We defer the discussion of the SDP protocol until the next section in this chapter. A typical SDP syntax that could be included in an S/MGCP command is:

v = 0
c = IN IP4 128.96.41.1
m = audio 3456 RTP/AVP 0

The session descriptor identifies SDP protocol version 0, an IPv4 network, IP endpoint address = 128.96.41.1, connection mode is set to audio, RTP port is set to 3456, using the user profile for payload type 0 (G.711 uncompressed 64K voice). (We discuss payload types in the RTP section later in this text.) We see actual packets captured in real time later during call flow analysis, for the syntax of SDP parameters in S/MGCP.

Packet Formats

As we mentioned before, S/MGCP is an ASCII text-based protocol. This makes the packet contents easy to display and understand, without the need for quick reference guides to remember bit positions and their meanings. In this section we show packet formats from the major protocols that were captured in a live trace using the Hewlett-Packard Internet Advisor (HP-IA). More information about the HP-IA and associated traces from signaling call setup can be found in the accompanying CD-ROM.

A typical S/MGCP packet captured on the HP-IA is shown in Figure 1.7. The packet shows a RQNT command sent across an Ethernet LAN segment, from IPv4 source address 10.1.1.65, to endpoint aaln/2 at IPv4 destination address 10.1.70.16. The command asks for a notification if the endpoint goes off-hook, and at the same time it sets and asks the endpoint to play the ringing tone.

The packet that appears on the Ethernet link is a standard IPv4 packet, with UDP payload. The UDP payload is the actual S/MGCP command data. The S/MGCP portion of the packet starts immediately after the checksum field of the UDP header. Note that each text line in the S/MGCP segment is separated by a single x'0A' (newline) character. The Request Identifier value sent to the MG for this RQNT will be returned in a NTFY message from the MG to the MGC when the requested event is detected. Also note that the

```
------------ ETHER Header ------------
ETHER: Destination: 00-90-A0-00-00-73
ETHER: Source: 00-A0-C9-D4-BC-35
ETHER: Protocol: IP
ETHER: FCS: 0937BA1E


------------ IP Header ------------
IP: Version = 4
IP: Header length = 20
IP: Type of service = 0
IP:     000. .... Precedence = Routine(0)
IP:     ...0 .... Delay = Normal (0)
IP:     .... 0... Throughput = Normal (0)
IP:     .... .0.. Reliability = Normal (0)
IP: Packet length = 85
IP: Id = c16a
IP: Fragmentation Info = 0x0000
IP:     .0.. ....  .... .... Don't Fragment Bit = FALSE
IP:     ..0. ....  .... .... More Fragments Bit = FALSE
IP:     ...0 0000  0000 0000 Fragment offset = 0
IP: Time to live = 128
IP: Protocol = UDP (17)
IP: Header checksum = 1DDB
IP: Source address = 10.1.1.65
IP: Destination address = 10.1.70.16


------------ UDP Header ------------
UDP: Source port = 2427
UDP: Destination port = 2427
UDP: Length = 65
UDP: Checksum = 1235


------------ MGCP Header ------------
MGCP: Packet Type = Command
MGCP: Command = Notification Request [RQNT]
MGCP: Transaction Identifier = 68
MGCP: Endpoint = aaln/2@10.1.70.16
MGCP: Version = MGCP 0.1
MGCP: Parameter = Requested Events [R:]
```

FIGURE 1.7 S/MGCP RQNT Packet Format (Courtesy of HP-Internet Advisor)

MGC has resolved the name of the endpoint into an IP address, with the syntax aaln/2@10.1.70.16. The endpoint name aaln/2 maps to port two of the media gateway, under convention.

Some implementations may supply both the \r (return) character and the \n (newline) as delimiters of the text lines. Before proceeding with more complex signaling examples, let's look at a brief overview of the Session Description Protocol (SDP).

1.2.1 Summary of the Session Description Protocol

Background

Regardless of the type of signaling protocol used in a domain, there is a need to assign session parameters to every user participating in a point-to-point or multipoint call. Required parameters for call management include the media payload types, which in turn may involve codec negotiation between endpoints. The Session Description Protocol (SDP) has the mechanisms and appropriate syntax to facilitate parameter passing between the MGC and the endpoints it controls through the MGs. The SDP syntax is straightforward and has been accepted as the coding method of choice for call parameter negotiation in the text based IP signaling protocols.

SDP Protocol Fundamentals

The Session Initiation Protocol is defined in RFC 2327. The RFC abstract states: *SDP is intended for describing multimedia sessions for the purposes of session announcement, session invitation, and other forms of multimedia session initiation.*

A multimedia session is defined by a set of multimedia senders and receivers and the data streams flowing from senders to receivers. A video telephony conference call is an example of a multimedia session.

Message Formats

In the S/MGCP protocol and its derivatives, SDP notation is used to carry session descriptions, without necessarily using the entire SDP protocol. Only the SDP syntax is used within the S/MGCP payload. SDPs, as they are commonly called, appear in S/MGCP messages at call initiation, and if modification of the session description is desired for the purposes of negotiating parameters mutually acceptable to all parties.

A session description is encoded as an ASCII string using an abbreviated message format as shown in the following. The v= line separates session descriptions, if multiple descriptions are being sent. All lines are separated by the newline or carriage return character.

v=protocol version
o=owner/creator and session identifier
s=session name
i=(optional) session information

u=(optional) URI of description
e=(optional) email address
p=(optional) phone number
c=(optional) connection information
b=(optional) bandwidth information

One or more time descriptions

z=(optional) time zone adjustments
k=(optional) encryption key
a=(optional) zero or more session attribute lines

Time description

t= time the session is active
r=(optional) zero or more repeat times

Media description

m=(media name and transport address)
i=(optional) media title
c=(optional) connection information - optional if included at session level
b=(optional) bandwidth information
k=(optional) encryption key
a=(optional) zero or more media attribute lines

Parameter Negotiation and Setting

The message in Figure 1.8 shows the method by which SDP syntax is used to signal session parameters to endpoints. The Ethernet and IP packet headers have been omitted for simplicity.

The S/MGCP packet payload shown is a Create Connection command (CRCX), which is telling the destination endpoint to establish a connection with endpoint 10.1.70.16 on UDP port 1029, media type is audio coded with PCM µLaw. The destination endpoint will select a Connection Identifier and respond with an ACKnowledgment. However, the requested media format may not be supported by the other endpoint, and a negotiation will take place.

The first element in the SDP is the protocol version (v = 0), which begins immediately after the newline character following the end of S/MGCP header. The SDP should be placed last in the packet. The connection information (c = ...) identifies INternet (IN) and the IP address of the call processor that created the session.

```
------------  UDP Header  ------------
UDP: Source port = 2427
UDP: Destination port = 2427
UDP: Length = 150
UDP: Checksum = F2F6
------------  MGCP Header  ------------
MGCP: Packet Type = Command
MGCP: Command = Create Connection [CRCX]
MGCP: Transaction Identifier = 57
MGCP: Endpoint = aaln/1@10.1.70.17
MGCP: Version = MGCP 0.1
MGCP: Parameter = Call Id [C:]
MGCP:    Value = 9999999999999999999
MGCP: Parameter = Local Connection Options [L:]
MGCP:    Packetization Period (ms): 20
MGCP:    Compression Algorithm   : G.711
MGCP:    Type of Network         : IN
MGCP: Parameter = Connection Mode [M:]
MGCP:    Value = sendrecv
------------  SDP Header  ------------
SDP: Version = 0
SDP: Mandatory Origin Field (o=) Not Found
SDP: Connection Field :
SDP:     Network Type = IN
SDP:     Address Type = IP4
SDP:     Address = 10.1.70.16
SDP: Media Field :
SDP:     Media Type = audio
SDP:     Port Number = 1029
SDP:     Transport Protocol = RTP/AVP
SDP:     Media Format = PCMU (0)
 Record #110      (From Hub To Node) Captured on 06.08.99 at 18:56:21.364751399
Length =    188
    00 90 a0 00 00 95 00 a0    c9 d4 bc 35 08 00 45 00    ........ ...5..E.
    00 aa f7 69 00 00 80 11    e7 85 0a 01 01 41 0a 01    ...i.... .....A..
    46 11 09 7b 09 7b 00 96    f2 f6 43 52 43 58 20 35    F..{.{.. ..CRCX 5
    37 20 61 61 6c 6e 2f 31    40 31 30 2e 31 2e 37 30    7 aaln/1 @10.1.70
    2e 31 37 20 4d 47 43 50    20 30 2e 31 0a 43 3a 20    .17 MGCP  0.1.C:
    39 39 39 39 39 39 39 39    39 39 39 39 39 39 39 39    99999999 99999999
    39 39 39 0a 4c 3a 20 70    3a 32 30 2c 20 61 3a 47    999.L: p :20, a:G
    2e 37 31 31 2c 20 6e 74    3a 49 4e 0a 4d 3a 20 73    .711, nt :IN.M: s
    65 6e 64 72 65 63 76 0a    0a 76 3d 30 0a 63 3d 49    endrecv. .v=0.c=I
    4e 20 49 50 34 20 31 30    2e 31 2e 37 30 2e 31 36    N IP4 10 .1.70.16
    0a 6d 3d 61 75 64 69 6f    20 31 30 32 39 20 52 54    .m=audio  1029 RT
    50 2f 41 56 50 20 30 0a    ca 13 66 e5                P/AVP 0. ..f.
```

FIGURE 1.8 S/MGCP CRCX Packet with SDP Parameters
(Courtesy Hewlett-Packard-Internet Advisor)

1.2.2 S/MGCP Summary

Voice over IP telephony and XoIP[4] services have placed a significant demand on efficient signaling between the service provider's media gateway controller and the media gateways serving the endpoints at the customer premise or at a carrier's point of presence. Offering primary line telephone service is much more involved than experimental voice telephony over the Internet. So, even though H.323 beat everybody to the punch, the needs of the service providers spurned a whole new research effort in the area of signaling. S/MGCP and SIP are the early signaling protocols intended for serious VoIP telephony signaling in the wide area, and both of them have been greeted by various degrees of acceptance in deployments. However, the standards bodies have come to the realization that if VoIP is to succeed it needs unity among the groups to gain wide acceptance in the industry. This observation will become increasingly important, when enough VoIP services from carriers have been rolled out and carrier interworking and interoperability across packet networks becomes a requirement.

The issue of protocol choice for the media streams seems to have been settled in favor of RTP, and little disturbance is expected in that for XoIP. However, much work is being done in this area as well for the purpose of establishing tractable means to offer quantifiable QoS in the ultimate scenario of supplying multiservice capabilities to the mass consumer market. The subject of end-to-end QoS measurement for voice media streams will be expanded upon in Chapters 4 and 5, where we will see quantitative measures of the delivered voice quality in reference topologies.

1.3 H.323 –AN OVERVIEW OF THE ITU-T APPROACH FOR VOIP TELEPHONY

Recommendation H.323 from the ITU-T is the pioneering umbrella specification for implementing packet-based multimedia conferencing over local area networks that cannot guarantee quality of service. Although substantial experimental work was in progress from the early days of IP-based call processing, using alternative means and protocols, the H.323 specifications found early adoption and proliferated in the enterprise. Later, the Internet served as a testbed for the viability of IP telephony in the worst possible case, a completely uncontrolled packet-based transport environment. Now the H.323 standard represents a very good working version of IP-based telephony over generic packet topologies. The documents of H.323 specify the protocols, methods

---

4.   XoIP is Anything over IP.

and network elements that are necessary to establish point-to-point multimedia connections between two endpoints (users), plus multipoint and bridged multimedia conferences with three or more parties. The case of point-to-point, two-party voice conferencing reduces to the commonly understood plain old telephone call, and is examined in detail in this section.

The basic network elements of an H.323 topology are terminals, gatekeepers (GK), multicast units (MCUs) and gateways (GW). MCUs are listed separately, but in practice they are most often part of a gatekeeper or a high-speed computer that acts as a terminal serving one or more users. Logical connectivity exists between the three element types and is used to facilitate call establishment and termination, as well as gathering of performance parameters which characterize the quality of operation of the underlying network infrastructure. H.323 has been extended to support efficient call processing across network segments through the PSTN, or generic IP packet network topologies. In this section we will look at the pros and cons of H.323 and offer some comparisons and performance expectations with respect to the other competing call signaling protocols. H.323 is one of the three major contenders for viable IP-based packet telephony, and although it is not a hands-down winner in any comparison, it offers capabilities that will continue to make it attractive, at least for call processing in the enterprise and controlled LAN environments.

The H.323 standard defines procedures for user (terminal) registration with a gatekeeper, call control, and logical channel capabilities negotiation between two or more parties that wish to enter into a multimedia conference. Registration, authentication, and status (RAS) and call control are defined in recommendation H.225.0, whereas logical channel capabilities negotiation (media control) is defined in recommendation H.245. The H.323 protocol stack is shown in Figure 1:11 on page 42, and we will look at specifics of call establishment and media type and format negotiation in simple call flows, using visual explanations as much as possible.

This treatise of the H.323 standard is not intended to be a substitute for the ITU specifications, but we hope the reader finds it easier to relate teachings of the standard to real implementation issues, using these descriptions. The reader is expected to develop familiarity with the key aspects of IP-based telephony, both in homogeneous topologies and in hybrid domains supporting multiple signaling standards.

Definitions and References

An H.323 terminal is a device that includes a signaling endpoint which supports one or more users who enter into real-time communication with one or more parties. In homogeneous H.323 environments the other parties will also be users of H.323 terminals, but in the general case one or more of the parties in a call may be in a dissimilar domain, such as a PSTN subscriber, SIP, or MGCP endpoint. The full H.323 call model is executed between two terminals, a terminal and a gatekeeper, or a terminal and a gateway.

A gatekeeper is the brain of an H.323 zone. An H.323 zone includes all the terminal gateways and multicast control units (MCUs) managed by one gatekeeper. There is *only one* gatekeeper per zone. A zone is a logical grouping of devices and can contain elements that may be part of a decentralized topology connected with switches and routers. In other words, a zone can span a wide geographical area. Figure 1.9 shows an extension of the general case of an H.323 zone.

Figure 1.9 shows connectivity between the gatekeeper and network elements in two LAN segments. Note that switches and routers are transparent to the H.323 network elements, that is, they do not see them or manage them as part of call processing or signaling management functions. There may also be more than one MCU in a zone, and their use is one of the functions performed by the GK. In the extended zone case, we show H.323 GK access to a residential gateway/hub, through switching and routing equipment. Such would be the case, for example, if a telephony service provider uses H.323 to offer basic telephone service as well as multimedia stream integration to remote and geographically distributed endpoints, such as residential gateways. This is merely a thought, and this type of service merging between the LAN and the WAN raises enormous design and implementation issues.

Gatekeepers can signal to other gatekeepers in other zones to access users in other domains in a manner transparent to the calling party. In enterprise scenarios this would be necessary to support distributed locations of a multinational corporation, or any other instance of geographical distribution between LAN segments. The gateways access the PSTN to offer call connectivity to POTS customers, but gateways also offer access to any dissimilar type of local segments, such as MGCP and SIP domains. We will delve into some of the issues associated with the general cases in this section.

System Components and Functions

The functions of H.323 call processing are divided into three basic areas: registration with a gatekeeper using the RAS protocol, call signaling using H.225.0, and media capability exchange with routing of the media channel using H.245. Figure 1.10 shows the possible methods for H.225.0 call signaling, and the impact on H.245 media routing.

The gatekeeper is optional in a domain, but if one is present its use is recommended. Absence of a GK in a domain means the domain *does not* constitute an H.323 zone. In other words, a domain is not necessarily a zone. Even

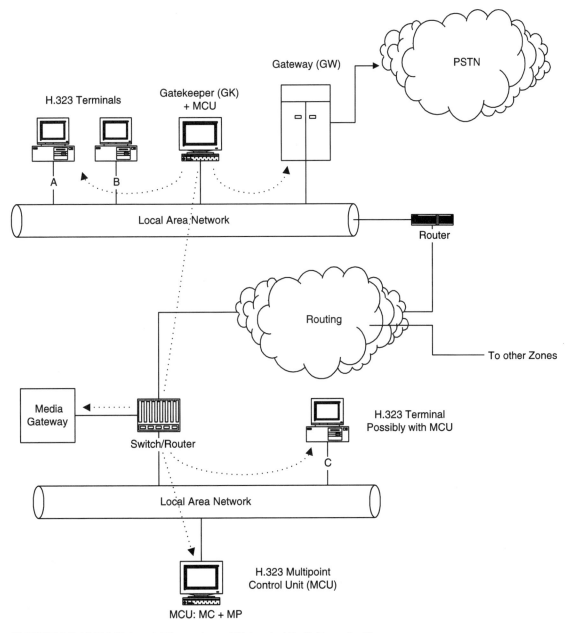

FIGURE 1.9 H.323 Network Elements and Extended Definition of a Zone

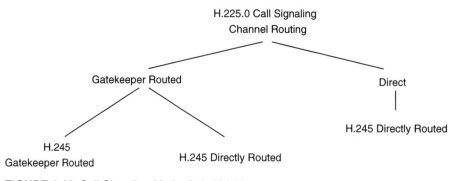

FIGURE 1.10 Call Signaling Methods in H.323

when a GK is present, the call model chosen during call setup may be that for direct call signaling routing. This decision is made during admission request by the endpoint to handle an incoming call itself. The GK provides address translation and is also in charge of assigning bandwidth for connections in response to requests from the endpoints. It is thus very important to keep the GK in a zone involved in the call model in some manner, in order to keep the overall network bandwidth utilization under control. In the direct routed model, the endpoints can request bandwidth changes as the needs for the call would demand in real-time, and the GK would be consulted and assignments would be made even though media streams between endpoints may not be flowing through the GK. Regardless of the call signaling routing model selected for H.225.0, media signaling with H.245 is normally direct, with an exception of bridged conferencing through an MCU. Routing directly has significant performance advantages in latencies, as well as robustness, since the gatekeeper can be a point of failure in the implementation platform.

In Figure 1.9 we saw an extended zone, and saw the gateway (GW) touching the PSTN. When such a topology exists, the most likely scenario for outgoing calls is for the calling party to signal through the GK, and for the GK to handle call processing with the GW. In this case the GW always acts as an endpoint, and the call model will consist of multiple call segments, each to be set up and terminated independently. There are issues of selection of TDM trunks based on digit analysis of the telephone number dialed, possible and most likely use of SS7 signaling by the GW towards the PSTN, other forms of signaling for special number dialing, etc., MF signaling for emergency 911 calls, 411 and x11 call routing, 800-number dialing, etc. In summary, there are several services offered by the PSTN today, and the use of a GW is required in H.323 networks offering PSTN access. This makes it difficult to select endpoint-to-GK direct call signaling routing, unless the GK is integrated with the GW. One of the most important features is operator services, which is not normally found in enterprise networks.

We briefly discussed the MCU, and we will see its use in the context of a call model a little later. The ITU loosely defines the MCU as a *bridge,* and its use is similar to a conventional bridge used for teleconferencing. It is an end-point in the network that allows the parties of a call to enjoy conferencing. Calls using the MCU need not start out as conferences, but they can evolve to such, with subsequent additions of other parties. MCUs contain an audio processor as a minimum to provide mixing and switching of the audio streams. MCUs consist of a multipoint controller (MC) and a multipoint processor (MP) at a high level. The MC handles the call control signaling, whereas the MP provides the mixing, switching and possible media translation to accommodate all parties. Actual implementations of the MC and MP and positioning of the MCUs in the network vary among topologies, and are not governed by standards at this time.

H.323 Protocols

The scope of the H.323 standard for audio, video, and fax applications is shown in Figure 1.11. Aside from H.225.0 for call signaling, RAS, and H.245 for media control, the H.323 standard also specifies RTP as the media transport protocol. RTCP is the companion control protocol to RTP and both are covered in detail in Chapter 2.

The protocol stack splits H.225.0 to run over UDP for RAS, and TCP for call signaling. H.245 runs only over TCP. The H.323 philosophy is robustness of call control, in non-robust environments. This comes at the cost of some performance degradation in setting up calls, and generally complex implementations for the brains of network segments, such as the GKs and the GWs. TCP offers a stateful approach to call signaling, but attaches performance restrictions that can be unacceptable for WAN telephony. Gatekeepers must keep all TCP connections up for the duration of the calls. Temporary issues with signaling lower-level channels can cause loss of the TCP connection, which will result in dropping the call. This may be acceptable in non-toll-quality voice telephony, but it creates issues when the objective is to achieve carrier-quality in distributed signaling domains.

One supported claim of the S/MGCP and SIP protocols is a much simplified call model. This is true in many cases, but simplicity comes at its own price. We will see this issue and similar others in the context of the H.323 call models. The H.323 protocols utilize the IP layer without caveats, that is, no proprietary extensions to IP. However, for QoS routing, H.323 recommends usage of RSVP (ReSerVation Protocol), which is defined in RFC 2205, but does not enjoy ubiquitous deployment in most networks. We will see RSVP

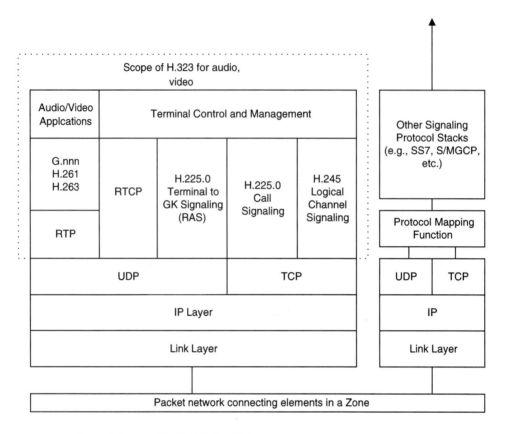

Legend: G.nnn = ITU-T, G-Series Codec

FIGURE 1.11 H.323 Protocol Stack and Protocol Interworking Architecture

and MPLS (Multi-Protocol Label Switching), for performance and reliability enhancement, in the Chapter 2.

The link layer protocol can be ATM, and the use of ATM in H.323 applications signaling has increased. In LANs the nominal link layer protocol is Ethernet, however ATM-based technology such as LAN emulation, multi-protocol over ATM (MPOA), plus the need to distribute H.323 signaling to remote endpoints, has mandated the need for a WAN link layer protocol to transport IP-based call control signaling. ATM lends itself nicely to the task, because of its different classes of service, reliability, and its own QoS mechanisms which enhance H.323 in quality and robustness. The physical layer in the diagram is a virtual layer and normally consists of a collection of point-to-point and broadcast segments across multiple network hops and types.

In Figure 1.11 we show, for reference only, an IP stack for protocol interworking between H.323 and SS7 or S/MGCP. The front end of the interworking protocol stack must support H.225.0 for call setup. Even though the lower layers look simple, the complexities in an interworking implementation are found in the mapping functions to properly extend the functionality of one set of protocols to another's domain, to the degree possible. For SS7 interworking, it is expected that the H.323 network segment will employ the network elements and procedures to control PSTN signaling and trunks, as we describe in the SS7 section of this book, in a manner transparent to the SS7 network; that is, the PSTN will not have knowledge of the call signaling and media transport mechanisms employed in the PSTN signaling point controlled by the GW.

Basic H.323 Call Model

The possible permutations of H.323 call model mixes is large, but there are may common elements with the direct routed and gatekeeper routed models. We will examine the direct routed model in the context of a point-to-point call, and the gatekeeper routed model in a multi-party conference.

The call model of H.323 consists of five phases.

1. Call setup (Phase A)
2. Initial communication between endpoints and terminal capability exchange (Phase B)
3. Establishment of audio/visual communication between endpoints (Phase C)
4. Request and negotiation of Call Services (Phase D)
5. Call termination (Phase E)

The signaling diagrams in Figures 1.12 through 1.14 capture the phases of a call in the direct routed model. This is a simple scenario of a point-to-point call originating in a zone within a private IP network controlled by GK at IP network address 10.0.0.1. Caller A at IP network address 10.0.0.10 wants to call user B, who is located in the same zone as A with IP network address 10.0.0.12. Caller A either knows the IP network address of B directly, or it is resolved via a DNS query sometime before the call signaling is initiated. DNS queries are usually done transparently to the signaling protocols.

The first set of exchanges shows the opening of a TCP connection between A and B's well-known TSAP. The TSAP is the H.323 Transport layer Service Access Point, which is TCP port number 1720. Once TCP-ACK has been returned by the calling party, indicating the connection is up, call signaling can begin. The TCP connection opening process is expensive in

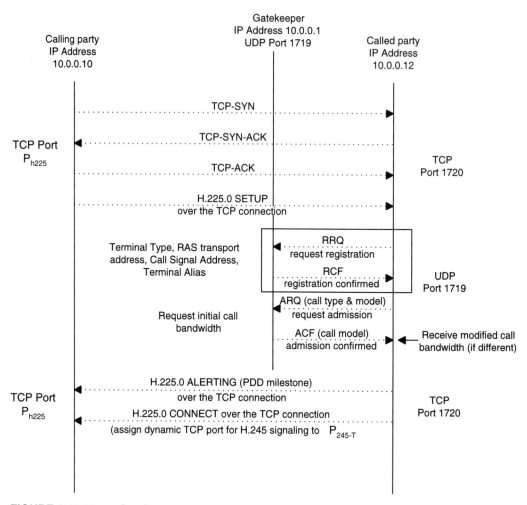

FIGURE 1.12 H.323 Call Setup, Phase A

terms of performance, because it requires one and a half round-trip times and the necessary protocol processing at both ends.

The first message over the new TCP connection is the SETUP message of H.225.0. The H.225.0 message set is a subset of the ITU-T Q.931 protocol. The message contains information about the type of call the originating endpoint is requesting, such as point-to-point or multipoint, possible establishment of a conference call, the transport address of the calling endpoint, security capabilities for the media channel (which has not yet been opened), and a possible request for a fast connect procedure, known as *fastStart*. We discuss the

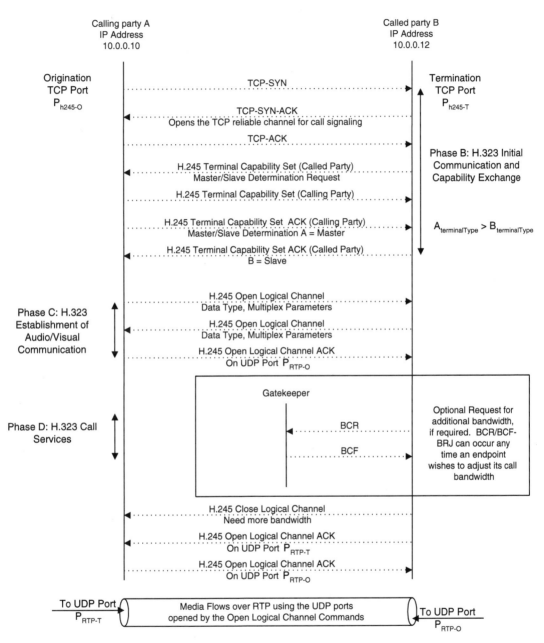

FIGURE 1.13 H.323 Call Setup, Phases B, C and D

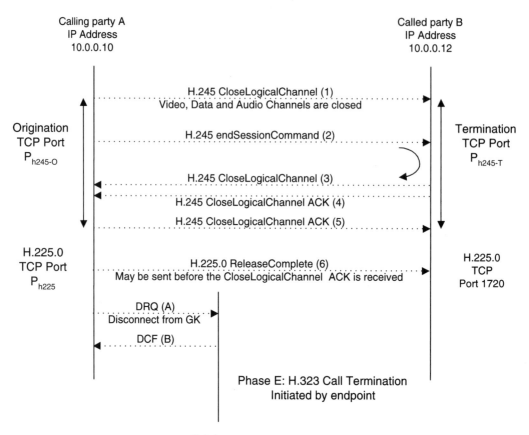

FIGURE 1.14 H.323 Call Setup, Phase E (Termination)

latter type of procedure a little later, but in this example, basic H.225.0/H.245 signaling is used throughout the establishment phase of the call.

If the terminal does not exist at that network address, for example, if it is powered off or disconnected from the network, the calling end's H.225.0 SETUP timer will expire and the call attempt will be dropped. If the terminal is reachable but is busy on another call, it will return a RELEASE COMPLETE with the reason for rejecting the call. If the terminal is not busy, the signaling process starts with one or more RAS message exchanges.

If the terminal has not already registered with a GK, this is a good time to do it with the RRQ (RegistrationRequest) RAS message. The RRQ/RCF exchange is not part of call processing, and normally happens when a terminal wishes to register with a gatekeeper upon startup or operator command. This method registers the terminal type, transport address, any aliases and call signaling addresses. The GK may reject the RRQ and send RRJ, in which case the terminal must find another GK to register with. The reason could be related to availability of resources inside the GK, but should not happen very often. Assuming the GK has accepted the registration, the receiving endpoint then sends a RAS admission request (ARQ) to the GK to ask for access to the network, bandwidth for the call, and a signaling model, either direct or routed signaling via the GK. UDP port number 1719 is the RAS transport address. The GK might not agree with the request, and might return a different call model in its reply ACF (admission confirmed). The GK could also reject the request for various reasons, such as unavailable bandwidth, and return ARJ (Admission Reject). If the request cannot be honored by the GK, the endpoint will release the call using the H.225.0 message RELEASE COMPLETE. In this example, the GK grants the request and the called endpoint sends H.225.0 ALERTING, indicating to the calling end that the phone is ringing. The ALERTING message indicates the mark for post dial delay calculations. In a real distributed topology, the message exchanges shown in Figure 1.12, beginning with the opening of the TCP connection up to the ALERTING message, can consume time on the order of several seconds. Finally, when the called party accepts the call, the CONNECT message is sent, which carries a very important quantity, the dynamic TCP port number for initiating H.245 signaling to set up the media channel. This completes Phase A of the call processing.

Phase B is the initial communication between the endpoints and capability exchange. Once again, a new TCP connection is required between the calling party and the TCP transport address of the called party that was supplied in the H.225.0 CONNECT message. It is necessary to establish a Master/Slave relationship between the two endpoints. The Master is looked upon to resolve any conflicts that may arise regarding resources required for the communication, or any other minor type of conflict. The terminal with the highest terminal type is determined to be the Master for the duration of the call. The more capability a terminal contains, the higher its number in the H.323 protocol. GKs, GWs, and MCUs capable of signaling for audio, video and fax are the highest. Terminals without MC capability are the lowest.

The Master/Slave determination message can be sent in the same TCP payload as the terminal capability set. There is more on H.323 message formatting later in this chapter. The call flow diagram shows two terminal capability set messages, one each from the originating and terminating endpoints. Each is acknowledged by the opposite end, and at the end of the exchange the capabilities of each terminal are known and any incompatibilities can be dealt with by the application. Let's look at the type of information included in a composite Master/Slave composite packet in Figures 1.15 through 1.18. The link layer and IP header information have been omitted for clarity. The data was captured from a live trace using the HP Internet Advisor.

```
------------ H245 Header ------------
H245: Multimedia System Control Message Type = Request
H245: | Request Type = Terminal Capability Set
H245: | | Sequence Number = 1
H245: | | Protocol Identifier = ITU-T.Recommendation.H.245.Version.2
H245: | | Multiplex Capability
H245: | | | H.225.0 Capability
H245: | | | | Maximum Audio Delay Jitter = 60 msec
H245: | | | | Receive Multipoint Capability
H245: | | | | | Multicast Capability = 0 (FALSE)
H245: | | | | | Multi UniCast Capability = 0 (FALSE)
H245: | | | | | Media Distribution Capability [0]
H245: | | | | | | Media Distribution Capability
H245: | | | | | | | Centralized Control = 0 (FALSE)
H245: | | | | | | | Distributed Control = 0 (FALSE)
H245: | | | | | | | Centralized Audio = 0 (FALSE)
H245: | | | | | | | Distributed Audio = 0 (FALSE)
H245: | | | | | | | Centralized Video = 0 (FALSE)
H245: | | | | | | | Distributed Video = 0 (FALSE)
H245: | | | | Transmit Multipoint Capability
H245: | | | | | Multicast Capability = 0 (FALSE)
H245: | | | | | Multi UniCast Capability = 0 (FALSE)
H245: | | | | | Media Distribution Capability [0]
H245: | | | | | | Media Distribution Capability
H245: | | | | | | | Centralized Control = 0 (FALSE)
H245: | | | | | | | Distributed Control = 0 (FALSE)
H245: | | | | | | | Centralized Audio = 0 (FALSE)
H245: | | | | | | | Distributed Audio = 0 (FALSE)
H245: | | | | | | | Centralized Video = 0 (FALSE)
H245: | | | | | | | Distributed Video = 0 (FALSE)
H245: | | | | Receive And Transmit Multipoint Capability
H245: | | | | | Multicast Capability = 0 (FALSE)
H245: | | | | | Multi UniCast Capability = 0 (FALSE)
H245: | | | | | Media Distribution Capability [0]
H245: | | | | | | Media Distribution Capability
H245: | | | | | | | Centralized Control = 0 (FALSE)
H245: | | | | | | | Distributed Control = 0 (FALSE)
H245: | | | | | | | Centralized Audio = 0 (FALSE)
H245: | | | | | | | Distributed Audio = 0 (FALSE)
H245: | | | | | | | Centralized Video = 0 (FALSE)
H245: | | | | | | | Distributed Video = 0 (FALSE)
```

FIGURE 1.15 H.245 Terminal Capability Set (1)

It is apparent the H.245 terminal capability exchange message is a complex entity, and the use of ASN.1 syntax makes the hexadecimal notation of the packet virtually impossible to decipher with the "naked" eye. The Internet Advisor offers the option of explicitly stating the multiplex capabilities, audio and video capabilities as stated in the capability table entries, delay

```
H245: | | | | MC Capability
H245: | | | | | Centralized Conference MC = 0 (FALSE)
H245: | | | | | Distributed ConferenceMC = 0 (FALSE)
H245: | | | | RTCP Video Control Capability = 0 (FALSE)
H245: | | | | Media Packetization Capability
H245: | | | | | H.261A Video Packetization = 0 (FALSE)
H245: | | Capability Table[0]
H245: | | | Capability Table Entry
H245: | | | | Capability Table Entry Number = 1
H245: | | | | Capability = Receive Audio Capability
H245: | | | | | Audio Capability = G.711 Ulaw 64k -- Parameter = 60
H245: | | Capability Table[1]
H245: | | | Capability Table Entry
H245: | | | | Capability Table Entry Number = 2
H245: | | | | Capability = Receive Video Capability
H245: | | | | | H.261 Video Capability
H245: | | | | | | QCIF MPI = 1 (1/29.97 Hz)
H245: | | | | | | Temporal Spatial Trade Off Capability = 0 (FALSE)
H245: | | | | | | Max Bit Rate = 7600 (100 bits/s)
H245: | | | | | | Still Image Transmission = 0 (FALSE)
H245: | | Capability Table[2]
H245: | | | Capability Table Entry
H245: | | | | Capability Table Entry Number = 3
H245: | | | | Capability = Receive Audio Capability
H245: | | | | | Audio Capability = G.711 Alaw 64k -- Parameter = 60
H245: | | Capability Table[3]
H245: | | | Capability Table Entry
H245: | | | | Capability Table Entry Number = 4
H245: | | | | Capability = Receive Audio Capability
H245: | | | | | Audio Capability = G.728 -- Parameter = 60
H245: | | Capability Table[4]
H245: | | | Capability Table Entry
H245: | | | | Capability Table Entry Number = 5
H245: | | | | Capability = Receive Video Capability
H245: | | | | | H.261 Video Capability
H245: | | | | | | CIF MPI = 1 (1/29.97 Hz)
H245: | | | | | | Temporal Spatial Trade Off Capability = 0 (FALSE)
H245: | | | | | | Max Bit Rate = 7600 (100 bits/s)
H245: | | | | | | Still Image Transmission = 0 (FALSE)
```

FIGURE 1.16 H.245 Terminal Capability Set (2)

restrictions in the media stream, multipoint capabilities for conferencing, and the terminal's simultaneous capabilities. The ACK messages simply confirm the Set messages were received by the respective endpoints and no conflicts were encountered. They also carry the Master/Slave resolution.

Once the capabilities have been exchanged and the Master/Slave relationship has been determined, Phase B is complete and we are ready to start opening logical channels for media transport.

```
H245: | | Capability Descriptors[0]
H245: | | | Capability Descriptor Number = 0
H245: | | | Simultaneous Capabilities[0]
H245: | | | | Alternative Capability Set[0]
H245: | | | | | Capability Table Entry Number = 1
H245: | | | | Alternative Capability Set[1]
H245: | | | | | Capability Table Entry Number = 3
H245: | | | | Alternative Capability Set[2]
H245: | | | | | Capability Table Entry Number = 4
H245: | | | Simultaneous Capabilities[1]
H245: | | | | Alternative Capability Set[0]
H245: | | | | | Capability Table Entry Number = 2
H245: | | | | Alternative Capability Set[1]
H245: | | | | | Capability Table Entry Number = 5
```

FIGURE 1.17 H.245 Terminal Capability Set (3)

```
H245: Packet Length = 11
H245: Multimedia System Control Message Type = Request
H245: | Request Type = Master Slave Determination
H245: | | Terminal Type = 30
H245: | | Status Determination Number = 100342
```

FIGURE 1.18 H.245 Master/Slave Determination (via terminal type identification)

Phase C begins with either party sending an H.245 OpenLogicalChannel message. Logical channels in H.323 are unidirectional (half-duplex), and therefore a channel must be opened in each direction for two-way communication.

The H.245 message contains information shown in Figure 1.19 and shows data type and multiplex parameters, such as selection of G.728 audio with 60 ms delay and the UDP port set to 5005.

One or more logical channels can be opened simultaneously using attributes from the terminal capability set that was exchanged previously. Hopefully the attributes selected by each terminal will result in bandwidth utilization within the limits of the initial RAS admission request exchange with the gatekeeper. If not, Phase D procedures take effect as shown in the call flow, whereby the receiving endpoint will do a bandwidth request (BCR) RAS exchange with the GK. If the GK can honor the request, a BCF will be returned, but the logical channel that created the bandwidth discrepancy will need to be closed and re-opened with the new multiplex parameters. If there is no bandwidth discrepancy, Phase D need not be invoked, and at the end of the OpenLogicalChannel message exchanges, media will flow on the UDP ports selected by those messages. Phase D call services also include status updates, ad hoc conference expansion from an MC point-to-point conference to multipoint, supplementary services, multipoint cascading and third party

```
------------    H245 Header   ------------
H245: Packet Length = 23
H245: Multimedia System Control Message Type = Request
H245: | Request Type = Open Logical Channel
H245: | | Logical Channel Number = 1
H245: | | Forward Logical Channel Parameters
H245: | | | Data Type = Audio Data
H245: | | | | Audio Capability = G.728 -- Parameter = 60
H245: | | | Multiplex Parameters
H245: | | | | H.225.0 Logical Channel Parameters
H245: | | | | | Session ID = 1
H245: | | | | | Media Control Channel
H245: | | | | | | Transport Address Type = Unicast Address
H245: | | | | | | Address Type = IP Address
H245: | | | | | | | Address = 10.0.0.10
H245: | | | | | | | Port = 5005
```

FIGURE 1.19 H.245 Open Logical Channel

rerouting. Such features are useful for announcements that may precede completion of a call, such as those we often hear when we dial into an area served by a PBX.

We have finally arrived at mid-call in H.323.

Call termination is handled in Phase E in the life of a call. Either party can send an H.245 CloseLogicalChannel command, which will close the video, data and audio channels. This command is then followed by an end-SessionCommand, after which the endpoint will not send any more H.245 signaling messages. The receiving endpoint will also send a CloseLogical-Channel command to close the logical channels in the other directions (remember, H.323 channels are half-duplex!), and as soon the respective CloseLogicalChannel ACK messages have been exchanged, an H.225.0 RELEASE COMPLETE command is sent by the disconnecting endpoint, and the call is terminated.

In the Phase E call flow of Figure 1.20, we show the calling endpoint having been registered with its gatekeeper, to demonstrate the use of the DisengageRequest (DRQ) RAS command. The DRQ command informs the GK that the endpoint is being dropped. DRQs cannot be sent between endpoints, and this command cannot be used in place of the RELEASE COMPLETE command. The GK may reject the DRQ with a DRJ, if the endpoint was not registered in the first place.

Conferencing Capabilities and Methods

So far we have seen the direct routed call model for H.323 point-to-point calls. H.323 provides extensive support for conferencing, which is as robust

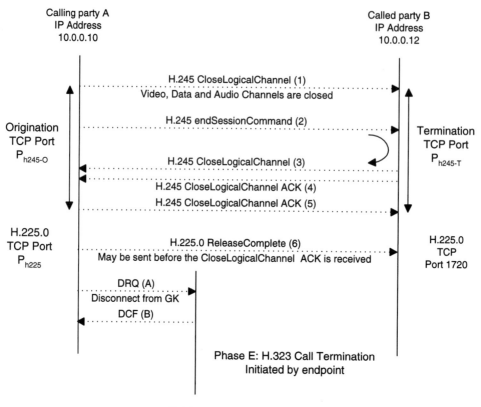

FIGURE 1.20 H.323 Call Termination (Phase E)

as it is complex, and we now discuss a basic conference call setup using the gatekeeper routed call model.

The basic call signaling process starts in very much the same way as if it were a point-to-point, two-party call. The call flow is shown in Figure 1.21. For purposes of simplicity we will assume the GK possesses an MCU, so that call redirection is not necessary to complete the conference call. Otherwise, the call is directed to the MCU of the GK's choice and the call flow resumes normally with the MCU handling call signaling. The conference call in the example flow starts as a two party call, and later a third party joins in.

During Phase A, the originating endpoint invites user B, through B's or A's gatekeeper (depending on if they are in the same zone or not, and if either, or both use gatekeepers). In the SETUP message, the caller inserts a conference ID and indicates *Create* in the message. The called party acknowledges the call setup, and by the end of Phase B we have media flow-

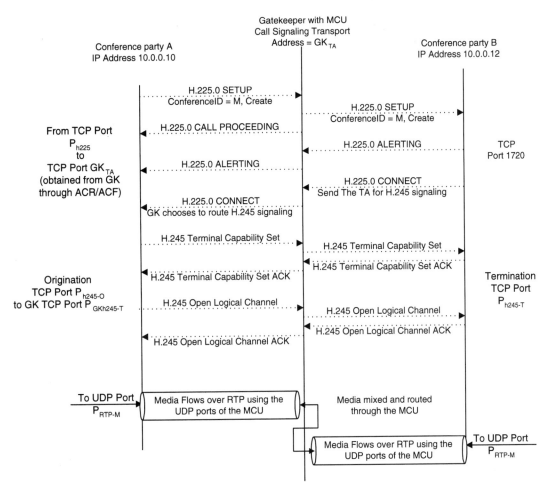

Phase A

FIGURE 1.21 H.323 Gatekeeper Routed Conference Call Model, Initiation

ing over the transport address of the MCU that has been designated to handle the call (the GK may have one or more MCUs). At this point this is a simple call and the MCU is performing null mixing, until a third party decides to join the conference, as shown in Figure 1.22.

When party C sends a SETUP message to endpoint B, it includes the conference ID it wants to join, and indicates *Join* in the message. Endpoint B cannot grant this request because it does not have a MCU, so it declines the offer with an H.225.0 FACILITY message, indicating *routeCallToMC*. This would have also been the case had endpoint C dialed into a GK without MCU

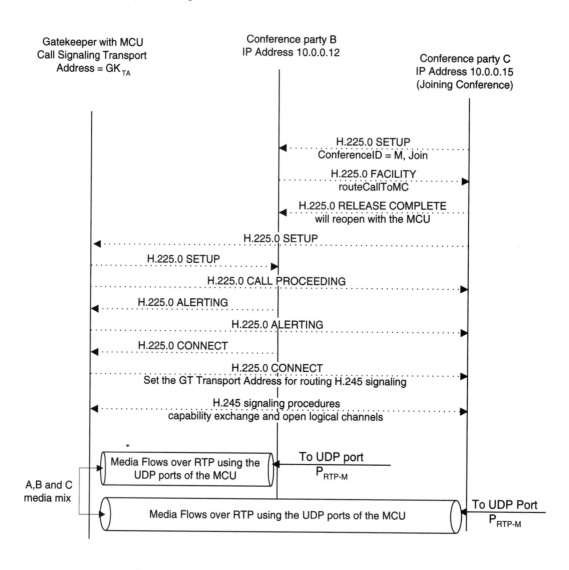

Phase A

FIGURE 1.22 H.323 Conference Call Model, Third Party Joins the Call

capabilities. The FACILITY message causes sending of RELEASE COMPLETE by the calling endpoint, and re-initiation of the call attempt using the transport address parameter returned in the FACILITY message.

Signaling through the GK handling the conference now proceeds as in the case of the original two parties who joined in the call. The H.245 transport address supplied is the same as the one used by the original two endpoints, and the embedded MCU in the GK performs mixing and switching of the media stream to all parties.

A party already in a conference can invite a third party to join in by sending a SETUP command with the *Invite* indication and the correct conference ID. The call flow then proceeds as in the other cases.

In unicast mode, transport addresses are exchanged between the calling endpoints and the MCU in H.245 signaling (openLogicalChannel). However, when multicast mode is used for conferencing, the MCU is responsible for multicast address distribution to the endpoints, using the *communicationModeCommand* of H.245.

H.323 QoS – RSVP

An endpoint requesting admission by a gatekeeper can indicate its ability to reserve resources in the ARQ RAS message, using the *transportQoS* field. H.323 specifies the RSVP protocol as the mechanism for providing QoS control of calls. We discuss RSVP in Chapter 2, but it is important to note that RSVP reservations can be made only by network elements directly on the media path of the call. This places a requirement on the endpoints to support RSVP in order to attempt to control the path of the media flow during call setup. RSVP is not ubiquitous, which leaves H.323 without a solid mechanism to control the quality of the media stream. This is a generic issue for the new VoIP call signaling protocols and is not unique to H.323.

Monitoring of QoS is accomplished with the help of RTCP, but the RTCP information is communicated only between endpoints in the call. Use of RTCP data to make inferences about QoS is not reliable because of the sometimes low bandwidth allocated to RTCP signaling. Real implementations use other means such as SNMP to collect performance data, and the diagnostic data obtained can be correlated with RTCP to reach accurate conclusions about the performance of the network and its individual elements.

Telephony Features

Common telephony features include services we can purchase from our local carrier, such as call forwarding, call waiting, three-way calling, call trace, etc. All these and many more telephony features are supported in today's "dumb" TDM network, but the "smart" packet signaling protocols and implementations are still lagging in this area. The reason is the origin of packet telephony was in the enterprise network and the Internet after that, where customer demand for Class 5 and Intelligent Network call features was not a priority.

H.323 allows for call re-direction, using the FACILITY Message of H.225.0 and the *alternativeAddress* field. More telephony features are supported through the implementation of supplementary services.

Protocol Failures, Robustness, and Reliability

The use of TCP for transporting H.245 signaling has serious implications for reliability. The transport protocol is very reliable, but if the TCP connection is lost, the call will be torn down by the endpoints. This is an interesting issue, because in mid-call there is no call-control signaling taking place between the communicating endpoints, so a failure not associated with any part of H.323 can cause the calls to be dropped.

The method for terminating a call in the case of a lost TCP connection is the same as if any of the parties had intentionally disconnected from the call. H.225.0 also uses a different TCP connection, which creates other interesting scenarios when the call signaling channel is lost but the media control channel is still alive. Sometimes an attempt to re-establish the broken TCP connection can be made, if it is detected by the GK, followed by a status request. If the endpoint detects the broken TCP connection, it can choose to drop the call or try to re-establish the call signaling channel with the GK, or endpoint, depending on the call signaling routing model.

In practice, TCP connections are broken because of timeouts and failure to exchange keepalive messages due to some link layer failure, or equipment malfunction. Since both TCP connections for signaling originated at the same endpoint, it is likely both will be lost more often, rather than just one of them. So, it is a good guess that failure to keep the TCP connections up in a reliable manner will result in dropped calls.

Performance Issues, Scalability, and Comparisons

Call setup in H.323 did not attempt to make sure there was a media path before it declared the call completed. There can be a very complex network between the endpoints, even in the same zone and domain, and even in the enterprise. Thus, the GK is fairly oblivious to QoS issues arising from the user experience in a call. RTCP conveys QoS information between endpoints, but there is no consistent mechanism to signal to the GK any issues that may come up. Furthermore, the call signaling model may be direct routed and the GK may be out of the picture for the duration of the call, after it is established.

One thing that is hard to determine in the new generation of packet signaling protocols is the voice quality experienced by the users in an end-to-end connection. If the call spans zones and domains, or touches the PSTN, it is likely there will be voice transcoding at the domain boundaries, which will reduce the voice quality. In a scenario of a call between two packet domains across the PSTN, there will be instances of possibly two transcodings and significant delay due to the need for de-jitter buffering to connect the dissimilar domains at the boundaries. Therefore, even a modest 60 ms request for end-to-end delay may not be achievable in the general case. VoIP is susceptible to quality degradation due to excessive delays, which accumulate quickly even in networks of modest size.

H.245 offers a method for determining the health of endpoints in a call. An endpoint can send a *roundTripDelayRequest* H.245 message, to find out if the connection is still alive. The remote endpoint will send *roundTripDelayResponse*, with the same sequence number, from which a rough estimate of round trip times for the signaling channel can be estimated. This number is not associated with the media round trip delay except in the direct routed signaling model, and includes queuing and computational delays, which can range in the tens of milliseconds. Therefore, using this quantity for estimating the round trip delay for media flow can lead to erroneous conclusions. H.323 also offers the capability to place a logical channel in loopback mode for diagnostic purposes, using the *mediaLoop* command.

The direct signaling call model can scale sufficiently within reasonable size domains, but the GK routed model scales as well as the GK itself. Any time centralized signaling is implemented the issue of scalability comes up, and for moderate and larger H.323 signaling topologies, distributed network implementations of the GK may be necessary to handle scaling of the endpoint population. A distributed implementation of the GK would involve modular expansion of the computing capabilities of the GK to handle capacity increases while keeping call signaling delays invariant. This is very important because of the need to support MC-based conferencing, which by its nature requires centralized call signaling.

In supporting media transport with invariant QoS as the population increases, H.323 suffers from the scaling shortcomings of RSVP. However, as we mentioned earlier, this is not unique to H.323. When we have discussed the Session Initiation Protocol, we will also see some of the intriguing functional differences between text-based and binary call signaling, among the major three contending signaling protocols.

The Fast Connect Procedure

The reader must be convinced by now that H.323 call signaling is complex, and complex signaling requires computational power, which in turn takes time to execute at an endpoint or its server. The result is a rather high post dial delay for even simple H.323 calls. This has been recognized by the ITU, and in version 2 of the protocol,[5] a faster method to get going with the call establishment appeared. It is referred to as *fastStart*, and offers significant improvement over the standard call setup method we have discussed so far.

The fastStart procedure cuts down the time needed to set up a call to one round-trip delay, after the basic H.225.0 TCP connection has been set up. The idea is to include a series of *openLogicalChannel* structures in the UUIE of the SETUP command, with all the parameters necessary for the logical channel to be opened in one step. The logical channels represent "suggestions" to the called end, from which the called end can pick the one(s) that suit it best. If the remote endpoint supports *fastStart*, it also returns a *fastStart* with the CONNECT message, otherwise the endpoints revert to the standard H.245 logical channel signaling procedures that we discussed earlier. If the remote endpoint decides to go ahead with *fastStart*, it returns the logical channel parameters it wants to use in the ALERTING, CALL PROCEEDING, or more likely the CONNECT message. Called endpoints are not supposed to initiate *fastStart*, unless they received a *fastStart* from the calling endpoint.

The calling endpoint must be prepared to receive media stream as soon as it sends a *fastStart*, just in case the command is accepted by the called endpoint. This is important to note, because the caller must be ready to receive on ANY of the logical channels it proposed to the remote endpoint. Therefore, software associated with transport addresses of the logical channels in a terminal must all be set up and ready prior to sending *fastStart*.

H245 signaling procedures can be invoked at any time after *fastStart*, but once they are invoked they remain in effect until the call is terminated. Call termination using *fastStart* is accomplished with a single RELEASE COMPLETE message. If H.245 procedures had been invoked, the standard Phase E completion process is used. The *fastStart* approach will be seen in the context of mixed network signaling in the next section.

H.323 Call Establishment in a Mixed Network Topology

For calls originating and terminating within one H.323 zone, H.225.0 signaling is sufficient to initiate call setup, with H.245 performing the bearer negotiation of capabilities for all endpoints participating in the call. However, life is rarely this simple, and in most cases protocol mapping may be necessary for terminals implementing H.323 signaling to be able to dial users on non-H.323-capable terminals, or plain old telephones across the PSTN.

A further complexity is introduced by the potential implementation approach of the gatekeeper. There are obvious architectural similarities

---

5.   Version 3 of the H.323 protocol was not ready when this text was created. H.323 is moving towards a more streamlined operation which will make it a difficult protocol to compete against, with its rich functionality and large installed base.

between a gatekeeper and a media gateway controller (MGC), and the natural temptation in some cases would be to combine the functionality of an H.323 gatekeeper with the functionality of a media gateway controller, which may be based on the IETF MEGACO protocol, or S/MGCP. The result would be a reference diagram similar to the one shown in Figure 1.23.

The Media Gateway Controller supports all the necessary signaling protocols to allow for H.323-capable terminals to set up calls with S/MGCP endpoints and POTS telephones. The call flows that apply to this topology are simultaneously the most generic and broad in the detail required to support IP-based telephony. There are several performance issues associated with this topology and the types of backbone networks used to transport signaling and bearer channels, which we are discussing in general terms in this chapter. But first, we will look at some of the idiosyncrasies of H.323, H.225.0, and H.245, and see how they can be used in conjunction with other signaling protocols in a single heterogeneous zone and across a backbone network.

In Figure 1.24 we construct a call flow between a H.323-capable terminal and an endpoint signaled to via S/MGCP by the MGC. We assume a single MGC connects to the Media Gateway and an H.323 gateway[6] on the signaling plane and supports both signaling protocols. The necessary mapping between protocol stacks is performed transparently to any type of terminal or endpoint.

In this scenario, the user at the Media Gateway wishes to dial a user at an H.323-capable terminal. The call agent has primed the RGW endpoint to look for Off-Hook (RQNT (1)) and when the user goes off-hook, digits are collected ((3) through (10)), and a half-duplex connection is established with the originating endpoint. In steps (11) through (14a), the call agent opens a TCP connection with the remote endpoint[7] and performs a RAS signaling admission request (ARQ), to which it receives *AdmissionConfirm* (ACF), with a direct call signaling option. Using direct call signaling option the two endpoints complete the setup of the call. The GW functional portion of the GK acts as an endpoint for the call, proxying and translating signaling for the user at the RGW.

It should be noted here that other RAS messages could be exchanged between the GKs, for instance bandwidth request (BRQ), to which the GK could respond with bandwidth confirm (BCF). The parameters of the ARQ message are numerous, but the most important ones are the call type, call

---

6.   The gateway functionality could be implemented as an integral part of the MGC device, either in a central or distributed design.

7.   This connection may be internal to the same server, if a single box is used to be the MGC and GW server functions in a domain which is also an H.323 zone. In distributed implementations, the TCP connection is external and between the two servers.

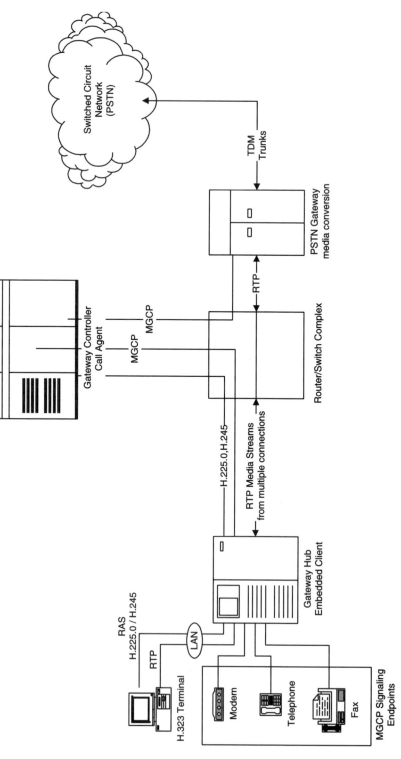

FIGURE 1.23 Composite Reference Diagram for Mixed H.323 and S/MGCP Signaling

60

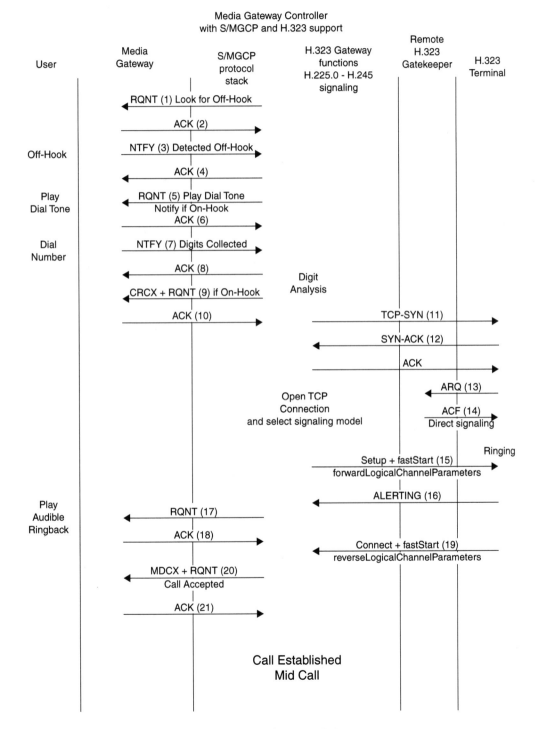

FIGURE 1.24 Media Gateway to H.323 Signaling for Call Establishment

model, the requested bandwidth of the connection, and the transport QoS. The call type refers to point-to-point or multipoint, the call model could be either direct between the two endpoints or routed through the gatekeeper, the bandwidth is the initially requested bandwidth, and the QoS is an indication of the endpoint's ability to reserve resources for supplying deterministic QoS.

The gateway then sends an H.225.0 SETUP message directly to the endpoint, which contains the *fastStart* option in the User-to-User Information Element. H.225.0 call SETUP defines the use of the UUIE Information Element (IE) to facilitate signaling operations specific to the H.323 protocol. Signaling using *fastStart* was discussed earlier in this section.

The ALERTING message is sent by the endpoint as an indication that it is in alerting mode, that is the virtual "phone" at the H.323 endpoint is ringing. Once ALERTING is received by the call agent from the H.323 gateway side, it instructs the S/MGCP endpoint to play ringback (steps (13) and (14)). The ringback is the audible ring we hear when the remote phone is ringing, but with the S/MGCP protocols it is possible to generate audible ringback locally via a command from the call agent to the MG endpoint.

When the called user "picks up," a CONNECT with *fastStart* option is sent to the gateway (step (15)), which causes a protocol exchange on the S/MGCP side to convert the connection to full duplex with an MDCX command (step (16)), and perform the bearer stream cut-through. The MDCX command can have piggybacked notification requests (RQNT), as shown in the call flow. At that time both users can hear each other and we have arrived at mid-call.

Call termination is simple and is shown in Figure 1.25. In this case the calling party went on-hook first. Steps (1) through (4) show the notification of the on-hook event to the MGC, and the subsequent deletion of the connection (DLCX). The MGC signals to the endpoint a RELEASE COMPLETE to terminate the call. The *ReleaseCompleteReason* code in the release complete message indicates normal completion (user went on-hook). The remote H.323 gateway then sends a disengagement request (DRQ) and receives disengagement confirm (DCF). This signals to the gatekeeper that the endpoint is being dropped, and it is followed by the closing of the TCP connection.

Messages of the H.225.0 Protocol

Call control messages are sent over TCP connections as we have seen. H.225.0 supports a Q.931/Q.932 message subset, which is listed in Table 1.11 for reference. The call establishment phase follows the procedures of the Circuit Mode Connection Control of I.451/Q.931. The discussion on messages, information elements and their use is informative only. The ITU specifications contain the exact definition and encoding of the messages.

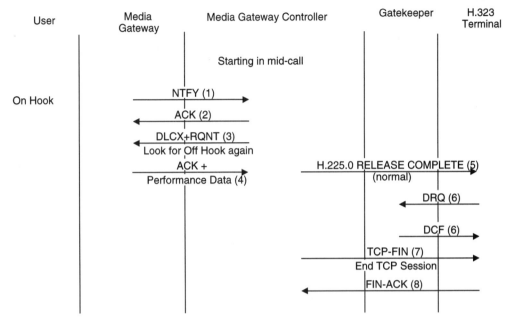

FIGURE 1.25 RGW to H.323 Call Termination

TABLE 1.11 H.225.0 Message Set

Q.931/Q.932 MESSAGE	TX SUPPORT	RX SUPPORT	SIGNIFICANCE
Alerting	M	M	Global
Call Proceeding	O	Conditional	Local
Connect	M	M	Global
Connect Acknowledge	Not Allowed	Not Allowed	N/A
Progress	O	O	Global
Setup	M	M	Global
Setup Acknowledge	O	O	Local
Disconnect	Not Allowed	Not Allowed	
Release	Not Allowed	Not Allowed	

TABLE 1.11 H.225.0 Message Set (Continued)

Q.931/Q.932 MESSAGE	TX SUPPORT	RX SUPPORT	SIGNIFICANCE
Release Complete	M	M	Local
Resume	Not Allowed	Not Allowed	N/A
Resume Acknowledge	Not Allowed	Not Allowed	N/A
Resume Reject	Not Allowed	Not Allowed	N/A
Suspend	Not Allowed	Not Allowed	N/A
Suspend Acknowledge	Not Allowed	Not Allowed	N/A
Suspend Reject	Not Allowed	Not Allowed	N/A
User Information	O	O	Endpoints only
Congestion Control	Not Allowed	Not Allowed	N/A
Information	O	O	Local
Notify	O	O	Access Endpoints
Status	M	M	Local
Status Inquiry	O	M	Local
Facility	M	M	Local
Hold	Not Allowed	Not Allowed	N/A
Hold Acknowledge	Not Allowed	Not Allowed	N/A
Hold Reject	Not Allowed	Not Allowed	N/A
Retrieve	Not Allowed	Not Allowed	N/A
Retrieve Acknowledge	Not Allowed	Not Allowed	N/A
Retrieve Reject	Not Allowed	Not Allowed	N/A
Legend: O = Optional, M = Mandatory.			

The RAS Protocol

We have seen some of the functions of the RAS (Registration, Admission, and Status) protocol already in the context of call flows. RAS is a straightforward protocol used by endpoints to register with a gatekeeper for the purposes of call setup with a H.323 endpoint.

RAS provides functionality that is missing from the signaling capabilities of H.225.0. H.225.0 uses a subset of Q.931 messages, which have their roots in the TDM PSTN network As such, services such as user identification and authentication, terminal capabilities, alias naming, dynamic bandwidth requirements, and management functions are not possible with H.225.0 call signaling. RAS fills the capability void between H.225.0 call signaling and H.245 logical channel control in H.323. As a comparison, the SIP signaling protocol offers RAS-type capabilities as an integral part of the protocol specification.

Most RAS transactions involve one round-trip message exchange with the gatekeeper. Remember, presence of a gatekeeper in a network is not mandatory. However, if a gatekeeper is present, all endpoints need to use its services. Gatekeepers provide call-control signaling (proxy signaling) for the endpoints, or simple call signaling routing between the endpoints. The mode is selected at the time an *AdmissionRequest* (ARQ) message is sent from the endpoint to the GK, as we saw already. Note that an endpoint need not necessarily refer to a physical endpoint. Terminals, servers, and gateways present multiple endpoints to a gatekeeper, each of which executes the procedures of the RAS protocol to set up calls in the gatekeeper's zone. A computer terminal serving multiple users could present multiple endpoints to the GK and other signaling entities in the network.

The basic services defined by RAS are address translation, admission control, bandwidth request, and management functions in the gatekeeper's zone. The annotated set of RAS messages are shown in Table 1.12.

A Few Words on RAS Timers

RAS specifies a general timeout value of three seconds for every message, except GRQ and LRQ. The GRQ and LRQ recommended timeouts are five seconds. Retry counts for each message are set to two seconds, except for URQ and IRQ, which is set to one.

Long timeout values and high retry counts affect call setup performance and can hinder a gatekeeper's ability to handle large numbers of endpoints, especially in a distributed implementation. The RIP message allows the flexibility to endpoints to "tell" the GK what the expected time for producing the desired response would be. When the requested response becomes available, the endpoint sends it to the GK immediately. This type of deferred response

TABLE 1.12 RAS Protocol Messages

RAS MESSAGE	ENDPOINT TX SUPPORT	ENDPOINT RX SUPPORT	GK TX SUPPORT	GK RX SUPPORT	NOTES
GRQ	O			M	*Gatekeeper Request.* Any GK receiving this message please confirm.
GCF		O	M		*Gatekeeper Confirm.* The GK responding identifies itself.
GRJ		O	M		*Gatekeeper Reject.* Reason is included.
RRQ	M			M	*Registration Request.*
RCF		M	M		*Registration Confirm.*
RRJ		M	M		*Registration Reject.* Reason is included.
URQ	O	M	O	M	*Unregistration Request.* The terminal wishes to break its connection to the GK.
UCF	M	O	M	O	*Unregistration Confirm.*
URJ	O	O	M	O	*Unregistration Reject.* Reason is included.
ARQ	M			M	*Admission Request.*
ACF		M	M		*Admission Confirm.*
ARJ		M	M		*Admission Reject.* Reason is included.
BRQ	M	M	O	M	*Bandwidth Request.*
BCF	M	M	M	O	*Bandwidth Confirm.*

TABLE 1.12 RAS Protocol Messages (Continued)

RAS MESSAGE	ENDPOINT TX SUPPORT	ENDPOINT RX SUPPORT	GK TX SUPPORT	GK RX SUPPORT	NOTES
BRJ	M	M	M	O	*Bandwidth Reject.* Reason is included.
IRQ	M	M	M		*Information Request.*
IRR	M			M	*Information Response.*
IACK		O	Conditional		Sent if the IRR requested an Acknowledgement, and the result was positive.*
INAK		O	Conditional		Sent if the IRR requested an Acknowledgement, and the result was negative.
DRQ	M	M	O	M	*Disengage Request.* Informs the GK that an endpoint is being disconnected and the call is being dropped (if one had been active).
DCF	M	M	M	M	*Disengage Confirm.*
DRJ	M	M	M	M	*Disengage Reject.* Sent by the GK if the named endpoint was not registered with this GK in the first place.
LRQ	O		O	M	*Location Request.* The GK is asked to provide the transport address of the destination endpoint.
LCF		O	M	O	*Location Confirm.* Returns transport address of the called endpoint.

67

TABLE 1.12 RAS Protocol Messages (Continued)

RAS MESSAGE	ENDPOINT TX SUPPORT	ENDPOINT RX SUPPORT	GK TX SUPPORT	GK RX SUPPORT	NOTES
LRJ	O	O	M	O	*Location Reject.* Reason is included, probably can't find the endpoint.
NSM	O	O	O	O	*Non-Standard Message.* Carries data not defined in Recommendation H.225.0.
XRS	M	M	M	M	*Unknown Message Response.* Sent by an endpoint whenever it receives a message it does not understand.
RIP	Conditional	M	Conditional	M	*Request in Progress.* This message is sent by an endpoint if the actual response to a message cannot be generated prior to the expiration of the RAS timer for the message.
RAI	O			M	*Resource Availability Indication.* Sent by a gateway to a GK to signal its capacity for each H-series protocol and corresponding data rates for the protocol.
RAC		O	M		*Resource Availability Confirm.* The GK's response to RAI.

* IACK and INAK applies IRRs sent to gatekeepers of version 2 or higher, with the needResponse Boolean field set TRUE.

gives an idea to the GK as to the magnitude of message execution delays it will be dealing with in the zone.

As a design practice, protocol timeouts and retries should not be part of procedural mainstream signaling operation. In other words, the expected signaling process between endpoints, gatekeepers and gateways should not include the use of retries and timeouts for normal operation, but it should be an exception to be looked at by the network administrators for possible reasons for the degradation of system performance.

1.4 SIP—SUMMARY OF FEATURES OF THE SESSION INITIATION PROTOCOL

The Session Initiation Protocol (RFC2543) is a text-based signaling protocol used for creating and controlling multimedia sessions with two or more participants. It is one of the three major contending signaling protocols for VoIP services[8] and has been adopted in substantial implementations. In simple terms:

> SIP is a client-server protocol transported over either TCP or UDP, but the most common implementations use SIP over UDP for simplicity and speed.

SIP sessions include multimedia conferences or simple telephone calls and can be unicast or multicast. Sessions can be set up among parties in an enterprise network, or across multiple network segments, as long as there is reachability of the segments over IP. Parties can be invited to new sessions or to join existing ones. Sessions may be advertised with other means, such as the Session Announcement Protocol. SIP is a much simpler protocol than H.323, but is at least as functional, and draws its roots from earlier text protocols such as HTTP.

Topology diagrams of networks using SIP signaling are very similar to those for S/MGCP and H.323. The network in Figure 1.26 shows two domains connected via a routing cloud, each implementing SIP signaling. We will see the basic call models in the context of this diagram, which looks very similar to the one we saw in the discussion of H.323.

Like its other two competitors, SIP can interwork with gateways that provide signaling protocol and media translation across dissimilar network seg-

---

8.   The others being S/MGCP and H.323.

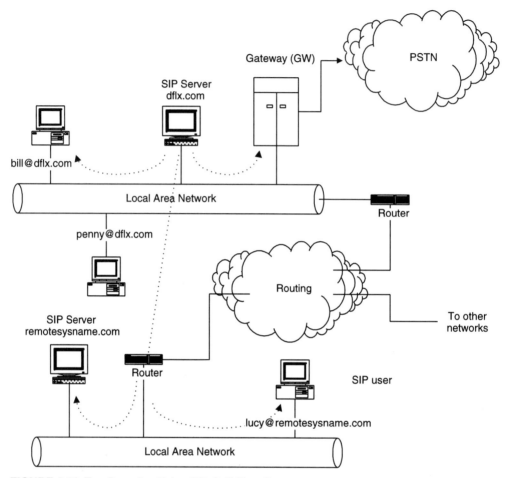

FIGURE 1.26 Two Domains Using SIP Call Signaling

ments. Such segments can be the PSTN with its SS7/ISUP signaling and TDM trunks, S/MGCP domains, or H.323 zones. The possible permutations of signaling protocol interworkings have been implemented in some form or another in the last few years, but there is still much to be learned from network and service deployments. H.323 has found by far the most widespread adoption thanks to its success in Internet telephony, but it is not necessarily the front-runner in telephony service deployment in the public network. SIP has major performance, flexibility, and scalability merits, and is considered a viable contender for major signaling applications, including call control for carrier-quality VoIP telephony in the public network. S/MGCP is also a major contender in the VoIP public network through the NCS standard used in telephony service offerings over cable.

SIP supports features of the Advanced Intelligent Network (AIN), such as name mapping, call forwarding and call redirection. This is very useful if SIP is to gain acceptance as a signaling protocol in the public network, where telephony feature offering is major part of the business of telephone companies. Another significant feature of SIP is support for user mobility. One loose definition of mobility is the ability of users to access their subscribed capabilities from any terminal and any location, and the network's ability to identify and authenticate users as they move from location to location. This concept is not new, and is supported to a large degree with H.323. Cellular telephone users have enjoyed this (expensive) roaming feature for years, and now it appears to have momentum to become a major attraction of the next generation of VoIP networks. This type of operation will require some kind of remote user login to a service node for purposes of identification and authentication. In this section we examine SIP in the context of examples using its basic call models, and offer explanations and comparisons with the other major contenders where applicable. But first we need to take a look at some protocol fundamentals.

SIP System Elements and Features

A SIP system consists of user agents (UA) and one or more servers. SIP systems can be either dedicated network segments, network segments connected across the public Internet, or logical groupings of devices in enterprise networks that also support other IP signaling protocols. For example, it is not unthinkable for SIP clients and servers to operate on LAN segments which also accommodate H.323 and/or S/MGCP endpoints. Naturally, users at endpoints implementing one type of call signaling protocol cannot call users of other types, unless there is protocol interworking available somewhere in the network. This is one of the features that can be offered by integrated servers in new environments, but the technology has not yet matured, due to several factors. One factor is the success and penetration of H.323 applications. Another factor is the targeting of the streamlined text-based protocols toward basic telephony services on the public network. It is unlikely H.323 and text-based protocols will co-exist in a telephony service offering from the same carrier. The more likely scenario is for each carrier to make a protocol choice and the winner to take all for the carrier's new service offerings.

SIP servers can operate as *proxy* or *redirect* services. Proxy servers execute call signaling on behalf of the parties they serve. Redirect servers determine the current location of the called party and instruct the calling party to initiate signaling with the called party directly. Both call signaling concepts are similar to H.323 gatekeeper-routed and direct-routed models, respectively. In both cases the servers search for the current location of the user, and in the case of the redirect call model they inform the calling party of the called party's current location.

Following are the five key aspects of SIP for facilitation of call establishment and maintenance in summary form:

1. **Call setup:** SIP is self-contained in setting up point-to-point and multipoint conferences as well as simple calls.

2. **User location services:** Users have the ability to move to other locations and access their telephony features from remote locations. This is the service equivalent provided by RAS in H.323.

3. **User capabilities:** Determination of the media and media parameters to be used. SIP uses the SDP protocol format for negotiating media parameters, much like S/MGCP. H.323 uses the H.245 signaling mechanism.

4. **User availability:** Determination of the willingness of the called party to engage in communications. SIP defines very explicit response codes to provide detailed information about a user's current availability.

5. **Call handling:** Includes transfer of an established call, telephony call features and simple termination of calls. This is important for telephony services in the public network.

SIP uses uniform resource locators (URLs) to identify the source, current destination, ultimate destination, and specify redirection (forwarding) addresses. The email-style name encoding of the format bill.douskalis@dflx.com can be host-dependent or independent. UDP port numbers can be included in the URL. The well-known UDP port for SIP is 5060.

SIP signaling functionality and proper operation of the protocol does not depend on other protocols such as RSVP, RT(C)P, or RTSP (Real Time Streaming Protocol) used for establishing multimedia conferences, QoS control and signaling. However, malfunctions at the media transport level or the system hardware affect the overall system operation. The involvement of SIP to detect and report exceptions is largely implementation dependent. In several cases the use of diagnostic reporting mechanisms such as SNMP are implemented, and they operate in parallel with SIP.

Like the other two protocol contenders, SIP also specifies the use of RTP for media transport and RTCP for monitoring the quality of calls and gathering important statistical data. The data produced by RTCP can be made available to the server through design considerations of the signaling platform.

SIP Signaling Methodology

SIP uses six methods for signaling that are shown in Table 1.13. They are INVITE, ACK, OPTIONS, BYE, CANCEL, and REGISTER. Other methods have been proposed in the IETF working groups, reflecting knowledge acquired from actual implementations, but have not been adopted in RFC status at this time.

TABLE 1.13 SIP Methods

SIP METHODS	
INVITE	This is the first message sent by the calling party in the call processing cycle. It contains information in the SIP header, which identifies the calling party, call-ID, called party, call sequence number, among other things (see SIP header definition). Basically, it indicates a call is being initiated. It can be sent during a call to modify the call's operating state (e.g., place a party on hold). The INVITE message usually contains an SDP description of the call parameter, such as media type and transport addresses. When a multiple choice of SDP parameters is offered, the ones chosen are returned with the success (200) code in the response message.
ACK	The calling agent responds with ACK only to INVITE requests that have been successfully accepted with a 200 code. ACK indicates the calling party has received confirmation to an INVITE request. The body of the ACK message may contain the SDP description of the media type capability of the called party. If the success response contained no SDP description, the session description parameters of the initial INVITE message are used for the media connection.
OPTIONS	This message is sent to query the capabilities a call agent. This is a nice tool for determining which media types a remote user supports before placing a call.
BYE	The client sends this message to the call agent to release the call. The sending endpoint terminates media flow and considers the call terminated regardless of a response from the far end. A return BYE from the other party is not necessary.
CANCEL	This method cancels a request in progress, but has no effect on an established call when no requests are in progress. The CANCEL method must explicitly identify the call via the Call ID, Call Sequence (Cseq), To and From values in the SIP header.
REGISTER	A client uses the REGISTER method to register the address listed in the To header field with a SIP server. A user agent may register with a local server on startup by sending a REGISTER request to the well-known "all SIP servers" multicast address "sip.mcast.net" (224.0.1.75). Registration can be done by the user or by a third party on behalf of the user. This will be shown in the From field.

Before we look at specifics of the SIP message headers and response messages, let's look at the basic call models supported by the protocol. I hope this approach makes it a little easier to understand header description and response code details.

The SIP Call Model

Let's look at a call made by penny@dflx.com to lucy@remotesysname.com in our reference diagram. The call flow for the most basic call model is shown in Figure 1.27. In the first example, the user agents operate directly and an INVITE command is sent from the originator (penny@dflx.com) to the called party (lucy@remotesysname.com). This means the user agent for penny@dflx.com (endpoint A) has resolved the name of lucy@remotesys-

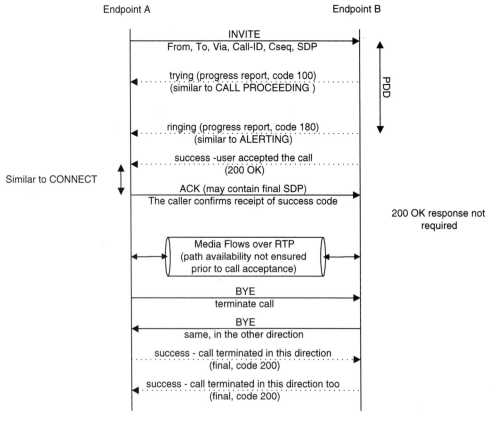

Signaling performed using either UDP or TCP

FIGURE 1.27 SIP Basic Call Model –direct Signaling Between Agents

name.com (endpoint B) into an IP address via a DNS query accessible through her own domain.

The INVITE command is sent to the well-known SIP UDP port (5060), and contains the Call-ID, Cseq and SDP of the media format, in addition to routing information, such as the From, To, and Via information. The TRYING informational response (100) from lucy's CA—Call Agent—is analogous to the Q.931 CALL PROCEEDING message, and indicates the call is being routed. In the direct call model, a TRYING response is unlikely, but in the proxy and redirect models it is very useful in keeping track of the call progress.

When the call has reached the remote endpoint and the (virtual or real) phone is ringing, a new informational response is sent to the called indicating RINGING (180). This is analogous to the Q.931 ALERTING message. The time between the user's dialing the last digit on the phone (or pushing the call button with lucy's name on it in terminal A), and the time RINGING is received by user A is the post dial delay (PDD) for SIP call setup. If penny@dflx.com can dial lucy's number as in a standard plain old telephone, there would also be a need to translate the dialed digits into an IP address. This can be done by a server, or some computing equipment the server has access to, but for simplicity it is not shown here. Assuming there is a "click to call" element (such as an icon) on penny's terminal, the PDD clock starts to tick as soon as penny clicks to call lucy.

When lucy picks up the phone a 200 response is sent to penny's User Agent. The UA sends one more request (ACK) recognizing the successful response to the INVITE request, and at that time media begins to flow on the transport addresses of the two endpoints. The ACK is not superfluous, and it is a request as much as it is an acknowledgment to the INVITE. It may carry the final SDP parameters for media type and format, as suggested by the receiving endpoint. If the ACK does not contain an SDP description, the original SDP in the invite message is used. The combination of the success response to the INVITE and following ACK is loosely analogous to the Q.931 CONNECT message. ACKs do not require a response.

It is very simple, but we have arrived at the SIP mid-call point. Media flows over RTP, with RTCP providing the monitoring of the quality of the connection and statistics.

A BYE request from either party terminates the call. Since all messages are sent over UDP, there is nothing else to do.

A SIP call with a proxy server is a little more complex. In this case the MGC of penny@dflx.com is configured with the name of Lucy's SIP server (sip.remotesysname.com). An INVITE is sent to lucy's SIP server, indicating lucy@remotesysname.com in the To field. The call flow in the proxy case is shown in Figure 1.28 as a generic flow between two endpoints. Server

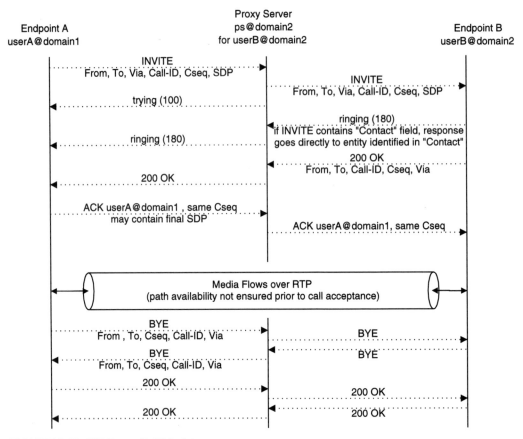

FIGURE 1.28 SIP Proxy Call Model

sip.remotesysname.com first needs to find out if lucy is registered with the server, and if she is, her current location. The user location service is part of the platform design of any network that supports the mobility feature, such as the next generation VoIP public networks.

Once the sip.remotesysname.com server has located lucy, it propagates the INVITE request without altering the header fields of the request, except for adding its own server name in the Via field. Note that multiple servers may be involved in the process. For example, if lucy had left her administrative domain altogether, but registered a new server name with sip.remotesysname.com, then the INVITE will be propagated one more time by the remote server, and a new Via field entry will be added to the header. This is useful in troubleshooting accessibility problems in SIP systems, such as loops that were not caught by the network and transport protocols.

The server now needs to keep some state information about the call. This is done by correlating Cseq numbers, Call-ID and other elements of the headers as they go by. It sends back a TRYING informational response, which in this case has useful meaning. When lucy picks up the phone at her new location, the RINGING response is returned to sip.remotesysname.com, via the remote server. Both servers will have Via entries in the response message to penny@dflx.com. The rest of the call flow, up to and including the ACK request, is a very simple request and response, proxying by sip.remotesysname.com. When the call is established, media will flow between penny@dflx.com and lucy@remotesysname.com directly, as was the case with S/MGCP and H.323. Call termination with propagated BYE requests is also very simply done with proxy signaling.

There are some important issues regarding user mobility in SIP. The called party can be logged in at multiple locations at once, having registered all of them with sip.remotesysname.com. This situation will result in the server most likely propagating the INVITE to all names on the list until the first successful conclusion (RINGING), or the user cannot be found. State information needs to be kept, and if lucy allows for automatic call answer in more than one terminal, this would create an interesting implementation problem for the network.

The redirect call model (Figure 1.29) reduces to the direct model after the initial INVITE message is sent to sip.remotesysname.com. The server will return a redirection response to the INVITE, with code 301 or 302, indicating lucy can be found at the location listed in the Contact field of the message body. Penny's MGC then closes its signaling business with sip.remotesysname.com, and initiates another INVITE to the location returned in the redirection response. From then on, the call flow is the direct model.

If lucy is registered in multiple locations, the redirect server will return a list of names to be contacted. It is up to the caller to traverse the list in a manner of its choosing.

The Contact field can be returned as part of a 482 response (ambiguous name supplied). If the URL does not resolve to an address, a list of all similar URLs may be returned by the server to assist the calling party in making a selection.

SIP Call Modification

SIP allows modifications to a stable call in progress. This capability is important for implementing telephony features, for example, the ability to place a party on hold. If lucy wants to put penny on hold, she pushes the "hold" button. This causes an INVITE to be sent to penny, with the same SDP description but with the c destination address set to all zeroes. The effect of this

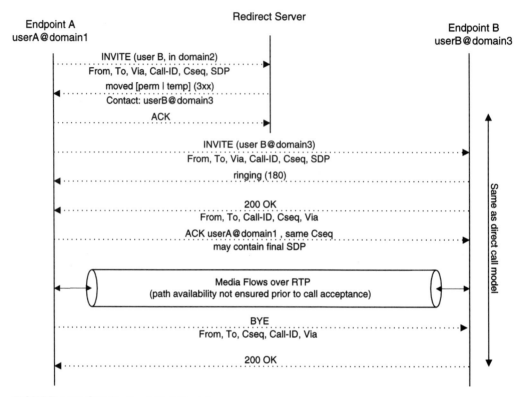

FIGURE 1.29 SIP Redirect Call Model

request is to stop the media stream temporarily. When lucy picks up again, the INVITE is sent again with the original SDP description indicating the proper network address.

The OPTIONS request is used to query a user agent server as to its capabilities. This means proxies and redirect servers have no input to this field and they simply forward the message. This request is useful for determining which SIP methods are supported by the call agent. All SIP entities need to support (parse, interpret, and properly respond) the OPTIONS request.

SIP Conferencing

SIP is independent of the conference size and model (References [3] and [4]). SIP user agents can provide both unicast or multicast addresses when they invite a party to join a call in progress. A two-party conference call or a conference with many participants are established in the same manner. H.323, on the other hand, offers more extensive involvement from the signaling protocols with the provisions of H.245 and H.332.

SIP Responses

SIP defines six types of responses to messages. Each type of response uses a code from a range as listed in the response code tables. Several of the returned codes require explicit reaction from the servers and endpoints, and several others result in implementation-specific system behavior.

1. Informational (code range 100–199). Proceeding with the execution of the request. Valid codes are:

CODE	MEANING
100	Trying – Analogous to the Q.931 CALL PROCEEDING, and will probably be returned from a proxy server, or other intermediate SIP server in the signaling path of a call.
180	Ringing – Has similar meaning to Q.931 ALERTING. Means the "virtual" or real phone is ringing.
181	Call forwarding – If a proxy server returns this code, it may also identify where it is forwarding the call in the message body.
182	Queued for service – This is useful for applications that can defer answering the call until they have serviced the calls ahead of it in the queue. Customer service departments of large corporations are major users of this feature.

2. Success (code 200). The request was successfully parsed and executed by the called party.

CODE	MEANING
200	Request executed successfully (OK). This is not the same OK as the S/MGCP ACK. (Do not confuse them.)

3. Redirection (code 300–399). The call needs more processing before it can be determined if it can be completed. The defined codes are:

CODE	MEANING
300	The address in the request resolved into more than one choice. The multiple choices are returned and the caller can pick from the list and redirect the call. This is another way of saying "ambiguous" but ambiguous name resolution results in its own error code.
301	The called user has moved permanently and the calling party should try the new location which is returned in the response header (Contact: field). It is possible to receive a list of possible locations, and the caller can make a choice about the order in which it traverses the list to make the call. If the server cannot find any information about the called party in its store, it returns a NOT FOUND error code.
302	The called user has moved temporarily and can be found at the returned address. This is useful for manual call forwarding because the server is not forwarding the call.
305	The called user cannot be accessed directly but the call must be handled through a proxy. Only Call Agents can send this reply.
380	The service requested is not available but alternative services are possible. This is an unlikely message. SDP parameter mismatches are covered with another code.

4. Client request failure (codes 400–499). The request cannot be parsed by the server or cannot be serviced. The request must be modified before being attempted again.

CODE	MEANING
400	Bad request due to syntax error. This means the message text could not be parsed by the far end. ANY syntax error should return this code. System behavior is implementation specific.
401	The user requires authentication before making this request. Special rules apply to message formatting when this error code is received (e.g., no SIP compact message format).
402	The user owes money. (For future use.) Good feature for telephone companies. Actions not specified, but one could guess.

(Continued)

CODE	MEANING
403	Forbidden request—do not reattempt. The message was parsed but the request will not be honored. If you attempt to call a number that does not accept calls from your number, you could get this message.
404	User not found. This message is sent either when the user never existed, or when the records have been purged from this server.
405	The encoded method in the message is not allowed for the called user. It is a good idea to allow all the methods, but this is an implementation decision.
406	The called endpoint will generate responses that will not be understood by the caller (code not acceptable). This response avoids the Tower of Babel syndrome from developing between endpoints if the call process continues.
407	Use Proxy Authentication first, before proceeding.
408	The server cannot produce a response within the time requested by the caller in the request header. Busy network servers could generate this response from time to time. The caller's reaction is implementation dependent.
409	There is a conflict between the current request and other conditions within the server, possibly due to existing registrations. Will get this response if a REGISTER request from a user conflicts with others.
410	The requested user or service is gone from this server and left no forwarding address. "I know that I used to know this person, but don't know what happened to them."
411	The server requires the caller to place the length of the message body in the header. Nit-picking response, but it must be accounted for by the application.
413	The size of the request is too large for the server to handle. Can't imagine what type of SIP message can cause this response, short of a malfunction by the process that creates the messages in the caller agent.
414	The server has difficulty interpreting the Request URI because of its large size. Keep the URLs shorter. There is no other way out of this error.
415	The server cannot accept the request because of its encoding. The server may indicate the proper method to encode the request.

(Continued)

CODE	MEANING
420	The server does not understand the extension of the SIP protocol being attempted by the caller. Upward compatibility is most likely the problem here.
480	Called party is temporarily unavailable. If the server recognizes the name but does not know where the party is now, it may send this message.
481	The server received a CANCEL for a request that does not exist, or a BYE for a nonexistent call. Discarded.
482	Loop in message routing detected. This is where the Via field is very useful, detecting loops that could be missed by the network and transport protocols. If a server sees itself in a Via field of an incoming message of an as yet uncompleted call, it is a good guess there is a server loop somewhere in the network. Time to get out the analyzers.
483	The hops required to reach the called party exceed the maximum allowed. This is a good protection against long and unstable routes, especially in the public network. Usually means the routers are not set up properly.
484	Address incomplete. This is a code used as a trick for a caller to obtain the exact address length of a party. Partial addresses are supplied of incrementally increasing lengths, until successful resolution occurs and the error codes stop.
485	Ambiguous address for the called party. The server may wish to offer alternatives to the caller. The usual scenario is multiple choices to be returned to the caller.
486	The called party is either busy or unwilling to take the call. May reply with a better time to call later. This is an implementation detail.

5. Server failures (code range 500–599). The request may have been valid, but the server cannot execute it.

CODE	MEANING
500	Server Error. This could be hardware, software or any internal error.
501	The server cannot service the request because the service is not implemented.

(Continued)

CODE	MEANING
502	Bad response received by the server from a gateway or server on the call path to the endpoint. This could be a typical failure for calls spanning multiple network segments and servers.
503	Service temporarily unavailable, probably due to processing overload or resource exhaustion.
504	The server timed out while accessing a gateway on the call path to the endpoint. The call request is probably still traveling somewhere.
505	SIP version not supported. Upward compatible designs will probably avoid sending this error. Older servers and call agents may do so when they see a newer version of SIP in the message header.

6. Global failures (code 600 series). The user request cannot be serviced by any server.

CODE	MEANING
600	The called party is busy. The response may indicate a better time to call back.
603	The called party declined the call.
604	The called user does not exist anywhere.
606	The user is willing to accept the call, but there are incompatibilities in the requested media or elsewhere, and thus cannot accept the call. For example, if the only choice given to the called agent is for G.728 voice compression and the called party supports only G.711, it is a good guess that this message would be received. The called party may simply decide not to accept the call.

SIP Header Definitions

SIP is rich in the amount and types of information it supplies to servers and user agents. This richness is achieved with a significant number of message headers, most of which are optional in most messages. Table 1.14 lists the headers that have been defined in RFC2543. The sign column indicates sig-

TABLE 1.14 SIP Headers

HEADER	MESSAGE TYPE	ACK	BYE	CANCEL	INVITE	OPTIONS	REGISTER
Accept	Request	n/a	n/a	n/a	o	o	o
Accept	415	n/a	n/a	n/a	o	o	o
Accept-Encoding	Request	n/a	n/a	n/a	o	o	o
Accept-Encoding	415	n/a	n/a	n/a	o	o	o
Accept-Language	Request	n/a	o	o	o	o	o
Accept-Language	415	n/a	o	o	o	o	o
Allow	200	n/a	n/a	n/a	n/a	m	n/a
Allow	405	o	o	o	o	o	o
Authorization	Request	o	o	o	o	o	o
Call-ID	General, copied from request to response	m	m	m	m	m	m
Contact	Request	o	n/a	n/a	o	o	o
Contact	1xx	n/a	n/a	n/a	o	o	n/a
Contact	2xx	n/a	n/a	n/a	o	o	o
Contact	3xx	n/a	o	n/a	o	o	o
Contact	485	n/a	o	n/a	o	o	o
Content-Encoding	Entity	o	n/a	n/a	o	o	o
Content-Length	Entity	o	n/a	n/a	o	o	o

TABLE 1.14 SIP Headers (Continued)

HEADER	MESSAGE TYPE	ACK	BYE	CANCEL	INVITE	OPTIONS	REGISTER
Content-Type	Entity	*	n/a	n/a	*	*	*
CSeq	General, copied from request to response	m	m	m	m	m	m
Date	General	o	o	o	o	o	o
Encryption	General	o	o	o	o	o	o
Expires	General	n/a	n/a	n/a	o	n/a	o
From	General, copied from request to response	m	m	m	m	m	m
Hide	Request	o	o	o	o	o	o
Max-Forwards	Request	o	o	o	o	o	o
Organization	General	n/a	n/a	n/a	o	o	o
Proxy-Authenticate	407	o	o	o	o	o	o
Proxy-Authorization	Request	o	o	o	o	o	o
Proxy-Require	Request	o	o	o	o	o	o
Priority	Request	-	-	-	o	-	-
Require	Request	o	o	o	o	o	o
Retry-After	Request	-	-	-	-	-	o
Retry-After	404, 480, 486	o	o	o	o	o	o
	503	o	o	o	o	o	o

TABLE 1.14 SIP Headers (Continued)

HEADER	MESSAGE TYPE	ACK	BYE	CANCEL	INVITE	OPTIONS	REGISTER
	600, 603	o	o	o	o	o	o
Response-Key	Request	-	o	o	o	o	o
Record-Route	Request	o	o	o	o	o	o
Record-Route	2xx	o	o	o	o	o	o
Route	Request	o	o	o	o	o	o
Server	Response	o	o	o	o	o	o
Subject	Request	-	-	-	o	-	-
Timestamp	General	o	o	o	o	o	o
To	General, copied from request to response	m	m	m	m	m	m
Unsupported	420	o	o	o	o	o	o
User-Agent	General	o	o	o	o	o	o
Via	General, copied from request to response	m	m	m	m	m	m
Warning	Response	o	o	o	o	o	o

nificance of the header. Most are end-to-end, however some have hop-by-hop significance. Mandatory headers are indicated with an m, while optional are noted as o.

SIP Compact Message Format Overview

SIP uses a compact text message format for use with UDP and authentication, such that the complete message will not run into MTU fragmentation problems along its path to the destination. The compact format looks similar to the format used in SDP specifications. Table 1.15 lists the abbreviations used for protocol parameters. The notation c means Conditional, n/a means Not Applicable, m means Mandatory, and o means Optional.

TABLE 1.15 SIP Compact Notation

SHORT NAME	LONG NAME
c	Content type
e	Content encoding
f	From
i	Call ID
m	Contact (moved)
l	Content length
s	Subject
t	To
v	Via

An example encoding of a SIP INVITE message body using compact notation follows. An example of actual signaling with a call agent is given below the message with the bit-decodings of an actual real-time SIP trace.

```
INVITE sip:mark@nstd.hp.com SIP/2.0
  v:SIP/2.0/UDP 10.0.0.1;maddr=10.0.0.10;ttl=24
  f:sip:bill@dflx.com
  t:sip:mark@nstd.hp.com
  i:12345@10.0.0.2
  c:application/sdp
  CSeq: 1 INVITE
  l: length of message in bytes
```

```
v=0
o=me 55667234 768675669 IN IP4 10.0.0.2
s=Book Review
i=Discussion of Book Issues
e=wd@dflx.com
t=<start time> <stop time>
m=audio 4657 RTP/AVP 0
```

SIP Typical Packet Decodes

Figure 1.30 shows as decode of a REGISTER message using an HP Internet Advisor.

The REGISTER message has From, To, Cseq, Call-ID, and Via as mandatory parameters. The Cseq (command sequence) parameter identifies a session and helps servers and call agents tie requests to responses in a transaction. The INVITE message decode shown in Figure 1.31 also includes SDP description of the session parameters, as captured in the IA analyzer.

In this example, the caller is asking for an audio connection on RTP port number 20134, using a choice of one of three media stream encodings as shown in the Media field and described in the Attributes for the payload type under rtpmap. Payload types are defined in RFC 1890 – *RTP Profile for Audio and Video Conferences with Minimal Control*, and we discuss them in an overview in the RTP section, together with current work in progress in the standards groups in audio/video transport. The choices given to the called party in this example are:

- Payload type 5, encoded as DVI4, a sample-based encoding of 4 bits per sample, with 8 Khz clock rate
- Payload type 0, which is the basic PCM ULaw encoding at 8 Khz, and
- Payload type 7, Linear Prediction Coding (LPC), also with an 8 Khz clock rate.

Note that rtpmap is used to map all the payload types in this example, even though some payload types could be standard and it would not have been necessary to use rtpmap.

Concluding Observations

We have looked at the three major contenders for all the marbles in VoIP telephony signaling. The variables each of the protocols has optimized reflects the priorities of the industry at the time, but there are major and distinct differences between them. SIP has the ability to achieve significant market penetration because it is simultaneously rich and robust through elegant simplicity. As this author has seen many times, all the excitement is in the details of the platform implementation that provides telephony features via

```
------------ IP Header  ------------
IP: Version = 4
IP: Header length = 20
IP: Type of service = 0
IP:     000. .... Precedence = Routine(0)
IP:     ...0 .... Delay = Normal (0)
IP:     .... 0... Throughput = Normal (0)
IP:     .... .0.. Reliability = Normal (0)
IP: Packet length = 345
IP: Id = 9f
IP: Fragmentation Info = 0x0000
IP:     .0.. ....  .... .... Don't Fragment Bit = FALSE
IP:     ..0. ....  .... .... More Fragments Bit = FALSE
IP:     ...0 0000  0000 0000 Fragment offset = 0
IP: Time to live = 60
IP: Protocol = UDP (17)
IP: Header checksum = 3CDE
IP: Source address = 128.59.15.71
IP: Destination address = 208.135.224.13

------------ UDP Header  ------------
UDP: Source port = 5060
UDP: Destination port = 5060
UDP: Length = 325
UDP: Checksum = EC64

------------ SIP Header  ------------
SIP: Message Type = Request
SIP: Method = REGISTER
SIP: Request URI = sip:208.135.224.13
SIP: SIP Version = SIP/2.0
SIP: Via= SIP/2.0/UDP 128.59.15.71
SIP: Call-Id= 29633bf2-21634109-64d01d65@128.59.15.71
SIP: From= 5551112 <sip:5551112@208.135.224.13>
SIP: To= 5551112 <sip:5551112@208.135.224.13>
SIP: CSeq= 50 REGISTER
SIP: Content-Length= 0
SIP: User-Agent= MxSip/2.0r0.0a
SIP: Contact= 5551112 <sip:5551112@128.59.15.71>
```

FIGURE 1.30 SIP REGISTER Message

combinations of protocol signaling, configuration management, diagnostic and statistical data gathering, and accounting information. In the end it is the actual implementation of the signaling protocol in the greater scheme of things that will make the difference in a product offering.

Parsing of SIP messages is easy, and troubleshooting of signaling problems is more effective in getting to the issues. On the other hand, the use of ASN.1 by H.323 results in difficult-to-understand binary data and packet

```
------------ SIP Header ------------
SIP: Message Type = Request
SIP: Method = INVITE
SIP: Request URI = +9002@2.0.0.2
SIP: SIP Version = SIP/2.0
SIP: Via= SIP/2.0/UDP  2.0.0.1
SIP: From= +9001@2.0.0.2
SIP: To= +9002@2.0.0.2
SIP: Call-ID= ECDAF189 @2.0.0.1
SIP: User-Agent= ProtoRouter
SIP: Cseq= 100
SIP: Content-Type= application/sdp
SIP: Content-Length= 112


------------ SDP Header ------------
SDP: Version = 0
SDP: Origin Field :
SDP:      User Name = PrototypeVersion
SDP:      Session Identifier = 7340
SDP:      Session Version = 629
SDP:      Network Type = IN
SDP:      Address Type = IP4
SDP:      Address = 2.0.0.1
SDP: Connection Field :
SDP:      Network Type = IN
SDP:      Address Type = IP4
SDP:      Address = 2.0.0.1
SDP: Media Field :
SDP:      Media Type = audio
SDP:      Port Number = 20134
SDP:      Transport Protocol = RTP/AVP
SDP:      Media Format = 0
```

FIGURE 1.31 SIP Typical INVITE Message

encodings. This is significant in estimating development and maintenance costs.

Protocol signaling has a major influence on the direction of system implementation and the degree to which it can be adapted to specific application needs. All the contenders have significant advantages in their areas of optimization. Only time will tell if SIP will find its winning place in the marketplace.

CHAPTER 2

Media Transport in Packet Networks

2.1 RTP AND RTCP—DEFINITIONS FOR MEDIA TRANSPORT IN IP NETWORKS

Media transport in IP-based telephony is implemented with the Real-time Transport Protocol (RTP). It is the de facto standard mechanism specified in the three major signaling protocols we have already discussed, and it provides end-to-end transport of real-time data, such as audio and video, and data for non-real-time applications. RTP does not guarantee QoS and does not address resource reservation along the path of a connection. It also requires the use of a signaling protocol to set up the connection and negotiate the media format that will be used. Media transport requires Quality of Service considerations in the design of the service platform and the underlying network. One major issue in using connectionless IP services for media transport, which comes up early in the design cycle, is whether RTP can actually be configured and viewed as a connectionless transport service in cases where QoS is paramount. Quality of Service-based routing provides a mechanism to "pin" media paths end-to-end, thus removing the routing uncertainty of IP packets, resulting in deterministic QoS, at least from a network perspective.

Media encoding is explicitly identified in the RTP packet payload format with *RTP profiles*, which we will see shortly. RTP operates transparently with both unicast and multicast connections, and provisions have been made in the latest IETF draft proposals to offer user multiplexing capabilities and support for mixing of media streams and users behind firewalls. The functionality of

RTP is enhanced with the Real-time Transport Control Protocol (RTCP), which provides for end-to-end monitoring of data delivery and quality of service. RTCP is part of the RTP specification, and it is a good idea to implement it if the objective is interoperability among equipment from different VoIP manufacturers and collection of as much real-time performance data as possible. Both RTP and RTCP are scalable to a degree to support large multicast topologies, although there are limitations. RTP and RTCP are independent of the underlying transport and network layers.

> RTP and RTCP are most commonly used on top of UDP, using different ports. RTP must be assigned an even UDP port number and the corresponding RTCP is assigned the next higher numbered UDP port (odd).

RTP supports data delivery to multiple destinations if the underlying network supports multicast distribution. The details of the protocol are found in RFC 1889, with a host of proposed new and significant enhancements in the new IETF draft proposals. In this section we highlight the protocol features and concentrate on the use case of transporting media for voice telephony application. There is a lot of ongoing work in the standards groups on the subject of RTP media transport, and some of the material we discuss in this chapter represents work progress, which may change. The reason for presenting some of the material is to underscore the magnitude of the effort required to duplicate the capabilities of the PSTN, in addition to transport of integrated multimedia, before we even start considering next generation network features.

2.1.1 Background on Performance Concerns and Other Issues

We return to the subject of RTP operation for general purpose telephony later, but first we need to look at some very basic issues associated with packet-based delivery of media streams in general.

Use of IP as the network protocol has traditionally presented the problem of delay in media delivery due to the store-and-forward handling in routers and internetworking devices in general. In addition, there is high protocol overhead in each packet, which taxes the required bandwidth of a connection. The advent of IP switching technology[1] has addressed the store-and-forward problem from the speed perspective to a large extent, but some fundamental problems remain in using IP for real-time data transport. The terms *real-time* and *IP* have not yet become synonymous, and may never be fully synonymous, but if voice and video are to be transported in a network topology that includes IP-based packet portions, the media must be transported with as little delay as possible. This is currently a very big issue for the perceived QoS by the end user, and affects network design and service offerings greatly. IP has a couple of strikes against it in the area of latency. As packet technologies go, ATM made the most credible attempt to match the quality of the TDM PSTN network, via cell switching of 53-byte cells with nominal cell-tax,[2] the QoS classes it defined, and the traffic management mechanisms it specified for predictable network design in scalable topologies. Constant and real-time variable bit rate ATM classes of service can be used to bring toll-quality voice transport capabilities with minimum protocol overhead. IP can provide comparable qualities in integrated services with next generation network switching and routing equipment to establish predictability and reliability of end-to-end media transport.

IP solutions, using plain IP with uncompressed headers, suffer from the overhead of the network and transport layers before a single octet of user data is placed in the payload. Header compression is most often prescribed and used, but the required bandwidth to carry a simple G.711 (PCMU) call using RTP over UDP over IP[3] over ATM is significant, and we discuss this issue later. Tradeoffs are always being suggested, whereby latency is traded off for improved bandwidth utilization, but there are limits to delay above which voice quality becomes unacceptable, or the bandwidth utilization to transport low bit-rate voice is unacceptably high. This problem is further exacerbated by the network designers' desire to achieve bandwidth savings through statistical multiplexing of packet voice. But does this mean one can mix voice and data traffic through the same router using a single Call Admission Control (CAC) algorithm that can oversubscribe the capacity of the router? Probably not, and this is one of the issues that requires significant research in network design before a topology with predictable capacity under predefined QoS limits can be realized. It should also be noted that the current activity in the IETF working groups will probably result in methods to transport media using compression and multiplexing of RTP payloads that will not be backward compatible with existing routers. So it is fully expected that the issue of carrying media over IP-based packet technology will fuel a new generation of router designs, just to stay close to providing predictable QoS in more than rudimentary network topologies.

---

1.   This term is used here generically to refer to hardware-assisted methods for reducing intermediate packet delays in routers.

2.   Cell tax is the overhead per packet from the AAL service layer that produced it.

3.   Hopefully IP is the first protocol above ATM.

The same size payload using native ATM and IP results in vastly different bandwidth requirements, even with the compressed headers in the IP solutions. Furthermore, the compression scheme used for the headers may be proprietary, which renders all the standard header bit definitions useless if only a single type of router can decipher the header and route the packet.

An uncompressed packet header using RTP/UDP/IP results in 40 bytes of overhead per RTP packet. There is additional overhead depending on the link layer protocol used to transport the packet. For ATM, the standard overhead for RFC1483 encapsulation is 8 bytes (an additional 64 bits), plus the ATM header of 5 bytes. This represents an entire ATM cell of 48 bytes required per sample, before the first byte of payload is transmitted. A single voice sample therefore requires a minimum of 2 ATM cells to be generated, using uncompressed headers. We see later in this chapter that use of ATM native transport mechanisms results in higher packetization efficiencies.

Hope for the required bandwidth in IP lies in using header compression and user stream multiplexing in a single packet. The method to compress RTP/UDP/IP headers is described in RFC2809 (CRTP, Compressed RTP). We will not recite or explain the content of the RFC here, but some observations are in order to understand the impact of header compression in bandwidth utilization.

The effective bandwidth required for the connection is also dependent on the packetization rate. This is the frequency with which packets are formed and transmitted, and tends to be either 10 ms or 20 ms for most applications. Other rates can be used, depending on the tolerances of the application. We discuss this subject in "RTP Profiles."

Using Figure 2.1 as a reference, a simple calculation using compressed voice with various sampling rates is shown in Table 2.1. Link layer overhead is not used in the base calculation, because it will tend to vary between network types.

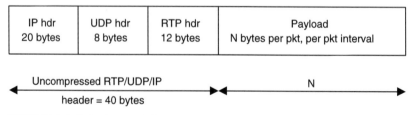

FIGURE 2.1 Calculation of Bandwidth Requirements for Media Transport Over RTP

TABLE 2.1 Voice Over RTP Nominal Bandwidth Calculations, No Link Layer Overhead Contributions

PAYLOAD FORMAT	NOMINAL RATE	PACKET RATE (MS)	PAYLOAD SIZE (BYTES)	REQUIRED BANDWIDTH, UNCOMPRESSED HEADERS (Kbps)	REQUIRED BANDWIDTH, COMPRESSED HEADERS (Kbps)
G.711	64 Kbps	20	160	80	64.8
G.711		10	80	96	65.6
G.729	8 Kbps	20	20	24	8.8
G.729		10	10	40	9.6

At every packet generation instant, the number of bytes that need to be transmitted is:

$$\text{Bytes per Media Sample} = 40 + N + \text{Link Layer Overhead}$$

The value of N is easily computed from the media encoding, that is, the type of voice encoder used in the application.

The link layer protocol will obviously contribute to the bandwidth requirement. If ATM is used as the link layer protocol the cell tax must be calculated, and the possibility of multiple cells required to transport a single packet. In the case of using AAL5 for link transport, the cell tax adds 64 bits of trailer overhead for control information and CRC. Plain G.711μLaw voice encoding with a 20 ms packetization rate would occupy a minimum of 5 cells in this example. The first cell would be dedicated to the RTP/UDP/IP and encapsulation overhead, while the remaining four cells would carry the 160-byte payload plus 8 bytes of trailer. The last AAL5 cell is partially filled with pad, but it still counts as a whole cell in the computation.

This simple case would result in a total bits per sample:

Bits per 20 ms packetization interval for G.711 over RTP/UDP/IP/ Encaps/AAL5 = 2120

The result is a requirement for 106 Kbps with 20 ms packetization rate and 5 cells, or 127.2 Kbps at 10 ms per packet with 2 cells. A similar exercise results in a bandwidth requirement of 42.4 Kbps to send a G.729 sample at 20 ms packetization rate, while the same encoding at 20 ms packetization results in exactly twice as much bandwidth requirement.

The PSTN may have a lot of flaws, but bandwidth allocation schizophrenia on trunks is not one of them. Consider also that the two examples we worked are very simple, and do not involve packet multiplexing.

It is immediately obvious that the use of plain, uncompressed RTP/UDP/IP headers can seriously undermine any savings gained by low bit-rate encoding of the voice stream. Statistical multiplexing gains are also meaningless at such high bandwidth numbers because they are not reliable enough to enter deterministic CAC algorithms. So this creates an early discrepancy using packet-based transport for voice in order to enjoy savings in bandwidth, which would otherwise be wasted in the PSTN. This issue is further exacerbated by two companion issues. The calculated bandwidth, even though it is large, still results in considerable end-to-end delay due to encoding, packetization, de-jitter buffering at the endpoints, and transcoding that may be required to hop across non-uniform topologies for media transport. Transcoding may also be required simply to support different user equipment capabilities when the voice session is set up. In the simplest case, it is mandatory when a session is set up using the PSTN, when either of the endpoints is not using G.711 encoding.

The numbers in the bandwidth table are indeed scary, but they can be improved with compression, mixing, and user multiplexing of user streams in a single RTP packet. But then the network designer may be faced with QoS routing issues of mixed and multiplexed streams. It can be seen that this is not an easy subject to tackle from a network design perspective. The main problem is how to engineer the capacity of the links connecting the routers, such that a simple and fast CAC algorithm can determine whether a call can be accepted.

In our list of issues with packet technology, one issue that needs to be addressed deals with the connectionless nature of IP itself. The question is: Can IP really be used as a connectionless service to transport voice telephony in a real deployment,[4] or does the network infrastructure need to support a nailed-up connection end-to-end once the call is established? If it is the latter, IP will undergo deterministic route lookup at each hop, for each packet of an RTP session, or bandwidth-inefficient source routing would need to be employed in small topologies. There are different schools of thought on this issue; we address some resulting problems from a different angle later and

---

4.   A real deployment in our nomenclature is one which guarantees service quality to the user with an SLA or other contract.

see the impact on voice quality due to packet loss. In connectionless IP service, packet loss for voice means either the packet really got lost, or it arrived out of sequence or late and cannot be used. Before we jump on the connectionless IP bandwagon, we need to take a look at this potential problem.

Compressed packet headers present the additional problem of the computational requirements in intermediate routing nodes, which invariably limits the number of RTP streams a router can handle in a timely manner. Scalability thus becomes a big issue even for moderate topologies, especially if QoS routing is used in the network with RSVP or other means. RTP does not concern itself with the issue of bandwidth utilization, but its use makes a case for propagation of packets with media payloads to their ultimate destination in an expedient manner. One major issue with compressed headers is presented with user multiplexing and stream mixing at intermediate points in the network. Header expansion and interpretation at intermediate points in the network can be a lengthy process, which further exacerbates the end-to-end latency issue.

Now let's take a tour of RTP and peek into some of the work in progress in the IETF, and see how it can be used in some basic topological examples.

In the call flow examples of Chapter 1, we observed media does not begin to flow until the proper connections have been set up with the endpoints. There can be more than two participants in a call, as in the case of the telephone conference call. RTP does not care about topological and administrative domain boundaries. It just hauls the payload. So it is up to the network designer to select an appropriate signaling mechanism to set up calls across different types of networks. The concept of a *session* is fairly abstract in RTP. It is a simple association of the participants in a two party or multiparty call Once the session has been started, packet generation and transfer begin. Each RTP packet needs to carry a certain minimum amount of information in the header for source identification and demarcation of significant points in the encoded media. The format of the basic RTP packet, with enhancements from application-specific usage, is described in the next section.

Packet Formats

The basic RTP header is small and consists of only 12 bytes. In Figure 2.2, only the fields up to and including the SSRC are part of the basic definition. ITU-T recommendation H.225.0 specifies modifications and non-standard extensions to the RTP header to satisfy application specific requirements. We see such an RTP packet a little later.

Let's look at the following packet parameter definitions with brief explanations of the use of each, and two real-time packet decodes captured on the network.

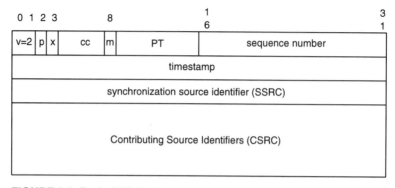

FIGURE 2.2 Basic RTP Packet Header

Version (V, 2 bits): This field identifies the version of RTP. The version defined by RFC1889 is two (2), but that may change when the current work in the IETF is completed.

Padding (P, 1 bit): If the padding bit is set, the actual data content of the packet is less than the size of the packet. If P = 1, the last byte of the padding is a count of how many bytes should be ignored. Padding may be needed by some encryption algorithms with fixed block sizes, or for carrying several RTP packets in a lower-layer protocol data unit.

Extension (X, 1 bit): If the extension bit is set, the fixed header is followed by exactly one variable-length header extension. The extension mechanism can be used by applications to pass control information without interpretation by intermediate nodes. The RTP extension header is two bytes long, and contains a right-justified 16-bit-length field that indicates the length of the extension. It must be inserted after the last valid field of the standard RTP header (which is either an SSRC entry or a CSRC entry, as we see later).

CSRC count (CC, 4 bits): The CSRC count contains the number of CSRC identifiers that follow the fixed header. This count is needed to support a capability called *mixing*. A mixer is a device that collects multiple media packets from multiple sources, combines them into a single packet, and forwards the packet to a destination. However, the sources whose packets have now been combined need to be explicitly identified in order for the resulting packet to be of use farther down stream. The first step is accomplished by identifying the number of contributing sources to this packet in the CC field. Only sources can be explicitly identified. There may be scalability issues involved with this concept, which may have other answers using multiplexing. The actual sources are identified in the CSRC list, which is described later. If there is only one SSRC in the stream, the CSRC Count field is set to zero.

Marker (M, 1 bit): The interpretation of the marker is defined by a *profile*. It is intended to allow significant events such as frame boundaries to be marked in the packet stream. A profile may define additional marker bits or specify that there is no marker bit by changing the number of bits in the payload type field. The M bit signifies the beginning of a talk spurt, or the end of a video frame. In the case of VoIP, it is then easy to know when the talk spurt ends and begin playout of comfort noise (CN).

Payload type (PT, 7 bits): This field identifies the format of the RTP payload and determines its interpretation by the application. A profile defines a static mapping of payload type codes to payload formats. Additional payload type codes can be defined dynamically through non-RTP means, that is, a signaling protocol. Once a session is set up, a sender cannot use different RTP payload types during the session; multiplexing of different media streams in the same packet is therefore impossible.

Sequence number (16 bits): The sequence number increments by one for each RTP data packet sent, and may be used by the receiver to detect packet loss and to restore packet sequence. Packet reordering is very hard to do and costs in voice and video quality, because it is virtually impossible to predict whether a packet is actually lost or is simply late in arriving. When coupled with QoS schemes that nail down an end-to-end path—and thus create a virtual connection-oriented IP session, that is, the oxymoron we touched on briefly earlier—the packets will flow from source to destination in sequence. The initial value of the sequence number must be a randomly selected number. The simple nature of the unpredictable sequence number, which increments predictably by one for each packet, makes it a good candidate to be eliminated when header compression is used.

Timestamp (32 bits): The timestamp is set at the sampling instant of the first octet in the RTP data packet. The sampling instant must be derived from a clock that increments monotonically and linearly in time to allow synchronization and jitter calculations. The resolution of the clock must be sufficient for the desired synchronization accuracy and for measuring packet arrival jitter, and could factor into the resolution of the end-to-end delay. The greater the clock resolution, the more accurate the view of the network performance parameters. The clock frequency is dependent on the format of data carried as payload and is specified statically in the profile or payload format specification that defines the format, or may be specified dynamically for payload formats defined through non-RTP means. For periodic RTP packet sending, the sampling instant is determined by the sampling clock, not the system clock. For speech telephony the timestamp clock would likely increment by one for each sampling period. If an application reads blocks covering N sampling periods, the timestamp would increment by N for each such block.

SSRC (32 bits): The SSRC field identifies the *synchronization* source, that is, the *sender*. This could be a machine, an announcement server, or a human. The value of the SSRC is chosen randomly, such that no two senders within the same RTP session will have the same SSRC identifier. Collisions, that is senders with the same identifier, can happen when a session is being set up, and when a collision is detected, a simple mechanism in RTP is specified to resolve it. When there is only one SSRC, the CSRC count field is set to zero.

SSRC collision resolution is simple in RTP. At first, each receiver of RTP packets needs to remember the source transport address associated with each SSRC. If an existing and active SSRC—not the receiver's own—is received from a new source transport address, the receiver ignores the packet and optionally updates statistics on collisions detected for the SSRC. If the receiver's own SSRC is found to be looped—that is, coming from a different source transport address—or it is determined that the receiver itself was the originator of the packet in the first place, then an RTCP BYE packet is sent on the looped SSRC and a new value is selected. The BYE packet effectively hangs up the participant from the current session.

If a source changes its source transport address, it must also choose a new SSRC identifier to avoid being interpreted as a looped source. This is an interesting problem which can occur when mixers and translators are present in the network. A mixer inserts its own SSRC, whereas a translator forwards the packet intact, although it places its own source transport address (IP Address + UDP port number) in the packet. A loop has closed when an endpoint receives the same SSRC values in RTP packets from two different source transport addresses. A loop is also closed when a source sees packets with its own SSRC, but also a collision in the initial selection has the same effect.

CSRC list (0 to 15 items, 32 bits each): The CSRC list identifies the contributing sources for the payload contained in this packet. This is meaningful only for packets that have been mixed. The number of identifiers is given by the CC field. CSRC identifiers are the original SSRCs of the packet sources, and are inserted by the mixers. The CSRC field is used for correct source identification when payloads are played out at the endpoint.

Let's look at a couple of decoded RTP packets to illustrate the use of fields in the header.

In Figure 2.3(a) shows a typical VoIP μLaw packet from a single source. Figure 2.3(b) shows an H.261 RTP video packet at a frame boundary (Marker Bit = 1), with a modification to the basic header to include profile-specific information. The data after the basic protocol header contains H.261 control information, before the payload begins. This type of header extension is allowed under the provisions of ITU-T H.323 requirements. (See reference

[1] for an example of a payload header format for H.323 video streams using H.263+.)

```
----------- RTP Header  ------------
RTP: Version = 2
RTP: P Bit = 0 (Padding Does Not Exist)
RTP: X Bit = 0 (No Extension Header Follows)
RTP: CSRC Count = 0
RTP: Marker Bit = 0
RTP: Payload Type = MU-Law Scaling (PCMU) (0)
RTP: Sequence Number = 19382
RTP: Time Stamp = 7241.899 seconds
RTP: Synchronization Source Identifier = 0x1C1A054A
RTP: 160 Bytes Of PCMU Payload Data


    00 90 a0 00 00 73 00 90    a0 00 00 95 08 00 45 00    .....s.. ......E.
    00 c8 00 37 00 00 78 11    a1 cb 0a 01 46 11 0a 01    ...7..x. ....F...
    46 10 04 02 04 05 00 b4    00 00 80 00 4b b6 03 74    F....... ....K..t
    05 58 1c 1a 05 4a ff ff    ff ff ff ff ff ff ff ff    .X...J.. ........
```

FIGURE 2.3(a) VoIP RTP Packet for PCM Voice (Courtesy HP, Internet Advisor)

```
----------- RTP Header  ------------
RTP: Version = 2
RTP: P Bit = 0 (Padding Does Not Exist)
RTP: X Bit = 0 (No Extension Header Follows)
RTP: CSRC Count = 0
RTP: Marker Bit = 1
RTP: Payload Type = H.261 (Video Codec) (31)
RTP: Sequence Number = 26118
RTP: Time Stamp = 18899.222 seconds
RTP: Synchronization Source Identifier = 0x6556BEC4
RTP: H.261 Header = 0xB5000000
RTP:     101. ....  .... ....  .... ....  .... .... Start Bit (SBIT) = 5
RTP:     ...1 01..  .... ....  .... ....  .... .... End Bit (EBIT) = 5
RTP:     .... ..0.  .... ....  .... ....  .... .... INTRA-Frame (I Bit) = 0
RTP:     .... ...1  .... ....  .... ....  .... .... Mot Vect (V Bit) = 1
RTP:     .... ....  0000 ....  .... ....  .... .... GOB Number (GOBN) = 0
RTP:     .... ....  .... 0000  0... ....  .... .... uBlk Addr Pred (MBAP) = 0
RTP:     .... ....  .... ....  .000 00..  .... .... Quantizer (QUANT) = 0
RTP:     .... ....  .... ....  .... ..00  000. .... Hor MotVectData (HMVD) = 0
RTP:     .... ....  .... ....  .... ....  ...0 0000 Ver MotVectData (VMVD) = 0
RTP: 1386 Bytes Of H.261 Payload Data
```

FIGURE 2.3(b) H.261 RTP Packet (Courtesy HP, Internet Advisor)

2.1.2 A Brief Overview of RTCP

The companion control protocol to RTP described in RFC 1889 is RTCP. RTCP is often mistaken as a signaling protocol, but it is not. RTCP packets convey end-to-end information about the quality of the session to each participant. Quantities like packet delay, jitter, packets received and lost, are very valuable for the network to use to assess its own health in real time. RTCP is useful as a heartbeat for monitoring whether data delivery is occurring at all, and for endpoints to decide whether parts of the corresponding RTP stream are being lost in cases of network malfunction. RTP and RTCP need not be routed along the same end-to-end path, but it may make a lot of sense to do so, if it can be done. If QoS routing is used, network design considerations may dictate that RTCP packets should not go through the same set of routers.

There are five types of RTCP packets:

- SR: Sender Report
- RR: Receiver Report
- SDES: Source DEScription
- BYE: Hangs up from a session
- APP: Application-Specific packet

The packet types of RTCP are defined here, with some observations of the usage of the protocol in real-time applications.

SR (Sender Report): Sender Report packets carry statistics from the active sender participants in a connection. SRs should be sent according to a bandwidth allocation algorithm specific to the network design in order to allow the flow of statistical information toward the most active packet generators in the network. Bandwidth allocation for SRs and RRs can be algorithmically derived, or set as part of the connection parameters when the session is being set up.

RR (Receiver Report): Receiver Report packets carry statistics from participants that are not active senders. The carving of the available session bandwidth for RTCP purposely favors receivers over senders in determining the RTCP packet transmission interval. A new draft proposal for extending RTP (Schulzrinne/Casner/Frederick/Jacobson, ietf-avt-rtp-new-03.txt, work in progress) suggests 5% of the session bandwidth be allocated for RTCP packets, of which 1.75% will go to senders and 3.75% will be allocated to receivers.[5] It is not immediately obvious, and it can be pretty hard to determine, how algorithmic bandwidth allocation can be dynamically maintained in real time over a large topology with multiple participants in a conference

---

5.   We discuss this proposed algorithm in order to illustrate issues in maintaining dynamically varying bandwidth assignments for RTCP packets.

call. However, for moderate-size conferences, the proposed algorithm scales the bandwidth quickly, and statistics keep flowing in a manner that favors those who receive the packet traffic over those who are creating it. Statically allocated RTCP bandwidth is most likely in simple situations, such as two-party basic telephony.

SDES (Source DEScription): Source Description packets allow the binding of the SSRC value in the RTP packet, with an actual identification of the user sending the data. The identification can be one or more of the user's name, email address, or user login identification on a host system. It is allowed to include other optional items such as a telephone number, location of the user, application used to produce the media stream, and possibly a note without stringent interpretation by the participants in the call. A mechanism to extend the SDES packet is also allowed in the work in progress of the AVT (Audio Video Transport) working group of the IETF.

Endpoints need to send an SDES packet at the beginning of the session such that each participant is explicitly identified. Mixers, which we discuss later, combine packets from all participants and produce a composite packet with as many "chunks" as there were packets originally.

BYE (ends a user's participation in a call): A bye packet tells all participants in the call that the user who sent it is departing. BYE packets cannot be mixed, because the departing user needs to be explicitly identified by the SSRC. Optionally, the application which is being used can identify the reason for leaving. Our observation on this point is that since BYE is used when a looped source or SSRC collision is detected, the BYE should contain the reason for statistics collection purposes. Another possible reason for disconnecting is a duplicate identification in the SDES packet, although this is not explicitly called for in the AVT work in progress. If there is a persistent reason for colliding SSRCs or duplicate user IDs in the SDES packets, knowledge of the cause for disconnecting will be useful in pinpointing the persistent problem.

APP (Application-specific RTCP packet): APP packets are intended to transport information between applications running at the endpoints, and are being proposed experimentally at this time. Possible uses could include the exchange of information for the remote instantiation of services when a user with certain privileges joins a call, but the industry is looking at more sophisticated methods for service instantiation and user access authentication, such as a CORBA environment.

As shown in Figure 2.4, the SR header includes the version of RTP (V = 2), possible padding at the end of the packet (P = 1), and the number of reception report counts present in the packet (rc). The payload type for the SR is 200, and the length of the packet is placed in the last 16 bits. If the P bit is set,

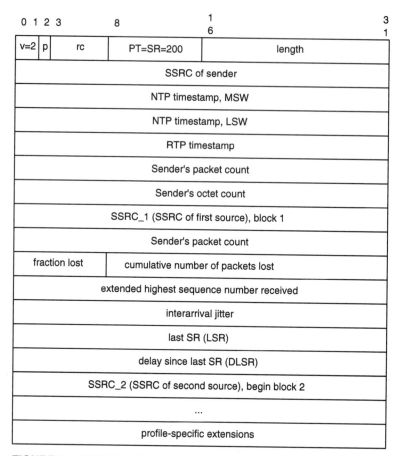

FIGURE 2.4 RTCP Sender Report Packet Format

the last byte in the packet indicates the number of bytes that should be ignored from this packet, including itself. As in the case of RTP packets, padding may become necessary if the RTCP packet is being encrypted.

The sending source of the SR is identified in the SSRC. The NTP timestamp field is the wall-clock time when the SR was issued, assuming the system that issued it has access to such time reading. If not, a value of zero may be set. The RTP timestamp is expressed in the units of that timestamp and is related to the NTP timestamp, rather than the timestamp of a particular media packet. This means that during the generation of the SR, the software looks up the NTP time and generates a corresponding RTP stamp. The sender's packet and octet counts are total counts for RTP packets and octets sent during this session, for as long as this sender has been using the SSRC identifier in the packet. If the SSRC changes due to collisions or loops, the count must change.

The *rc* field identifies the number of SSRCs for which statistics are included in the packet, up to a maximum of 32, and returns a report block for each source. For each SSRC, the fraction of packets lost since the last SR was sent is placed in the FL field in word 2 of the block.[6] The FL quantity is encoded as an integer representing the fraction of lost packets multiplied by 256, and must be non-negative. Care must be exercised in choosing this number.

If the number of packets lost was zero, but there was packet duplication which makes this number negative, a value of zero must be entered. However, if there has been both packet duplication and packet loss, the FL can convey erroneous information if not chosen properly. The implementation may want to look into not counting duplicate packets arriving in the receiver in the calculation of the FL.

The *cumulative packets lost* field represents the total number of packets lost since the beginning of the session. Lost packets are identified by gaps in the sequence number in the RTP frame.

The ex*tended sequence number received* field consists of two parts. The least significant 16 bits are highest sequence number received from $SSRC_n$, up to the moment the SR was generated. The most significant 16 bits contain the wraparound count of the sequence number since the last SR was sent. The measures that must taken to ensure valid sequence numbers are described in the algorithm presented in RFC 1889, including the establishment of a probationary period when a new source appears in a session before the sequence numbers from that source are considered valid. The probationary period is defined in number of RTP packets that must be seen from the new source with consecutive sequence numbers before the new source is declared valid.

Statistics during the probationary period of a new source are meaningless and should not be kept or sent in RTCP packets until the source is validated. If packets from a new source are lost or have other sequence number issues, the probationary period begins with the packet whose sequence number caused the inconsistency. It is recognized that stringent source validation with a required high number of initial valid packets can result in a delay to validate a source, which may be otherwise perfectly valid. Whatever algorithm for source validation is implemented by an endpoint, the use of RTCP packets

---

6.   The author realizes the tendency in the communications industry to use natural integers, that is, starting with 1, when counting bits, octets, etc. However, in this text we will use plain old integers to count, starting with 0.

received from the new source can enter the algorithm to reduce the number of required good packets before the RTP stream is declared valid.

The recommended *per-source* state information includes parameters used to estimate packets lost. All packets received are counted in the state information for the source. The number of lost packets is computed as the number of expected packets vs. received packets. One way to derive this number is to establish a parameter for each source for packets expected during the time interval for generating SRs. We need to warn you here about the difficulty associated with setting such an expectation if the RTCP packet generation interval itself varies depending on source participation in the call, as has been recommended. If an implementation chooses to accordion the RTCP generation interval, care must be exercised not to erroneously report missing packets as the interval expands, or set the wrong expectation when the interval contracts.

In the simplest case, the SR generation interval will be kept unchanged for a session and the payload type of the RTP packet can be used to set the expectation (we say more about the different payload types in the discussion of RTP profiles). It is a good idea to keep the expectation algorithm simple, and to this extent we are aided by the fact that the recommended packetization rates for most codecs in use have a least common divisor of 5 ms. Thus, when a session starts and a new source is validated, if we generate SRs every second, the expected valid number of packets is equal to 100 for each SSRC using 10 ms packetization. The packetization rates *can* be set by the signaling protocols to different values from those recommended in the RTP profiles.

It is not advisable, in this author's opinion, to count duplicate packets in the received valid packet count for the SSRC that generated them. The proper method to calculate intervals for issuing RTCP packets will not be known until ubiquitous interoperable RTP implementations appear, so we expect the intervals to be fixed with the first such instantiations of the protocol.

The *interarrival jitter* field contains the mean deviation in packet spacing measured at the receiver, per the algorithm we describe later.

The *last SR timestamp* (LSR) field for an SSRC is the middle 32 bits of the last NTP timestamp received from that SSRC, as long as one has been received. If no NTP stamp has been received, the field should be set to zero. Remember, a source may not have access to a wall clock or other acceptable elapsed time, so this field for a particular SSRC may stay zero for the duration of the session.

The *delay since last SR* (DLSR) is the time elapsed since this endpoint saw an SR from a sender. Each tick of this counter represents 1/65536 of one second.

```
------------   RTCP Header   ------------
RTCP: Version = 2
RTCP: P Bit = 0 (Padding Does Not Exist)
RTCP: Report Count = 1
RTCP: Packet Type = Sender Report Packet (SR) (200)
RTCP: Packet Length (in bytes) = 52
RTCP: SSRC Of Sender = 0x693A70D3
RTCP: NTP Time Stamp = 771919.3371499520
RTCP: RTP Time Stamp = 1765457244
RTCP: Senders Packet Count = 98
RTCP: Senders Octet Count = 19600
RTCP: SSRC Of Source 1 = 0x655662CC
RTCP:     Fraction Lost = 255
RTCP:     Packets Lost = 1638399
RTCP:     Extended Highest Sequence Number Received = 1664574
RTCP:     Inter Arrival Jitter = 253
RTCP:     Last SR Time Stamp (seconds) = 50964.7405
RTCP:     Delay Since Last SR (units of 1/65536 secs) = 310444

 Record #498      (From Hub To Node) Captured on 10.20.98 at 17:28:43.504756698
 Length =     98

   00 60 b0 f0 f5 9b 00 10    7b 48 36 c6 08 00 45 00     .`...... {H6...E.
   00 50 6a 33 00 00 1e 11    15 37 09 09 09 11 01 08     .Pj3.... .7......
   0a 12 05 fe 13 8d 00 3c    99 b8 81 c8 00 0c 69 3a     .......< ......i:
   70 d3 00 0b c7 4f c8 f5    00 00 69 3a bd 5c 00 00     p....O.. ..i:.\..
   00 62 00 00 4c 90 65 56    62 cc ff 18 ff ff 00 19     .b..L.eV b.......
   66 3e 00 00 00 fd c7 14    1c ed 00 04 bc ac 75 d4     f>...... ......u.
   32 8e                                                  2.
```

FIGURE 2.5 RTCP Sender Report Packet (Courtesy HP, Internet Advisor)

Figure 2.5 shows an RTCP SR packet from an audio conference. The link layer and network layer headers have been omitted for simplification.

The RR report packet, shown in Figure 2.6, conveys identical information as the SR from the endpoint, except sender information. An endpoint may choose to send either RR or SRs, but SRs contain overall packet and byte counts not reported in the RR.

SDES packets, shown in Figure 2.7 are necessary to bind an SSRC to the sender's real identification. Up to 32 participants can be explicitly identified by the sender of the SDES packet, in chunks. Endpoints will normally send a single SSRC (their own), but mixers will identify all the sources for which they mix packets.

SDES items contain the item identification, the length of the item and the item itself. The length field limits the SDES items to 255 bytes, plus 2 for item ID and length. There are only 8 SDES items currently proposed, as shown in Figure 2.8.

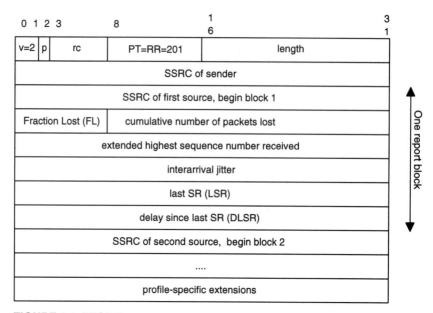

FIGURE 2.6 RTCP Receiver Report Packet Format

The combination of one SSRC/CSRC$_n$ + SDES items fields is called a *chunk*. The SDES packet is composed of a header and zero or more chunks, each of which is composed of items describing the source identified in that chunk. The items are described individually in subsequent sections.

Version (V), Padding (P), length: As described for the Sender Report packet.

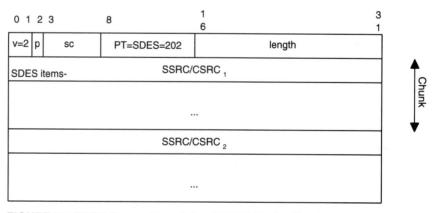

FIGURE 2.7 RTCP Source Description (SDES) Packet Header

Name = 2	Length = 8 bits	Variable length user name, i.e. George Doe

Email = 3	Length = 8 bits	Variable length user's email address

Phone = 4	Length = 8 bits	Variable length user's phone number

Location = 5	Length = 8 bits	Variable length user's geographical location

App Tool = 6	Length = 8 bits	The application used to generate packets for this session

Note = 7	Length = 8 bits	Some useful form-free note about the source.

Priv = 8	Length = 8 bits	Prefix Length 8 bits	Variable length private prefix text string

Variable length private string

FIGURE 2.8 SDES Item Description

Packet type (PT, 8 bits): Contains the constant 202 to identify this as an RTCP SDES packet.

Source count (SC, 5 bits): The number of SSRC/CSRC chunks contained in this SDES packet. A value of zero is valid but should not really be used.

The format of the BYE packet is shown in Figure 2.9.

2.1.3 Mixers, Translators, and Other Fun Devices

We have mentioned the mixers and translators and now is the time to see their intended functionality and usage. The simplest of the two is a translator. Its most likely function is to convert (that is, transcode) a payload type across a

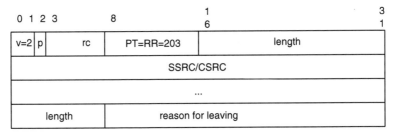

FIGURE 2.9 RTCP BYE Packet

network boundary where this is necessary. It does not alter the packet identification in any other sense, except to use its own transport address as the source of the packet. The original source of the packet is in the SSRC, which is globally unique everywhere, even across administrative boundaries.

If a translator needs more than one of the original packets in order to do proper transcoding, it must use new sequence numbers. Simply stated, this means it needs to create and keep session context for each source whose packets it handles. This type of activity will affect the timestamp of the resulting packet as well. It is not yet exactly clear how to deal with the issue of jitter calculation when multiple packets are combined into a new packet after transcoding. The receiver will know the arrival times, but the packet generation time of the new packet will be ambiguous unless correctly computed by the translator and inserted in the timestamp. If the translator absorbs jitter (that is, the new combined packet features a new timestamp), the quality of the network infrastructure in terms of delay and jitter is not known to the endpoints. It will be up to the translator to keep necessary statistics for interpretation by the network administrators.

Lost packets and packets arriving out of sequence also cause concern for the translator when it computes the new timestamp for the combined packet. We explain in the discussion of jitter calculations why this can be a problem.

A mixer is a packet-based funnel in many ways, and in its most basic form is shown in Figure 2.10. It takes in packets from multiple sources, it may perform media format conversion, it mixes the content in a manner spec-

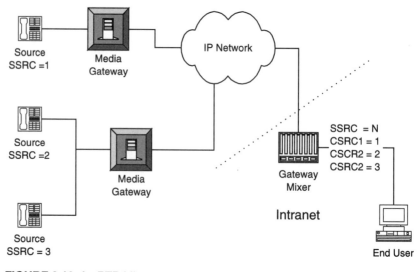

FIGURE 2.10 An RTP Mixer

ified by the application, and it proceeds to form a new packet and send it along to its destination. The mixer, due to its nature, provides synchronization for the new stream and has no choice but to add itself as the new SSRC. But the sources themselves are also identified in the CSRC list as we mentioned earlier. An issue can be the scalability of the mixer, given that only 15 contributing sources are identifiable. It is also impossible to prioritize sources through the mixer in cases when multiple sources become active simultaneously and occupy more bandwidth than is available at the output of the mixer itself. The IETF work in progress calls for a remote control mechanism to throttle individual streams through the funnel. This can be accomplished through existing functionality or extensions of a signaling protocol.

Mixers and translators are expected to be found as services offered in a gateway at the edge of the core network, or in some gateway capacity connecting an intranet with a public VoIP network. Mixing and translation is also expected to be provided in VoIP media gateways.

Discussion of issues with RTP and RTCP

It is important first to understand the spirit and purpose of RTCP before we look at some lurking issues with the performance of packet-based networks. RTCP is primarily responsible for providing statistics information to all the participants in a conference, in real time and with enough resolution that meaningful extrapolations can be made regarding the design quality of a topology. *Participants* here means the applications used to connect parties in a call, and those applications capable of taking action if statistical data indicates quality degradation below pre-set acceptable standards. Obviously, the services of RTCP are needed to identify a user with its SDES packets, which may be especially important in sessions spanning administrative boundaries or dissimilar networks (signaling protocols may not convey explicit user identification across multiple AS boundaries, beyond those in an SDES packet).

As an analogous example of the above potential issue, the reader is reminded of Automatic Name Identification in SS7. The new telephony services, with the use of RTP and RTCP, will have the ability to identify much more about users than simply their name.

The usage of RTCP in a session requires bandwidth. It is not immediately obvious how to allocate it in a simple manner, and how to scale it when session participation changes over time. One thought is to keep RTCP bandwidth constant as the session participation increases, but what is the minimum acceptable RTCP packet generation interval to satisfy interoperability among various implementations? The work in progress puts forth an algorithm and the reasoning behind it, but there are still unanswered questions and problems to be sorted out. The key issue with RTP/RTCP is lack of meaningful usage and performance data from an existence case study—that is, deployment over a topology of significant size and geographical area.

For RTCP to provide tangible added value in network deployments, endpoints and gateways need to act upon information carried in RTCP packets. But what can an endpoint or gateway realistically do if the RTCP statistics are not to its liking? For example, can a gateway reroute the call in progress if the jitter reduces the QoS below acceptable levels? This is nearly impossible as topologies scale to include large and dissimilar hops end-to-end. In simple terms, it seems the best usage of RTCP is in learning about the robustness of the network and dynamically implementing changes to constantly improve the delivered QoS. To this end other information will become paramount, to increase the knowledge of where the issues are in a topology. Simple end-to-end information is not sufficient to tell us where the QoS took a hit.

The driving concept for RTCP bandwidth allocation is session bandwidth. This is a number arrived at by some undefined means, especially if network administrative boundaries are crossed. In the simplest case of a point-to-point call, the session bandwidth per endpoint is the one-way bandwidth allocated to a single user. If an endpoint uses compressed voice, and when all is told the bandwidth for the media transport is X bps, then the initial recommendation is to allocate 5% of X for RTCP traffic, with some caveats regarding its partitioning. The bandwidth allocated to RTCP is directly related to the packet transmission interval and is averaged over the packet sizes generated by the SSRCs.

The first obvious question is what amount to give to a receiver vs. a sender, and why should the two be different? In any case, the telephony application at each endpoint must agree with the partitioning, otherwise there can be a problem resulting in premature timeouts at one extreme or excessive overhead in the other. This is a significant observation, because if VoIP is to become ubiquitous, RTP and RTCP must be implemented in an interoperable manner across every administrative domain to avoid surprises. Here the term administrative domain is extended to include telephone and cable companies (carriers) connecting to each other via IP, rather than with a hop through the PSTN. We are looking a bit forward to replacement of the TDM version of the PSTN with a packet-based version in which all carriers have POP connections to other carriers using IP trunks and a common signaling protocol at the boundary.

The new draft proposal for RTCP bandwidth allocation (which we briefly discussed earlier) specifies allocation of 1.25% of the session bandwidth to senders and 3.75% to receivers. In other words, the total bandwidth for a point-to-point connection becomes 105% of that required for carrying RTP media packets. A *sender* here means a sender of RTP packets—for instance, a talker in a conference call (not the sender of the RTCP reports). This remains the case until the number of senders increases to include more than 25% of all the participants in the call. The idea then is to divide the RTCP bandwidth equally among the participants.

One major advantage of this scheme is that it maintains constant control traffic in the network, independent of the number of participants. A disadvantage could be the speed with which the current active participant list needs to be updated and interpreted correctly by all the endpoints and new bandwidth numbers need to be computed in a consistent fashion across the board. We lack early implementation data on a wide scale to give us any insight on this potential issue.

Another issue is the actual computation of the session bandwidth. For multicast sessions and point-to-point calls, this is an easy and straightforward calculation. The number can be communicated via a signaling protocol, if not equal to the one-way bandwidth for the endpoint, or the endpoint can be programmed to compute it in a consistent manner. For conferencing applications, however, it is not that simple, but minimum RTCP packet transmission intervals are proposed, such that a high degree of resolution is maintained for the statistics.

A minimum RTCP packet transmission interval is available as an option, and the recommendation is to set it at 5 seconds. When this option is taken in the implementation, those endpoints are running the risk of being timed out too early by implementations looking for the algorithmically-arrived-at RTCP packet spacing. A method being proposed to reduce the minimum spacing is to use the result of 360/(session bandwidth) in Kbps. It is advisable to use the session bandwidth without link layer protocol overhead when using this calculation. The calculation results in more frequent RTCP packets being sent for sessions using more than 72 Kbps. But if the idea is to use compressed voice, with silence suppression to gain bandwidth efficiency, the result will be a minimum of 5 seconds per RTCP packet generation, per endpoint. A lesser value is obtained for transport of G.711 uncompressed voice over uncompressed RTP/UDP/IP, which is not expected in major deployments. The signaling protocol needs to be aware of the endpoints' use of RTCP, to make appropriate bandwidth assignments (or none at all).

Another small but potentially significant item to remember is the operation of mixers. The media stream may be mixed in a manner to meet some bandwidth limit on the hop from the mixer toward the endpoint. Although this can be done for audio, the RTCP report blocks from each SSRC *cannot* be mixed and reduced in size.

Consider an example of a mixer combining N RTP streams into one stream, for an audio conference session towards an endpoint. All the endpoints use PCM μLaw G.711 voice with 20 ms packetization period. Let's also assume each of the N RTCP sources sends SR reports with the nominal division of the RTCP session bandwidth—that is the inactive senders consume 3.75% of the RTP session bandwidth and the active senders consume 1.25%. The RTCP bandwidth in the direction of the endpoint, the sum of all the RTCP packets, is then:

$$RTCP_{SRBW} = N \cdot \frac{3.75}{100} \cdot Session\ BW$$

For N = 4 (5 participants in the call) the RTCP traffic towards an active sender through a mixer is roughly 15% of the RTP session bandwidth. Larger conference calls would run into a bandwidth problem. An application may run into scalability issues with RTCP traffic generation even in the most typical scenario.

This issue has been realized in the IETF working groups and a new SDP extension has been suggested for setting the RTCP bandwidth at an endpoint with out-of-band signaling. The format is:

b = RS:<bandwidth value>, for the sender report
b = RR:<bandwidth value>, for the receiver report

Both values are in bits per second to avoid using fractional notations. If the signaling protocol does not supply RTCP bandwidth values, the default descriptions we have discussed above apply in setting the minimum transmission interval for RTCP packets at the endpoints. For example, if the SDP attribute defines

b = RS

for voice using 32 Kbps, without setting the RTCP parameters, the 5% rule would allocate 1600 bps to RTCP packets.

RTP and User Profiles

RTP profiles were originally discussed in RFC 1890. There is, however, work in progress with draft contributions in the IETF to augment the original specification.

In this section we discuss elements of the work in progress, from the proposal in the AVT group entitled "RTP Profile for Audio and Video Conferences with Minimal Control." We will point out, from a signaling and call control perspective, some of the typical issues that surface in the desire to provide end-to-end IP-based telephony across independent AS domains, whether public or private. We might conclude that the control required to establish, maintain, and terminate such multi-party conferences in real life may be not so minimal after all.

As we pointed out, an RTP profile is a mapping of a media encoding to a payload format, but there are other implicit aspects to a profile that must be considered. Some of those we have discussed already in the context of RTCP control packet traffic generation. Others deal with the subjective voice quality in a basic two-party call, and to make matters more difficult, the measurable QoS for voice delivery in multi-party conferencing when not all endpoints in the conference support the same media encoding. Let's begin by listing all the supported payload formats for media encodings at the time of the writing of this text. The entries in Table 2.2 are an indication of the enormous effort

TABLE 2.2 Major Audio Stream Encodings and Basic Properties

MEDIA ENCODING S=SAMPLE, F=FRAME	BITS PER Sample	SAMPLING RATE	FRAME RATE	DEFAULT PACKET RATE	RTP PAYLOAD TYPE
1016 (f)		8KHz	30ms	30ms	1
CN (f)		Variable 8		Comfort Noise	19
DVI4 (s)	4	Variable or 16 KHz		20ms	5 at 8 KHz 6 at 16 KHz 6 at 16 KHz 6 at 16 KHz 17 at 22.050 KHz
G.722 (s)	8	16 KHz		20ms	9
G.723 (f)		8 KHz	30ms	30ms	4
G.726 $(16+8n^a)$ Kbps (s)	2+n	8 KHz		20ms	2 only for G.726-32
G.727 $(16+8n^b)$ Kbps (s)	2+n	8 KHz		20ms	Assigned via signaling
G.728 (f)		8 KHz	2.5ms	20ms	15
G.729 (f)		8 KHz		20ms	18
GSM (f)		8 KHz		20ms	3
GSM-HR (f)		8 KHz		20ms	Assigned via signaling
GSM-EFR (f)		8 KHz		20ms	Assigned via signaling
L8 (s)	8	Variable			

TABLE 2.2 Major Audio Stream Encodings and Basic Properties (Continued)

MEDIA ENCODING S=SAMPLE, F=FRAME	BITS PER Sample	SAMPLING RATE	FRAME RATE	DEFAULT PACKET RATE	RTP PAYLOAD TYPE
L16 (s)	16	Variable			10 for 2 channels 11 for one channel both at 44100 KHz
LPC (f)		8 KHz		20ms	7
MPA (f)		Variable			14 at 90 KHz
PCM ALaw (s)	8	Variable			8
PCM μLaw (s)	8	Variable			0
QCELP (f)		8 KHz			12
SX7300P (f)		8 KHz		30ms	Assigned via signaling
SX8300P (f)		8 KHz		30ms	Assigned via signaling
SX9600P (f)		8 KHz		30ms	Assigned via signaling
VDVI (s)	variable	Variable			Assigned via signaling
RED			.	See description in text	Assigned via signaling

a. n = 0…3
b. n = 0…3

by the research community to find the lowest possible bit-rate coding that delivers the maximum possible perceived quality to the user. The key word here is *perceived*, and we visit this subject in Chapter 4 of the book when we measure the impact on voice quality due to impairments typically found in packet networks. Speech clarity is the most important issue in packet voice over the public network, but delay and packet jitter are also factors that affect the perceived quality of speech. Delivered quality is what it's all about in the public network, so this is a major area of research and development in IP-based packet networks.

One of the major issues in packet voice technology is the minimum end-to-end delay that is imposed due to encoding and packetization. In Figure

2.11 we show a simple reference model to calculate end-to-end delay and determine acceptable values in a typical point-to-point or conference call.

Voice quality, and the overall user experience, will be affected by the delays introduced at the encoding and transcoding (media translation) points, as well as the core network. There are two cases to examine:

1. Calls across network segments that do not require media transcoding in an end-to-end call, and
2. A mixed topology with possible transcodings at network segment boundaries.

The first may be the best case, as the one-way delay consists of the sampling and packetization interval at each source, and buffering enough packets to de-jitter the arriving stream at each endpoint. Propagation delays will be due to distance and packet processing by network routers. The routers will add delay if compression and user multiplexing are used. Further delay is introduced if QoS routing is implemented, for example, RSVP.

A mixed network topology could be one of two sub-cases:

A. An IP-based topology end-to-end, using possibly different media encodings and signaling protocols at segment boundaries. Such would be the case, for example if gateway A is in an MGCP domain, and gateway B is in an H.323 domain, whereas the core network that connects them is using RTP media transport and RTCP for statistics distribution, or
B. The core network is the current PSTN.

In sub-case A, the problems with establishing an interoperable call model will be related to the signaling mechanism to initiate a session, and whether the media encoding options supported by user A are also supported by user B, and what to do if they are not. As common sense would dictate, a small list of commonly supported coding formats must be available at all endpoints in a packet-based telephony network. Using G.711 as the common format is fine, but G.711 over RTP/UDP/IP/LLP[7] is a bandwidth-expensive proposition as we have seen already. The RTP profile recommendation suggests the DVI4 format as a second alternative for endpoints (it is already supported by MAC computers), but one other encoding format from the G-Series of ITU-T recommendations is a better bet in the design of the access portion of the VoIP network.

In the second case, transcoding to and from G.711 format will always be necessary at the ingress and egress points to the PSTN respectively, with a notable exception. This is the case when G.711 has been selected as the

---

7.   LLP is the Link Layer Protocol that carries IP.

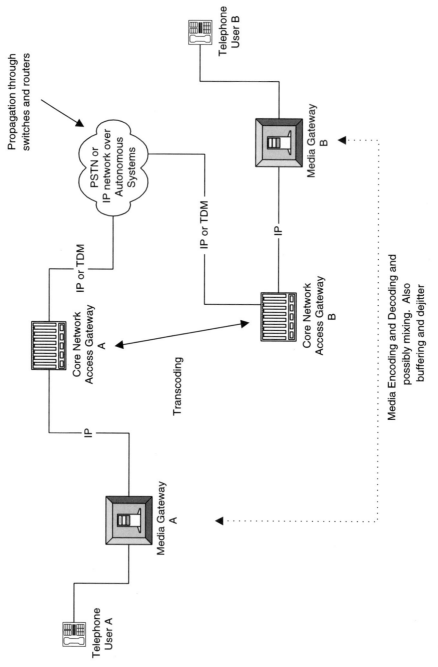

FIGURE 2.11 End-to-End Delay Measurement Reference Model

media format for the endpoints in the call, and the respective gateways do not require the media to be compressed in any network segment in the path of the call in order to conserve bandwidth.

Another possible problem with interoperating across multiple AS domains will be the types of routing protocols used, and whether QoS routing is at all possible. Here is what this issue can mean in the user experience: Today, when you pick up the phone, you will make a toll-quality voice call wherever the called party is on the PSTN (this does not apply to cellular calls, especially in the analog AMPS network). In other words, voice QoS negotiation is a simple parameter in an information element in an ISUP message, asking for a 64-Kbps channel to carry PCM µLaw voice. In the new world of packet-based VoIP telephony, matters are much more complex. Some aspects of a network connection affecting voice QoS will have to be negotiated up front with signaling means, especially if telephone carriers are involved and want to have packet POPs to other carriers, ILECs, CLECs, and IXCs. How this is going to be done between carriers will not be final until a cooperative effort is put in place between carriers and the equipment vendors, as the VoIP technology matures and gains market acceptance.

If QoS routing involves RSVP, for example, it may not be supported across administrative domains (that is, telephone companies). If it is not, then QoS will either not be an element of the session, or will be guaranteed only up to the boundary where it can be signaled and ensured. In either case, the end-to-end voice quality experience is not ensured, so even if G.711 µLaw encoding is used, all bets are off on what the carried speech will sound like in the presence of generic IP routing through an administrative domain. In Chapter 5 we construct a VoIP topology using industry standard and commercially available equipment to show a typical example of voice quality degradation in the presence of network impairments such as packet loss, or high bit-error rate.

In sub-case A, the best scenario is for the endpoints to support a common coding format, thus making transcoding unnecessary. Encoding and packetization delays in one direction are equal to twice the amount required at each endpoint, plus sufficient buffering to remove jitter from the voice stream must be provided. When QoS routing is not implemented and congestion periods cause large deviations in packet delay, the buffering size can add substantially to the overall delay. As an example, let's assume a coding format using 20-ms packetization and encoding, and a 10-ms one-way propagation delay. This could be something like a call across a few hundred miles through routers using RTP header compression. If the endpoints need to buffer 3 packets, the resulting one-way delay is:

$$D = 20 + 3 \cdot 20 + 10 = 90ms$$

It is obvious that the packetization rate has the biggest impact on the end-to-end delay. A 40-ms packetization interval results in a one-way delay of 170 ms, which would not be met with rave reviews from the user population.

In sub-case B, it is irrelevant whether the VoIP encodings at the endpoints as the same or not, unless it is G.711 at both ends. The respective PSTN gateways take care of the transcoding of the voice media, from the encoding used at each endpoint to PCM μLaw to hop on the TDM network, and vice versa. At first glance this appears to be a better case because of the presence of the fast switching network, which consists of DACS equipment. DACS in general can switch a TDM voice sample in microseconds, and their presence does not amount to much in the end-to-end delay contribution across the PSTN. But this scenario can be a much worse problem in end-to-end delay.

If transcoding is necessary at each gateway, this results in a total of 3 major delay points in the network. Dejittering is also required at the transcoding point converting from packet to TDM format, which can be 2 or 3 packets, with a 3-packet buffering being a more conservative design. At 20-ms packetization at the end points, and 2 dejittering points (all except the sender's endpoint), the one-way delay with the same common parameters as the previous example can be a minimum of:

$$D = 20 + 3 \cdot 20 + 20 + 3 \cdot 20 + 10 = 170ms$$

The reader can easily see the issue with a 30-ms packetization interval at the endpoints when the PSTN is placed in the middle of a call.[8] If jitter in the network can be contained to small values, a two-packet dejitter buffer is possible at each point, and this will minimize the end-to-end delay.

From the robustness perspective, the PSTN example has other issues associated with signaling across dissimilar networks. This deals mostly with the ability of carriers offering VoIP services in their domains (serving their subscriber base) to deliver features to subscribers of other competitive carriers through signaling means. If the pond in the middle is the PSTN, which uses SS7 signaling, the most common set of features will be those supported by SS7 and whatever support is common between the carriers through the Advanced Intelligent Network (AIN). In any case, the most commonly used

---

8.   These calculations are illustrative only and do not include look-ahead delays or other intrinsic delays due to implementation. The objective is to show the magnitude of the issue rather than an exact value of delay.

Class 5 telephony features will most likely be supported to a large degree in mixed carrier topologies, by each carrier through standard and proprietary means, even with telephony services provided through cable modems.

Robustness concerns dealing with call setup, post dial delay, FCAPS, billing, and support for wireless services across mixed networks are all valid and require further work in the standards groups before interoperable implementations are deployed.

A Few Words About the Encoding Formats

Minoli ([21]) does a very good job analyzing the various speech encoding schemes. Endpoints supporting all of the defined types are unlikely in the near term, although your PC has a pretty good selection already. Toll-quality voice, as you have known it on the PSTN, can be delivered with PCMU,[9] PCMA, or ADPCM coding, and minimum network impairments. ADPCM is supported via G.726-32 or G.727-32. The two formats are not bit-level compatible, but G.727 offers greater robustness in high speech quality because it can absorb packets lost due to network conditions. G.726 and G.727 range from 16 Kbps up to 40 Kbps in 8-Kbps increments.

The reader should not confuse low-delay encoding formats with the prescribed packetization delay in a session. Producing the encoded samples can be done quickly enough, but the generation of a packet is the dominant factor in the delay calculations. The upside is that if a network design wants to use excess bandwidth to minimize delay, the low-delay algorithms are more suited to the task. But at the same time, the efficiencies gained by packetized media are mostly lost, and network engineering of the links between gateways and exchanges becomes far more complex.

The G.723.1 series prescribes two types of encodings, one at 5.3 Kbps and one at 6.3 Kbps. *Both* encodings must be supported by an endpoint when it permits selection of G.723.1 during the signaling process.

RED uses redundancy in a clever form, by sending previous samples, but even more heavily compressed, together with new samples of encoded speech. If the endpoint is lucky enough to have one of those more heavily compressed samples when a real packet does not arrive, the voice waveform can be approximated from the later packet and produce a better user experience. This sounds (and is) hard to implement, and it is even harder to guarantee its effectiveness when jumping across dissimilar AS domains. It is also bandwidth-expensive, due to packet duplication.

The SX family of codecs produces encodings of 120 samples (15 ms intervals), with variable byte count per encoded block. SX7300 produces 14

---

9. PCMU is another name for μLaw encoding

bytes per block or 7467 bps, SX8300 produces 16 bytes or 8533 bps, and SX9600 produces 18 bytes, or a bit rate of 9600 bps.

RTP Payload Formats for Carrying DTMF Digits, Tones, and Events

In the PSTN, DTMF digits are carried from the telephone to the local exchange as in-band tones. In VoIP networks, DTMF digits are transported in RTP packets after they have been recognized, collected, and possibly even analyzed by the media gateway. Codecs in general have serious difficulty understanding compressed DTMF tones. This issue creates the need to transport DTMF tones between endpoints out-of-band.

The basic idea is to encode DTMF digits and tones in RTP packets using the same characteristics used for the encoding of the voice data. The RTP packets use the same sequence numbering as the voice packets, assuming timing alignment is not absolutely critical with respect to the voice packets. A drawback is in using RTP over an unreliable transport protocol to transfer control digits. The packet payload format and payload type must be dynamically assigned via the signaling protocol.

Issues to look for in DTMF recognition and transport deal with the manner in which to convey the duration of the pressed digit on the keypad, and the volume of the detected tone. The latter will be the volume detected at the originating endpoint and can be carried in a new payload format easily. The duration of the tone must be explicitly identified, such that the receiving endpoint can play it out. This presents a couple of problems. The first is that the entire DTMF tone, up to a cut-off point, must be detected and a packet must be generated. The extra delay may be undesirable if DTMF is used for user signaling, for instance, invocation of a Class 5 feature. In Chapter 4 we see measurements associated with the quality of tone generation and transport in a network.

RTP Support for Telephone Signal Events and Tones

Internet draft <ietf-avt- tones-00.txt>[10] defines RTP packet payload formats to transport telephone signals, tones, and events in RTP packets. The basic direction of the standards is to specify encoding of tone signal characteristics and transport them to the far end for tone re-creation.

The number of signaling events and tones that must be recognized is listed in Table 2.3, which we present here only as a reference and whose size is a testament to the magnitude of the problem of robust integration of class services and basic telephony in a general purpose, multi-national, IP-based network.

---

10. Work in progress, whose contents and status may change.

TABLE 2.3 RTP Payload Types for Tones and Signal Events

PAYLOAD ENCODING	DEFINITION	EVENT TYPE
DTMF Tones and Signals (the encoding name is **dtmf**, and the MIME name is audio/dtmf)		
0	(DTMF) 0	DMTF Tones through PT 16.
1	(DTMF) 1	The payload type in the RTP packet header must be assigned dynamically via a signaling protocol, and for each event category separately.
2	(DTMF) 2	
3	(DTMF) 3	
4	(DTMF) 4	
5	(DTMF) 5	
6	(DTMF) 6	
7	(DTMF) 7	
8	(DTMF) 8	
9	(DTMF) 9	
10	(DTMF) A	
11	(DTMF) B	
12	(DTMF) C	
13	(DTMF) D	
14	(DTMF) *	
15	(DTMF) #	
16	Flash Hook	
Fax Tones and Signals		
1	ANS (fax answer tone)	See the fax description section for the definition of these signals. Also see notes in the text of this section for additional comments.
2	ANSam (V.34 fax)	
3	CNG (Fax Calling Tone)	
4	V.21 channel 1, bit = 0 (calling station tx)	V.21 modulation at 300 bps. FSK is used by Group 3 fax stations to negotiate parameters of the transmission and control exchanges.
5	V.21 channel 1, bit = 1 (calling station tx)	
6	V.21 channel 2, bit = 0 (called station tx)	
7	V.21 channel 2, bit = 1 (called station tx)	Each V.21 bit has it own tone at 300 bps, and needs to be sent independently!

TABLE 2.3 RTP Payload Types for Tones and Signal Events (Continued)

PAYLOAD ENCODING	DEFINITION	EVENT TYPE
	Line Events	
0	Off-Hook	The reader should consult with ITU documents E.180/Q.35 and E.182 for more details on these tones.
1	On-Hook	
2	Dial Tone	
3	Internal PABX dial tone	
4	Special Dial Tone *User reminder of the existence of special conditions from the place of origination of the call.*	
5	Second Dial Tone *This is the tone we hear when we dial *NN service activation, *69 for user-originated call trace.*	
6	Ringing Tone	
7	Special Ringing Tone *Used for call waiting or call forwarding to alert the caller of the call progress.*	
8	Busy Tone	
9	Congestion Tone *Indicates to the caller that the network is busy and the call cannot go through (may also get a recorded announcement).*	
10	Special Information Tone	
11	Comfort Tone *Indicates that the call is progressing, don't hang up.*	
12	Hold Tone	
13	Record Tone	
14	Caller Waiting Tone	
15	Call Waiting Tone	

TABLE 2.3 RTP Payload Types for Tones and Signal Events (Continued)

PAYLOAD ENCODING	DEFINITION	EVENT TYPE
16	Pay Tone *Advises users of pay phones that payment is required.*	
17	Positive Indication Tone *Advises the calling party that the request for supplementary services can be granted.*	
18	Negative Indication Tone *Advises the calling party that a request for supplementary services cannot be granted.*	
19	Warning Tone *The conversation may not be private. Indicates the use of a recording device.*	
20	Intrusion Tone	
21	Calling Card Service Tone	
22	Pay phone Recognition Tone *Advises an operator the incoming call is originating from a pay phone.*	
23	CPE Alerting in CAS form	
24	Off-Hook Warning Tone *The loud tone you hear when you leave the phone off hook for a long time.*	
Country-Specific Line Events		
0	Acceptance Tone *Used in Kuwait, Mali, Saudi Arabia, Vanuatu.*	Source ITU-T E.180, Supplement 2.
1	Confirmation Tone *Used in the US, Canada, Israel, Jordan, Laos, Turkey and Brunei.*	
2	Recall Dial Tone *Used in Anguilla, Antigua and Barbuda, Austria, Barbados, British Virgin Islands, Canada, Dominica, Hong Kong, Iran, Iraq, Israel, Japan, Korea, Montserrat, Nauru, Nigeria, St. Kitts-and-Nevis, Saudi Arabia, Syria, Turks and Caicos Isl., and the US.*	

TABLE 2.3 RTP Payload Types for Tones and Signal Events (Continued)

PAYLOAD ENCODING	DEFINITION	EVENT TYPE
3	End of Three-Party Service Tone	
4	Facilities Tone *Used in Australia.*	
5	Line Lockout Tone *Used in Kuwait, Malaysia, and Oman.*	
6	Number Unobtainable Tone *Used in most countries, but not in the US.*	
7	Offering Tone *Used in Australia, Bhutan, Czech Republic, Hungary, Indonesia, Iran, Slovakia and Thailand.*	
8	Permanent Signal Tone *Used in Iran.*	
9	Preemption Tone *Used in Iran.*	
10	Queue Tone *Used in Finland.*	
11	Refusal Tone *Used in Kuwait, Saudi Arabia.*	
12	Route Tone *Used in most countries but not in the US.*	
13	Valid Tone *Used in Greece*	
14	Waiting Tone *Used in most countries to alert a caller that a called station has call waiting active when it is busy.*	
15	End-of-Period Warning Tone *Used in Brunei, Chile, Malaysia.*	
16	Warning PIP Tone *Used in Brunei.*	

TABLE 2.3 RTP Payload Types for Tones and Signal Events (Continued)

PAYLOAD ENCODING	DEFINITION	EVENT TYPE
Trunk Events		
0 – 9	MF Digits 0 through 9	Notes:
10	MF K0 or KP (signal to start digit outpulsing)	MF signaling is implemented between Central Offices. Following a Wink handshake, the sending station (for example, a PBX) sends KP followed by the collected digits from the calling party. Outpulsing of digits is indicated with the ST signal.
11	MF K1	
12	MF K2	
13	MF ST0 or ST (Stop digit outpulsing)	
14	MF S1	
15	MF S2	
16	MF S3	
17	Wink On	
18	Wink Off	
19	Incoming Call Seizure Attempt	
20	Return Seizure	
21	Unseize Circuit	
22	Continuity Test	
23	Default Continuity Tone	
24	Continuity Tone (single tone, loopback mode)	
25	Continuity Send (transponder mode)	
26	Continuity Return (verification tone)	
27	Loopback	
28	Old Milliwatt Tone at 1 kHz	
29	New Milliwatt Tone at 1.004 kHz	

Another possible means for transporting DTMF, other tones, and signaling events is to let the signaling protocol do it with out-of-band signaling. This approach, by itself, has the problem that it may not be supported across different domains, which may reduce to in-band DTMF payloads being the only option across network boundaries. But even so, the dynamically assigned in-band payload types may not be the same, or negotiable, across domains, and this can result in a big problem setting up a call or DTMF end-to-end signaling. Clearly, for now, for all Class 5 feature activation/deactivation, the local exchange needs to see the DTMF digits either in-band, or through out-of-band signaling and, in both cases, in a manner that it understands.

A possible caveat with general tone recognition and transport is the presence of an MF signaling trunk at the edge network, toward an endpoint. In this case, digits will appear coded in the MF pairs in-band. There is no out-of-band signaling protocol for MF trunks, and the gateway has no choice but to send DTMF digits arriving in-band as RTP payload, as MF tones of precise duration on the PSTN trunk. This implies knowledge of the in-band signaling requirements on the trunks by the gateways, and adaptation of the timing of the DTMF digits indicated in the payload to the timing of the corresponding MF tones.

RTP Jitter and Delay Calculations

One of the statistics conveyed by the RTCP sender and receiver reports is jitter. Jitter is defined as the timing difference between the actual of occurrence of an event and its expected occurrence. The jitter value for RTP packets is arrived at by smoothing a running average of packet interarrival delays. Jitter is calculated with the help of Figure 2.12.

The first thing the receiver knows about a packet's transit time is the difference between its timestamp and the current time in the receiver. The difference is:

$$\text{Delay}_{(n-1)} = \text{Received}_{(n-1)} - \text{Sent}_{(n-1)},$$

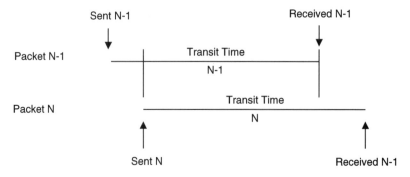

FIGURE 2.12 Calculating Interarrival Jitter in RTP

and represents its transit time and some of the machine time from when the packet was time-stamped to when it actually was sent on its way on the output link at the source. RFC1889 recommends the use of NTP to accomplish end-to-end synchronization of endpoints, although implementations exist with unsynchronized endpoints.

The incremental delay difference (second order effect) between packets N and N-1 is

$$D_{(n-1,\, n)} = [\text{Received}_{(n)} - \text{Received}_{(n-1)}] - [\text{Sent}_{(n)} - \text{Sent}_{(n-1)}]$$

The packet jitter is maintained as the smoothed running sum:

$$J_n = J_{n-1} + \frac{(|D_{n,\, n-1}| - J_{n-1})}{16}$$

Two traces from typical jitter measurements are shown in Figures 2.13(a) and 2.13(b).

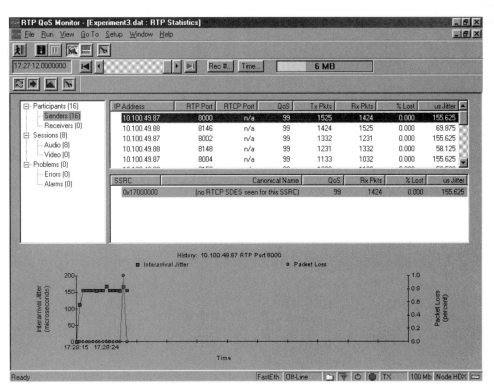

FIGURE 2.13(a) Typical RTP Packet Interarrival Jitter Calculations

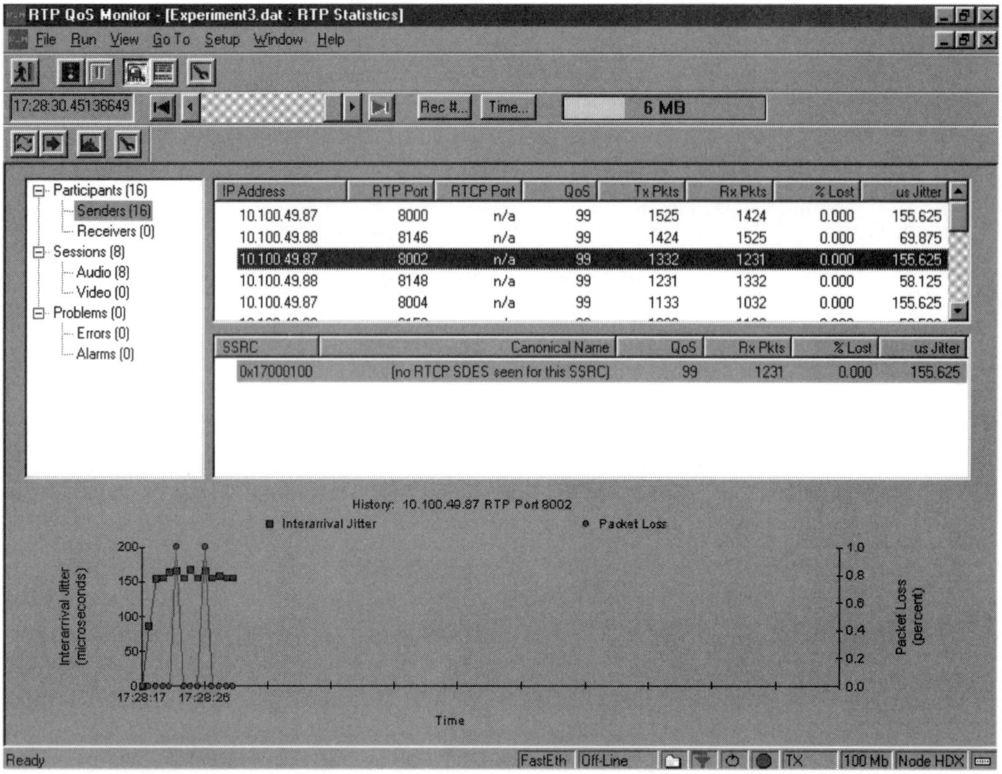

FIGURE 2.13(b) Typical RTP Packet Interarrival Jitter Calculations

Figures 2.13(a) and 2.13(b) were taken from a live trace captured with the HP Internet Advisor, and show packet loss data superimposed with jitter calculations. The data is from two senders of an audio conference, which experienced instantaneous packet loss at separate time instances. The QoS parameter can be set to weigh the jitter and packet loss figures, such that an objective measure can be established for the user experience. Such mapping is not yet standardized, but as the VoIP experience grows, de facto correlations of jitter and other parameters to perceived QoS will be made. Jitter is a very good metric, and can be related to the quality of the voice experienced by the participants. This relationship of metrics to delivered quality is discussed in Chapter 5, when we configure a reference topology, and simulate wide area network impairments and jitter characteristics, while observing objective measures of voice quality.

IP Performance Measurements

Many good concepts on the subject of test and measurement in IP networks are presented in RFC 2330.[11] In this segment, we want to visit some of the concepts and take insight into the meaning of metrics and measurements one step higher—that is, the telephony application using the IP network.

Packet network performance has been studied extensively in the industry, both in simulation and in real topologies running real applications. Some methods are biased and therefore incorrect, with dubious methodologies and equally dubious conclusions. Carrier-class quality telephony is the new term coined by the industry, which has not yet been characterized, beyond the hand-waving of MOS (mean opinion scores) results. We do not know the impact on the end-user experience of some fundamental assumptions that are being made regarding what is acceptable voice quality and what is not. One thing is for sure, and we will state it again in the context of psychoacoustic modeling of the human auditory perception and voice quality measurements (Chapters 4 and 5):

The speech quality delivered by the TDM network today is a hard act to follow by any type of public packet network.

The measurement methodology one chooses makes a big difference in whether the acquired data is meaningful for analysis, or simply dangerous because it results in erroneous conclusions.

Measurements must be taken via repeatable and consistent experiments, using calibrated instruments, stored samples of real or test-generated traffic, and an absolute timing reference.

A repeatable experiment results in consistent readings, but not necessarily the same results. This is key in understanding how to test IP networks. In general, almost all observations in a real packet network will be stochastic in nature and observed values will be represented by random variables rather than absolute numbers. This is the nature of performance measurement in packet switching applications, and it is recognized that several key character-

---

11. RFC 2330, *Framework for IP Performance Metrics*, V. Paxson et. al.

istics of a network will be represented by empirical or fitted distributions obtained via real-life measurements or simulation.

A *metric* is a quantity whose value we are trying to measure. A metric may be time-varying or time-invariant. A metric *can be a random variable*, and most recently *subjective* metrics have been introduced in VoIP quality analysis.

Some of the most important metrics in VoIP telephony are delay, echo, jitter, speech clarity, and perceived quality.

Establishing an absolute timing reference is sometimes easier said than done. A simple test to measure one-way packet transmission delay can result in a very complex setup. We will discuss this subject more in the test and measurement section of this text, which is presented in Chapter 5.

The use of a solid timing reference is extremely important. It is tempting to underestimate the impact of a 0.01% frequency difference between two hosts' clocks, but consider the following example. If a host transmits packets every 20 ms, and its clock is 0.01% slower than the receiver's, which expects them every 20 ms per its own clock, the receiver will starve every 3 minutes and 20 seconds.

However, hosts (which includes routers in the IP measurement methodology framework) normally take their timing reference from the PSTN network and are expected to be at least Statum-3 accurate, when their clocks happen to be free-running for a short time.

Sampling is important, as pointed out in the IP performance methodology framework. The observer needs to set a-periodic sampling intervals for data gathering. The term *sample* is used here in an extended sense to include a set of measurements, not just a single measurement. Many samples can be used to derive a statistic, examine its properties, and find out if the data fits a closed form theoretical distribution, via a goodness-of-fit test. The framework suggests use of the Anderson-Darling test for goodness of fit, but others are also useful. The chi-squared and Kolmogorov-Smirnov tests are other standard methods for fitting data into distributions. The key to classifying a collection of data is the hypothesis one will use to declare a fit to a distribution. A hypothesis is simply a statement regarding the probability distribution of a random variable. Hypotheses are not true or false. They are either accepted or rejected, based on limits posed when the statement is made.

The hypothesis statement is made regarding the set of parameters that uniquely define the distribution[12] and always contains an error probability, also known as *level of significance*. A hypothesis about the fit of a set of measurement data to a known distribution may be acceptable with 5% error probability, but may be unacceptable at the 2% level.

In general recurrent sampling is recommended, done at unpredictable intervals which can be generated using the simple Poisson distribution. However, a lot of performance metrics in packet networks are time-dependent (i.e., percent congestion at the busy hour of the busy day) and use of a periodic sampling interval may in fact be an objective.

Finally, we would like to include all types of IP packets in the metrics defined by the framework, such that packets with compressed headers can be included. Compressed header packets do not fit the strict definition of "standard formed packets."

Use of Compressed Headers in RTP

The purpose of using compressed headers in RTP streams is to reduce the overhead they represent as a percentage of the overall bandwidth. A lot of emphasis has been given to controlling the RTCP traffic to within 5% of the session bandwidth, but RTP overhead can exceed by far that of the corresponding RTCP bandwidth. The basic idea behind RTP header compression is presented in RFC 2508; and in this section we provide an overview and ask the reader to delve further into the RFC if a compliant implementation is being contemplated.

RTP header compression done in conjunction with UDP and IP header compression can reduce header size to 2 bytes if no UDP checksums are sent, or 4 bytes when operating with UDP checksums. It is obvious that by considering all three protocol headers simultaneously, the best possible compression efficiency is achieved. Header size during a session will vary anyway, in order to resynchronize compressors and decompressors in case of packet loss, or when members join or depart from a conference call. The observation that guides RTP header compression is that once a session begins and RTP packets begin to flow, little information in fact changes in the headers from packet to packet. Thus in steady-state on a reliable high-quality link, there is high redundancy that simply eats up bandwidth. Let's take a look at a combined typical IP/UDP/RTP header, shown in Figure 2.14, and follow the reasoning of RFC 2508 to arrive at the minimum possible encoding of a header.

---

12. For example, the mean of a Poisson distribution completely defines the distribution.

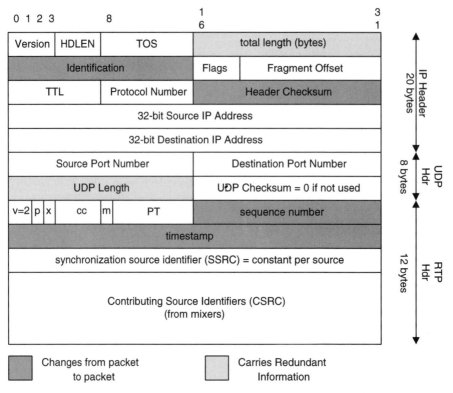

FIGURE 2.14 Combined RTP/UDP/IP Header

The length of the IP packet is identified in some form in the link layer protocol and the UDP packet length is immediately known as a result. If the UDP header checksum is not used, the field is always zero and can be omitted.

NOTE: The reasoning for arriving at this type of IP/UDP header compression has excluded IP options from entering the compression scheme.

The hashed fields in the RTP packet change, but both the timestamp and the sequence number change in a predictable manner. The sequence field increments by one and the timestamp can be inferred by the packetization rate, which is one of the session parameters. Since the difference in value between successive valid packets is known, the second order difference is zero. Mixers present a minor issue because they need to re-send the CSRC list if it changes during a session, but hopefully this will not happen very often during a conference call. Decompressors need to simply calculate the first order differences between successive good packets and maintain the value in the session context space for each source.

The remaining fields can be saved in the session context for this source by the decompressor, once a complete and uncompressed packet header has been seen. Therefore, it is important to somehow negotiate a Context session ID (CID) parameter between compressor and decompressor for packet identification. The CID can be either a 16-bit quantity, which allows for 65536 contexts to be identified, or an 8-bit quantity for 256 contexts. The former results in a minimum of a 2-byte compressed header, whereas the latter is only 2 bytes long.

What remains is the representation of the RTP sequence number in the compressed packet. A reasonable compression to 4 bits allows for expedient recovery for a moderate burst of lost packets; otherwise, a fully decompressed header exchange will be necessary to resynchronize compressor and decompressor.

Unfortunately, decompressors are required not only at the endpoints but in the network itself, which causes some performance and stability concern about the compression scheme in cases of network impairments, such as during periods of moderate congestion. In other words, specifying the sustained performance of RTP routers implementing header compression, so that a network engineer can reliably allocate generic RTP traffic volume through them, is sometimes easier said than done.

There is one more caveat. How does the protocol convey whether an RTP packet header is complete or partially compressed? Partial header compression is desirable to convey only elements of the particular header that need refreshing at the decompressor. This scheme relies on the link layer protocol to indicate four different compressed RTP packet formats. ATM doesn't make it because it is not suited for such accommodations. One possibility is to use the PPP protocol to transport compressed RTP, and the new model would be PPP/IP/UDP/RTP before the first bit of encoded voice data is transported. The link layer protocol or out-of-band signaling will also be required to negotiate RTP header compression.

The FULL_HEADER packet carries the complete uncompressed combined header, plus the CID and the 4-bit sequence number of the compressed header, as shown in Figure 2.15. The two additional fields are stuffed in the IP and UDP header length fields, respectively, for an 8-bit CID, or the opposite for the 16-bit CID, to avoid expanding the standard IP/UDP header sizes.

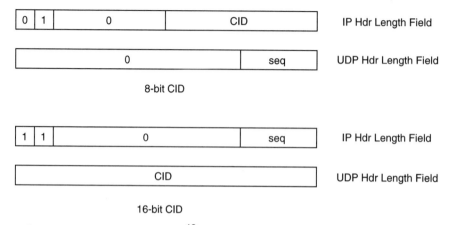

8-bit CID

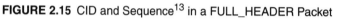

16-bit CID

FIGURE 2.15 CID and Sequence[13] in a FULL_HEADER Packet

The COMPRESSED_UDP packet format indicates that the IP and UDP headers are compressed, but there are differences in the RTP header (or any other protocol on top of UDP), which is being sent intact.

The COMPRESSED_RTP packet format is the normal header type when header compression is in effect and all headers are compressed. Minimum header is 2 bytes, and increases are based on deltas and differences that need to be sent to the decompressors.

The CONTEXT_STATE packet is sent by the decompressor back to the compressor to indicate contexts that are out of sync and need refreshing. This may be the case, for example, following a burst packet-loss error, whereby the second order differences in sequence numbering may not be zero and the context state needs to be restarted.

The optional COMPRESSED_NON_TCP packet format is sent if the desire is to send the IPv4 ID field uncompressed. This would increase the robustness of the compressed protocol in high packet-loss scenarios, but would make the compressed header a minimum of 4 bytes.

The resulting compressed RTP packet header is shown in Figure 2.16. The fields in dotted lines are not sent during normal transmission of compressed header packets.

---

13.   We assume IPv4 implementations in this discussion. If the reader is contemplating an IPv6 implementation of RTP, there are additional requirements in the RFC which must be adhered to carefully in the design.

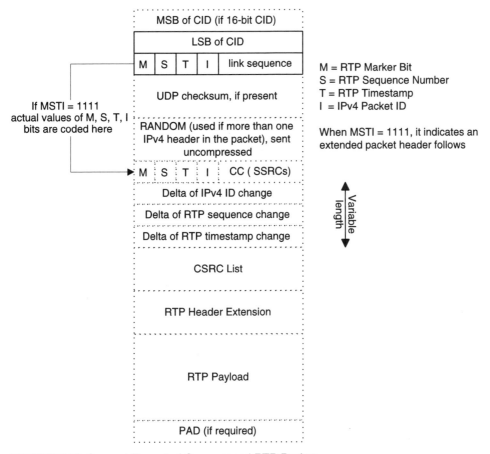

FIGURE 2.16 General Format of Compressed RTP Packet

Changes in RTP fields that are supposed to be constant during a session mandate sending an uncompressed RTP header with the COMPRESSED_UDP packet format, shown in Figure 2.17, which leaves the IP and UDP headers compressed if they do not require updating.

RFC 2508 defines a method for encoding the delta differences in compact form, but it also recommends a table-driven delta encoder, which is more robust and allows more flexibility in negotiating the encodings for each session. The issue is the length of the delta sequence in compact form when an update is needed. In the RFC, the reader will notice that the encoding of the first nibble of the first byte in the delta field can be used to show the length of the delta field. The delta compacting process of changed values, which is shown in RFC 2508 (section 3.3.4), is not unlike Huffman encoding.

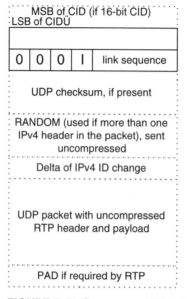

FIGURE 2.17 Compressed UDP Header and Packet Format

Recovering From Errors and Context State Negotiation

Contexts become invalidated when the sequence field in the compressed RTP header increments by more than one. (If it increments by 1mod16, the errors will go unnoticed by the decompressor unless the link layer protocol issues notification to the IP layer.) Context invalidation prompts the decompressor to return a CONTEXT_STATE packet, shown in Figure 2.18, and request sequence field updates for the contexts contained in the packet.

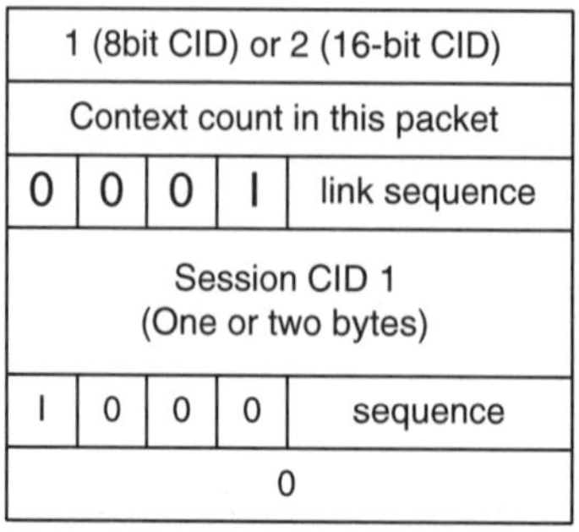

1 (8bit CID) or 2 (16-bit CID)			
Context count in this packet			
0	0	0	I	link sequence
Session CID 1 (One or two bytes)			
I	0	0	0	sequence
0			

FIGURE 2.18 CONTEXT_STATE Packet Format

If I = 1 in the packet, the decompressor is requesting a FULL_HEADER packet for that source.

Recovery from error is disruptive and can take some time in the presence of network congestion. What is more disturbing is the presence of multiple invalid contexts on a low-speed link whose full update can possibly cause more transitory congestion until all the updates have been made.

Compression of RTCP Packets

RTCP packet content cannot be compressed, and it is better to leave RTCP packets alone and away from compression schemes. As we discussed already, the total bandwidth allocated to RTCP is about 5% of the session bandwidth, or a fixed amount usually less than 5% anyway, so compression offers little benefit in terms of bandwidth savings and efficiency.

Finally, when traversing multiple AS domains, it is possible to run into packet fragmentation. The thinking is that large packets carry large payloads and the impact of the header size on large packets is less pronounced as a percentage of the total. Our advice is to avoid compression completely when large packets are being sent, and keep the total packet length to the minimum supported by the AS (that is, avoid fragmentation as well). The effort required at the decompressor to deal with potentially out-of-order packets due to fragmentation occurring somewhere in the network is too risky and its derived benefits minimal.

RTP Payload Multiplexing

RTP payload multiplexing increases the bandwidth usage efficiency between gateways. The format of a multiplexed RTP packet containing payloads from two sources is shown in Figure 2.19.

The Channel ID (CID) is the channel number and the length indicator is used to determined the last byte of the payload for the CID. T is a transit bit used for negotiating the kind of processing for the contained packet, and R is a reserved bit. CID is similar in concept to the CID used in AAL2, and it is expected to be assigned by out-of-band signaling.

Multiplexed packets can be compressed using the standard compression algorithm for RTP, but they signify packets from a single SSRC, the one in the main RTP header. Channel identification significance is meaningful only at the endpoints which de-multiplex the payload.

2.1.4 Summary and Technology Outlook

RTP is the transport mechanism that will bring us integrated multimedia with basic telephony service. In this section we looked at RTP and its companion

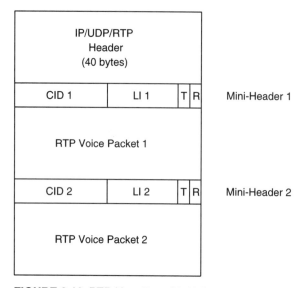

FIGURE 2.19 RTP User Data Multiplexing

protocol RTCP, which are accepted by H.323, S/MGCP, and SIP, even though H.323 has allowed payload header definitions, especially for video transport, which may carry into the other signaling protocols when they cross the same bridges. There are large numbers of unknowns in networks deploying packet telephony, but the belief is that once the big decision to deploy is made, the solution to the technical problems that arise will be part of the VoIP evolutionary process. The expectation is that any major technological deployment will have "glitches" that can be annoying sometimes, but the added value of the new networks will mitigate any minor user annoyances in the meantime.

Voice over IP is the first service to be deployed on a large scale from all the major carriers, who have their eyes on value added services. As such, great emphasis is given to match as closely as possible the look and the feel of the simple two-party telephone call we enjoy on the wireline PSTN. VoIP can come close to this experience at the expense of high bandwidth utilization for a simple PCM call and network overlays for different media types, but as time goes on compressed voice over IP for integrated service access will become a reality, at least as a service option. A driver would be the availability of high bandwidth at the home or small office for data applications, sharing the narrow bandwidth of access links. Only time will tell how many new business drivers will emerge as the new services are deployed, some of which nobody has thought of as of this time.

2.2 RSVP – THE RESOURCE RESERVATION PROTOCOL

2.2.1 Background

The ReSource reserVation Protocol—RSVP—is defined in RFC 2205, with several other RFCs detailing its usage with link layer protocols such as ATM. RSVP is IP signaling for the purpose of establishing a path between two endpoints, with the goal of delivering high QoS on a media stream. RSVP does not guarantee the QoS, but it does its best to treat packets of a certain classification according to the rules of the classification, such that end-to-end delivery is a predictable process. The protocol is also well-suited to accommodating multicast applications and as such it has inherent complexities. It is under strong consideration as a QoS signaling protocol for delivering IP-based telephone service in the new public network.

RSVP fixes a path to be used by IP packets flowing between two endpoints. There is an immediate and obvious question: How does one force a path selection between two endpoints in a network based on QoS, when routing at the IP level is based strictly on the destination IP address? A secondary consideration is how to handle the case where the predetermined path cannot offer the required QoS and alternative routes need to be examined before a call setup fails.

The IP community had a noble goal in mind when they decided to pursue a protocol that pins a path between two endpoints in a connectionless service. This may sound like a contradiction, but without a specific transport path for the duration of a call, all bets are off for achieving any meaningful QoS regardless of the service. But stitching an end-to-end path for the connectionless IP protocol is easier said than done.

The protocol abstract from the RFC states:

"RSVP provides receiver-initiated setup of resource reservations for multicast or unicast data flows, with good scaling and robustness properties. The RSVP protocol is used by a host to request specific QoS from the network for particular application data streams or flows. RSVP is also used by routers to deliver QoS requests to all nodes along the path(s) of the flows and to establish and maintain state to provide the requested service. RSVP requests will generally result in resources being reserved in each node along the data path."

A key aspect of RSVP is that reservation of resources cannot be guaranteed in the general case. Think of this as analogous to SS7 signaling (we see this in Chapter 3) not being able to find TDM segments along the path between exchanges. The big difference is that it is easy to find out whether or not in there is a TDM trunk the public telephone network. The trunk is reserved in the forward fashion, without strings attached in the reverse direction. Circuit reservation in the PSTN is a binary decision. On the other hand, resource reservation in VoIP telephony will depend greatly on the type of capacity algorithms implemented in the routing products running RSVP, and whether an adjacent device can tell in advance if an RSVP request is going to succeed or not. At first glance this can result in excessive signaling with high probability of failure during periods of high service utilization.

> RSVP is not a routing protocol. RSVP is not traffic management. RSVP is intended to operate with current and future unicast and multicast routing protocols. RSVP is a transport layer control protocol, like IGMP and ICMP or any routing protocol, but it does not transport data.

Protocol Fundamentals

The RSVP protocol is characterized by the following high-level attributes:

- It is receiver-oriented, that is, the actual reservation of a path "proposed" by the sender is done by the receiver. The main reason is support for multicast applications. This is where it differs greatly with SS7 signaling for circuit reservation to set up a simple telephone call. The added functionality for multicast support has an immediate price for the simple application.
- It supports heterogeneous reservations per multicast session. It allows receivers in a multicast session to request different QoS.
- It offers dynamic QoS per reservation. Receivers have the ability to modify an existing QoS on a path between endpoints. This flexibility can cause other problems with ATM signaling if ATM is the transport network.
- It supports multiple reservation styles for different needs of different applications, for instance, audio and video. This is critical for conserving resources in a network, such as VCs, in cases where explicit sender identification is not always necessary.
- It is a simplex protocol. This means that in a two-way call, both receivers need to establish and fix their paths independently of each other.
- The protocol maintains a soft state for each reservation inside each RSVP router. This state needs to be periodically refreshed by the sender and receiver with appropriate messages. The soft state expires if it does not receive a refresh.

RSVP treats the sender separately from the receiver, even in cases of a single application being both the sender and receiver, as would probably be the case for telephony services in an MGC. The protocol requires receivers to request a specific QoS. This means that for packet-based telephony, if one were to use RSVP for QoS purposes, both the sender and the receiver have to request the QoS serially, which affects performance in the time it takes to set up a call. The QoS requests execute serially because they travel along the reverse path from the origination of the data transmission. Thus the path selection begins from the calling party toward the called party. The called party begins the reservation process in the reverse direction, while at the same time trying to establish a path for its own transmission toward the calling party. Finally, the calling party reserves the path toward the called party and, if all goes well, a connection is established.

Quality of service is implemented for a particular data flow by mechanisms collectively called *traffic control*. These mechanisms shown in simplified block diagram form in Figure 2.20 include (1) a packet classifier, (2) policy and admission control, and (3) a packet scheduler or some other link-layer-dependent mechanism to determine when particular packets are forwarded. The packet classifier determines the QoS class (and perhaps the route) for each packet. For each outgoing interface, the packet scheduler or other link-layer-dependent mechanism achieves the promised QoS. Through these functions, traffic control can implement the desired QoS service capabilities.

During reservation setup, an RSVP QoS request is passed to a local decision entity,[14] policy and admission control. Admission control determines whether the node has sufficient available resources to supply the requested QoS. Policy control determines whether the user has administrative permission to make the requested reservation. If both checks succeed, parameters are set in the packet classifier and in the link layer interface (for instance, in the packet scheduler) to obtain the desired QoS. If either check fails, the RSVP program returns an error notification to the application process that originated the request.

RSVP protocol mechanisms provide a general facility for creating and maintaining distributed reservation state across a mesh of multicast or unicast delivery paths. RSVP itself transfers and manipulates QoS and policy control parameters as opaque data, passing them to the appropriate traffic control and policy control modules for interpretation. The structure and contents of the QoS parameters are documented in specifications developed by the Integrated Services Working Group; see RFC 2210. The structure and contents of the policy parameters are under development.

---

14. Policy and admission control could be implemented as separate entities.

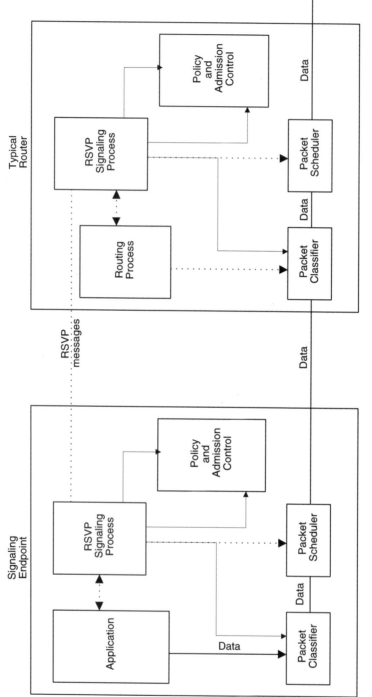

FIGURE 2.20 RSVP Reference Models for Signaling Endpoints and Routers

Since the membership of a large multicast group and the resulting multicast tree topology are likely to change with time, the RSVP design assumes that state for RSVP and traffic control state is to be built and destroyed incrementally in routers and hosts. For this purpose, RSVP establishes "soft" state; that is, RSVP sends periodic refresh messages to maintain the state along the reserved path(s). In the absence of refresh messages, the state automatically times out and is deleted.

Finally, the reader should remember that *all* the routers in the path of a call must support RSVP in order to have predictable delivery of the media packets. This detail is expected to create either a huge market for RSVP such that all carriers will offer this type of routing, or the industry will continue its research to find a best-suited QoS routing protocol to integrate the needs of simple telephony, and the services promised by the new packet networks.

Reservation Styles

RSVP defines four different reservation *styles*. Reservation styles are options for handling traffic types in a router. There are two types of senders identified in the styles: explicit and wildcard. Explicit is self-explanatory and identifies a specific sender in an RSVP session for a specific QoS. Senders are not grouped even for the same destination, and even if the QoS is the same. In ATM networks, each sender is assigned to a specific VC in the outbound direction. The wildcard style encompasses all the senders in an RSVP session with the same QoS, and for ATM networks all such senders share a VC. There are also two types of reservation that are supported by RSVP, shared and distinct. Table 2.4 summarizes the different reservation styles.

TABLE 2.4 RSVP Reservation Styles

SENDER	DISTINCT RESERVATION	SHARED RESERVATION
Explicit	Fixed Filter (FF)	Shared Filter (SF)
Wildcard	No definition for this style	Wildcard Filter (WF)

The fixed filter (FF) style identifies a specific sender with an outbound VC. This results in the maximum VC usage and may have other processing implications inside the router as well. For large-scale unicast applications, such as voice telephony, it is expected that QoS will be done with FF-style reservations, which will invariably limit the number of calls that can be handled by a router. This type of reservation is also appropriate for video transmission from multiple senders, as in a videoconference.

The shared filter (SF) style improves on the efficiency of the network and the routers by grouping "similar" senders and placing them on a single VC in the outbound direction. The receiver explicitly identifies the senders to share the reservation. Shared reservations are appropriate when all the senders are not expected to start sending simultaneously. Such is the case for the audio streams of most conference calls.

The wildcard filter (WF) style is used when all senders in an RSVP session can be combined and placed in a single VC toward a receiver. The upstream senders' flows are all shared for the reservation. As new senders appear in the session, their flows are also shared in the same manner. A WF style can be used when there is a large number of senders in a session and its use would result in less processing overhead in the routers along the way than an SF style for the same purpose.

It must be remembered that all three reservation styles are mutually incompatible for a given reservation and cannot be combined among themselves.

Usage in Call Models

Figure 2.21 shows the three possible reservation styles between endpoints in a session.

How does RSVP really work? A fundamental concept of RSVP is the *session*. An RSVP session is a data flow with a destination, using a particular transport protocol. It is defined by the set [destination address, protocol ID, destination port], the last of which is optional. The destination address is the IP address of the endpoint and can be either unicast or multicast. The destination port would be the UDP or TCP port, if either of those protocols is used as transport.

An RSVP reservation request is characterized by a *flow descriptor*. The flow descriptor consists of the flow specification and the filter specification, or flow spec and filter spec, respectively. The flow spec defines the desired QoS for the session for this reservation. This information is used by the router's packet scheduler to ensure compliance. The filter specification defines which packets from the sender will receive the specified QoS. This information is used by the packet classifier in the router. Since packet classification uses the TCP/UDP port number, it is imperative that fragmentation does not occur anywhere along the path to the receiver. This presents a problem for multicast trees because the minimum MTU must be computed for the tree. RFC 2210 elaborates on a method to compute the minimum MTU.

RSVP has two fundamental message types for making reservations. These are the PATH and RESV messages. There are also TEARDOWN, RESVERR, and PATHERR messages. All RSVP messages are sent as raw IP packets with protocol number 46. PATH messages travel from the sender downstream to the

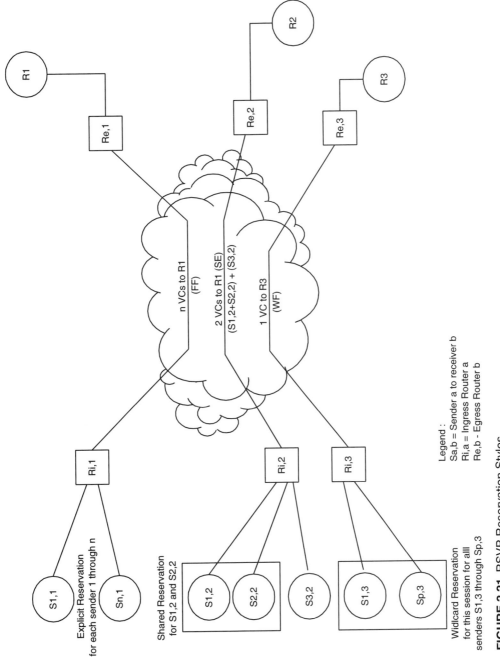

FIGURE 2.21 RSVP Reservation Styles

Legend :
Sa,b = Sender a to receiver b
Ri,a = Ingress Router a
Re,b - Egress Router b

n VCs to R1
(FF)

2 VCs to R1 (SE)
(S1,2+S2,2) + (S3,2)

1 VC to R3
(WF)

Explicit Reservation
for each sender 1 through n

Shared Reservation
for S1,2 and S2,2

Widlcard Reservation
for this session for alll
senders S1,3 through Sp,3

receiver. The routers store a PATH STATE at each intermediate routing point. This state includes the unicast IP address of the previous router (hop) from which the PATH message was received. The state information is used to route the RESV messages originating from the receiver along the same set of routers that were visited by the corresponding PATH message.

Table 2.5 shows the information included in PATH messages.

TABLE 2.5 RSVP PATH Message Information Parameters

INFORMATION	MEANING
Sender Template	Defines the types of data packets that will be sent by the sender during this session. It can be used as a qualifier to allow the receiver to distinguish the packets from this sender from other packets possibly in the same session.
Sender Tspec (Traffic Spec)	Defines the traffic characteristics of the data that will be sent. Used as input to admission control algorithms along the way.
Adspec (Advertisement spec)	This is used in cases of One-Pass with Advertising (OPWA) information. This approach is used for the receiver to find out the result of a QoS request. The summary advertisement of the path's abilities is updated along the way and travels downstream to the receiver. The receiver then has a good idea whether the desired QoS can be accommodated and can make adjustments as necessary.

PATH messages are sent with the source and destination addresses, the same as the data packets. This ensures correct routing through areas that do not support RSVP. On the other hand, RSVP RESV messages travel one hop at a time.

RESV messages contain a *flow descriptor list, policy data,* and *confirmation requests.* The confirmation requests let the receiver know that a request was executed successfully all the way back to the sender. Policy data is carried as input to policy control at each intermediate point to provide usage feedback or authorization. The flow descriptor list carries the flow spec and filter spec (for FF styles), or the flow spec and filter spec list (for SE styles), or simply the flow spec for WF styles.

PATH TEARDOWN messages are originated by the senders and travel toward the receivers. When a router receives a path teardown message, it removes the matching path state for the reservation. These messages must be routed along the same route as the path messages; otherwise, intermediate segments of the path will not be torn down.

RESV TEARDOWN messages are originated by the receivers, and delete the matching reservation state at each intermediate point.

RESV CONF messages are sent to the unicast address of the receiver for the session.

PATHERR messages communicate errors associated with the processing of path messages. They are routed backward toward the sender, following the established path state. They include the IP address of the node that experienced the error, and optional policy data to assist in decoding the error.

RESVERR messages communicate errors associated with the processing of RESV messages in the routers along the path. They are routed a hop at a time, using the established reservation state. They also include the IP address of the node that experienced the error, and optional policy data to assist in decoding the error.

Potential Issues with RSVP

We mentioned earlier a possibly major issue in selecting routes for a packet not based on the IP address in the packet header. Protocols and architectures such as MPLS (multiprotocol label switching) address this issue in a satisfactory form.

There are a couple of "killer" reservation problems that have been identified, with recommendations for workarounds.

The first problem deals with a receiver making a new reservation Q1, which happens to be greater than an existing reservation Q0. The result of merging the reservations could be rejection by admission control in an upstream node. If this occurs, this situation must not adversely affect the existing reservation.

The second problem deals with a persistent request Q1 from a receiver, which may be failing in some intermediate node, thus precluding acceptance of a smaller request Q0 from a different receiver that would otherwise be accepted if it were not merged with Q1. This is handled via the *blockade state*, established in each router traversed by the ResvErr message. The blockade state in effect prevents the router's merging process from including the failing request in the merge, thus allowing a smaller request to be considered by admission control and be accepted. There is an extensive set of recommendations in RFC 2205 regarding the creation and use of the blockade state.

Traversing Non-RSVP Networks

The rule of thumb for PATH messages travelling through a non-RSVP network is to carry the IP address of the last RSVP router they encountered prior to entering the non-RSVP cloud. This in effect renders the non-RSVP cloud invisible to the RSVP-capable portion of the network, but with a big caveat. The caveat is that the desired QoS may not be compliant through the non-

RSVP hops, as there is no way to signal it to those routers. As a result, a "non-RSVP" flag is sent to local traffic control when non-RSVP routers are present and Adspecs are formed and sent to the receiver(s) using OPWA[15] so they can make appropriate choices in QoS requests.

Naturally, the presence of a non-RSVP segment in the path of a call will cause uncertainty as to the resulting end-to-end QoS. However, if two RSVP network segments touch the PSTN at both ends, for example, two carrier VoIP networks not directly connected over IP, the resulting quality will be of the highest possible.

2.3 A QUICK LOOK AT AAL2 FOR VOICE TRANSPORT

The battle to bring high bandwidth from the local carrier to the home and small office is very much alive. ISDN Basic Rate Interface (BRI) did not see the success its proponents were hoping for, partly because of some of the cost and scalability issues now being addressed by IP technology. ISDN is basically a circuit switched service, with substantial costs to the local carrier. Scaling of ISDN BRI means buying more and more circuit capacity in Class 5 systems, and the resulting cost structure has priced BRI out of the range of most consumers. In comes Digital Subscriber Loop (DSL) technology, generically known as xDSL, in many flavors and capacities. DSL technology modulates the copper in the "last mile" with digital means to deliver high bit rates, as long as certain distance restrictions from the local exchange carrier office are met. Symmetric versions of DSL, such as HDSL and SDSL, offer promise of T1-equivalent bit rates for the home and small office, but it is the asymmetric version, or ADSL, which holds the bigger promise for wider deployment to the home.

ADSL can support 6–8 Mbps bandwidth in the downstream direction, and upward of 600 Kbps upstream. It is an ideal solution for accessing the Internet and downloading large files, but there is an obvious discrepancy in the speeds if you need to send your downloaded files somewhere else, when integrated multimedia applications are simultaneously active. Still, ADSL is much more promising than ISDN BRI, and the hope of the industry is that it will become ubiquitous as a service in the next couple of years.

At first glance, ADSL pilot programs and early service deployments have shown good performance, with as much as an order of magnitude more bandwidth to the home at reasonable pricing than is currently feasible with ISDN BRI service. However, when we account for call features that the PSTN sub-

---

15. One Pass With Advertising.

scriber is used to with the current SS7 network, and the desire for high speed data access to the Internet, the access bandwidth is not so large after all. For simple residential solutions for one or two users, the bandwidth is more than adequate, but as users and features are added, including Intelligent Network features of the future, one has to be careful how the bandwidth is used.

The natural inclination is to use compressed voice instead of simple G.711 64K μLaw[16] or ALaw. This solution has its own merits and drawbacks. Although bandwidth utilization can be improved, there are user-perceptible voice QoS concerns that must be addressed. Simple G.711 over RTP/UDP/IP/ATM is a headache and inefficient, as we already discussed. It offers acceptable latency for low packetization periods, but bandwidth demands skyrocket because of protocol overhead.

Simply stated, if rate adaptation is allowed on the link, there can be uncertainty as to how many calls to accept from the subscribers at any given time. The scenario becomes confused when a number of calls are up using uncompressed voice in a down-speed situation, using all but, let's say, 40K in the uplink. Then another subscriber served by the media gateway dials a number. During signaling for the new call, the proper codecs are not negotiated with the far end, or the call is off net to a PSTN user and the call defaults to G.711. Thus the call will not be accepted (MGCP would most likely return an "insufficient resources" error code, H.323 would complain with an ARJ, and a SIP implementation would return a warning code 370). There can be service level agreement issues if the service guarantee was to accept all calls from all subscribers at all times. Obviously, careful network and service design are paramount for a good all around experience.

2.4 EDGE BANDWIDTH MANAGEMENT—A LOOK AT AAL2

AAL2 is the latest ATM adaptation layer, which provides for variable length packet payload multiplexing within a single virtual circuit, for applications with end-to-end timing requirements. The structure of AAL2 is very simple and consists of two low layer stacks (sublayers). Layer CPS sends and receives packets from specific channels, which connect to a service specific convergence sublayer or directly to the application that produces the payloads. Figure 2.22 shows the protocol relationship of the two sublayers of AAL2, which is specified in ITU-T recommendation I.363.2 (reference [34]).

Managing voice, voiceband, and non-real-time data in the same physical medium can be challenging enough, but it doesn't stop there. If compression

---

16. μLaw.

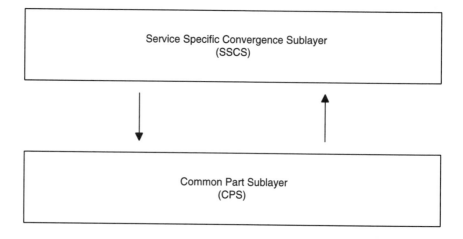

Structure of AAL2 protocol layers

FIGURE 2.22 AAL2 Protocol Structure

is used, the task of bandwidth management gets another twist when a trunking protocol is in use. If, for example, AAL2 is used as the multiplexing mechanism for multiple media streams, then support for voiceband (fax, modem) connection poses the problem of accommodating expansion of the payload to G.711 when a fax is sent or when someone uses a modem for dialup access. Bandwidth expansion for support of voiceband calls is a recommended action in the ATM VToA specification (reference [36]).

When compression with silence suppression and echo cancellation are used simultaneously on a connection, the call processing hardware and software must be agile enough to respond to indications of voiceband signals, such as the 2100 Hz answer tone being detected. A method is necessary to immediately inform the endpoint it controls to remove echo cancellation and echo suppression, while at the same time expanding the virtual time slot (Channel ID, in AAL2 terms) occupied by the connection. Some sophisticated equipment can react to voiceband tones and expand the payload, but the system elements need to intervene to shut down echo cancellation and silence suppression. The new accommodation will presumably last for the duration of the call.

Performance is significantly increased over plain IP-based transmission for two reasons. First, the protocol overhead per bit of payload is drastically reduced. Second, this method allows for payload multiplexing at the link layer, which has advantages over network and higher layer multiplexing in performance and capacity.

The packet format supported by the CPS sublayer is shown in Figure 2.23.

Each contributing source of payload information is assigned a CID (channel ID). The length indicator is a zero-based length of the packet, which is either 45 bytes maximum or can be dynamically set on a per channel basis up to 64 bytes. Channels sharing a virtual circuit need not be assigned the same packet length. However, a channel within a VC maintains its assigned length once the assignment has been made by the system's signaling processes. The CID value is bi-directional, and may be either statically or dynamically assigned.

The user-to-user information field carries codes of significance only to the endpoints of the channel, whereas the HEC field is simple header error control.

PDUs begin with a start field (STF), which consists of an offset field, a sequence field, and a parity bit. The offset field simply specifies where the next PDU in the ATM begins. This is necessary to accommodate the non-uniform packet length multiplexing performed by the protocol. Field SN is a simple sequence number, which simply toggles from 0 to 1, and P is a parity bit, maintaining odd parity across the 8-bit STF.

In the general case, packets of different lengths will be multiplexed in a single VC. This is true even for plain voice transport, due to the different packet lengths generated by the various compression schemes. Figure 2.24 shows an arbitrary example whereby three PDUs from three different contributing sources are multiplexed on a VC.

In Figure 2.24, multiplexing of PDU A and B in one cell is not feasible and we end up crossing cell boundaries. The start field of the first cell points to the packet header which is located immediately after the STF. In the second cell, the last 12 bytes of PDU B are placed immediately after the STF, but the STF points to the first byte of the packet header of PDU C, which also does not fit within the same cell and we cross cell boundaries again.

In the last PDU, the STF points to the beginning of the padding bytes (zeros), after the remaining 11 bytes of PDU C are placed at the beginning of the PDU.

Error recovery in cases of cell loss is very simple in AAL2 and is done via resynchronization of the endpoint CPS sublayers. If an intermediate cell is lost, the SN will not toggle and it is easily seen that we had an odd number of packets lost. Partially received packets are discarded and the process restarts at the next reliably established packet payload boundary. This transport mechanism produces excellent delay characteristics for voice and voice-band applications.

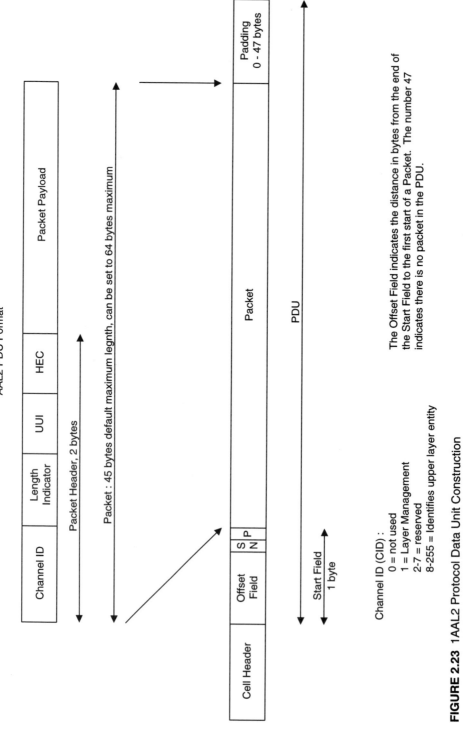

AAL2 PDU Format

Channel ID	Length Indicator	UUI	HEC	Packet Payload

Packet Header, 2 bytes

Packet : 45 bytes default maximum legnth, can be set to 64 bytes maximum

Cell Header	Offset Field	S N	P	Packet	Padding 0 - 47 bytes

Start Field
1 byte

PDU

Channel ID (CID) :
    0 = not used
    1 = Layer Management
    2-7 = reserved
    8-255 = Identifies upper layer entity

The Offset Field indicates the distance in bytes from the end of the Start Field to the first start of a Packet. The number 47 indicates there is no packet in the PDU.

FIGURE 2.23 1AAL2 Protocol Data Unit Construction

154

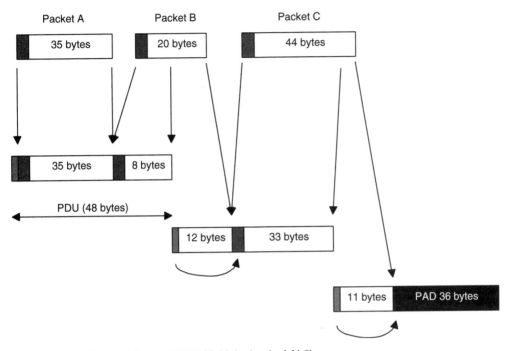

FIGURE 2.24 General Case of PDU Multiplexing in AAL2\

What are the challenges for fax and voiceband transmission that are addressed with AAL2? When a user whose subscription profile indicates compression dials a remote terminal, the initial connection will be made using the codec selection in their profile, for example, G.726. The connection will stay in this mode until the remote fax number is dialed and the CED tone is placed on the line by the remote terminal. At that time, the interworking functions between the access point and the network need to select a bit rate which can reliably transport the voiceband signal end-to-end. This means the channel in the VC carrying the fax call data will expand to 64 Kbps when the 2100 Hz tone is detected. The expansion will remain in effect until the fax has been transmitted or the modem signal modulation has been turned off. Expansion must be quick and reliable so that equipment timing considerations for signal handshakes are not violated.

AAL2 defines three packet types. Type 1 packets—also referred to as unprotected—are used as the default and carry the compressed image of a fax transmission. Type 2 packets—also known as partially protected packets—contain an internal header and CRC protection field at the beginning of the payload. The header field is 19 bytes and CRC occupies the remaining 5 bits of the 3 header bytes. The remaining part of the payload is unprotected.

Type 3 packets—also known as fully protected packets—are used to transport dialed digits (DTMF signals), CAS bits, fax demodulation control data, and alarms. Type 3 packets can be used to expand the bit rate of a channel detecting CED from a remote fax terminal.

Less critical, but still mandatory requirements at the access portion of the network deal with the call model used when trunking has been implemented between the MGs and the media gateway controller. Access trunking is mostly necessary for SOHO and business applications for voice. Factors such as CID assignment, static or dynamic, can affect post-dial delay and the overall quality of the user's experience with the call. Static CID assignments at the access offer the advantage of less overhead at connection time, since the virtual slot in the virtual trunk for a particular endpoint does not need to be negotiated or assigned for every call. Dynamic allocation on a per call basis offers flexibility and reduced latency and is considered desirable for some applications.

2.4.1 Converging Media Streams in the Backbone

When all the access streams have converged inside the cloud, the age-old issue of add and drop multiplexing (ADM) needs to be addressed again. If the backbone is ATM-based, the use of AAL2 simplifies the problem somewhat, with the only complication being the accordion effect of voiceband streams on compressed connections. Other backbone technologies have also worked ADM schemes with various degrees of efficiency, flexibility, and latency. These technologies and signaling issues for intra-network media stream routing are beyond the scope of this text.

CHAPTER 3

Basic Call Control for Voice Telephony

In the previous chapters we discussed the basics of signaling and the media transport mechanism in VoIP networks. We also saw some reference topologies and basic call flows between the central office and equipment on the customer premise. It is now time to review the signaling mechanism of the PSTN for call establishment and termination, and look at some basic signaling exchanges at network boundaries with signaling interworking. We begin this chapter with a look at the fundamentals of Signaling System 7, and then we will take a look at basic call flows across networks employing different signaling mechanisms.

3.1 AN OVERVIEW OF SS7

Signaling System 7 (SS7) is the current suite of protocols used in the North American public network to establish and terminate telephone calls. SS7 is implemented as a packet-switched network, which in most cases uses dedicated links, nodes, and facilities. In general, SS7 is a non-associated, common channel, out of band signaling network. However, SS7 signaling may traverse circuits—real or virtual—on links that also carry voice traffic.

Complete coverage of SS7 has appeared in the literature and its full treatment is a very detailed and lengthy subject. The reader can find excellent in-depth descriptions of SS7 in the references, which cover the individual protocols in considerable detail. Our interest in this section is to understand the basic signaling functions and interfaces of SS7, because they may influence the implementation of interworking between IP-based telephony and the PSTN.

3.1.1 SS7 Network Topology

SS7 network topologies are constructed using three types of components, arranged throughout the network in a manner that offers maximum reliability, flexibility, and speed for accomplishing several instrumental tasks in providing telephone service. The fundamental elements of the signaling capabilities offered by SS7 include the following:

- Establishing and terminating calls between telephone service subscribers.
- Accessing back-office systems to obtain subscriber information directly or indirectly related to the completion of a telephone call.
- Accessing back-office systems for customer billing information.
- Accessing back-office systems for the translation of toll-free numbers, toll numbers, and other advanced network features.
- Supporting mobile network features, such as wireless roaming and authentication.
- Supporting local number portability (LNP), which allows consumers to select different telephone companies without having to change their telephone number.
- Providing access to advanced telephone service features such as call forwarding, calling party name and number identification, and three-way calling.

The components of the SS7 signaling network are shown in Figure 3.1(a) and an example simplified topology that uses them is shown in Figure 3.1(b). An SSP is the local exchange that provides telephone service. It consists of a voice switch and equipment to monitor and manage the individual circuits and trunks connected to other exchanges. It can also be a tandem office. SSPs communicate with other SSPs across the SS7 network for the setup and termination of calls. SSPs also have interfaces and access to back-office functions for configuration, billing, performance monitoring, error reporting, and technical support. These back-office functions are collectively known as FCAPS, which stands for failure, configuration, accounting, performance, and security.

SSPs are assigned point codes (PC), which are IDs that uniquely identify them in the SS7 network. Most SSPs have one point code, but implementation requirements in packet telephony may result in more than one PC per SSP. Such is currently the case for international signaling points, which have two point codes, one for domestic use and one for identification internation-

Service Switching Point
The local telephone exchange,
which employs subscriber circuits
and trunks connecting to other
exchanges. It connects directly to
STPs to establish calls using SS7
signaling

S.S.P.

Signaling Transfer Point
Offers transfer and routing services
of SS7 messages originating at the
SSP. STPs connect directly to
other STPs, SSPs, and SCPs

S.T.P.

Service Control Point
The SCP offers access to the
telephone companies' data bases
via the STP network.

S.C.P.

FIGURE 3.1(a) Components of the SS7 Signaling Network

ally. PCs are 24-bit quantities in the North American network and 14-bit quantities in networks using the ITU version of SS7. Messages between the North American and ITU-compliant networks require routing through translation points.

STPs are computers with embedded router functionality. They receive signaling messages from their local SSP or other SSPs over the SS7 network, and are responsible for properly routing these messages to their ultimate destination. There are two types of signaling messages: end-to-end user signaling, and signaling associated with trunks that carry subscriber voice conversations or voiceband data such as modem and fax. One of the major functions of the STP is Global Title Translation (GT), that is, the translation of a dialed digit string to a routable number in the public network. Toll-free 800 and toll 900 numbers are such a global titles. If the STP that is local to

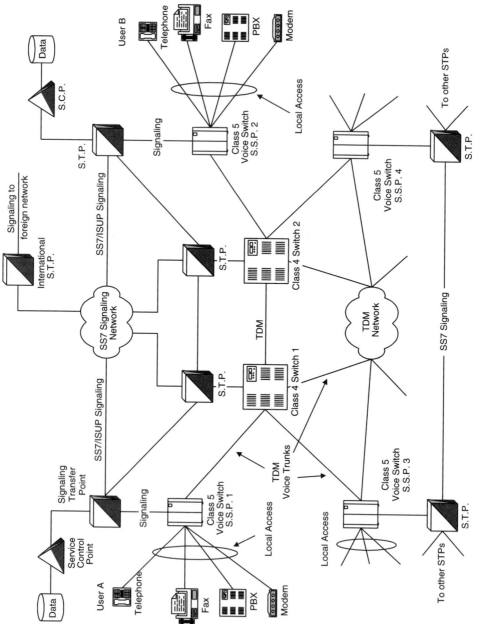

FIGURE 3.1(b) Simplified view of SS7 component topology

the SSP that received the dialed digits cannot perform the GT translation, it forwards the request along to an STP with the translation capability. The STPs also monitor the health and status of the signaling links, and are responsible for ensuring signaling connectivity in the network via changeover procedures when links become unstable or fail.

The SCP is a host computer or distributed computer network attached to an STP, with access to a database that contains information necessary to process an incoming call to an exchange. Such information may be the translation of toll-free or toll 900 numbers, billing and credit card information, and routing information for numbers that have been ported to another carrier. A "ported" number is a number that has been moved to another carrier, as is the case when a subscriber selects a different long distance company.

Numbers that have been ported present an interesting problem for the completion of long distance calls by the inter-exchange carriers (IXCs). When the user dials a number on the telephone keypad, the originating local exchange (OLE) analyzes the digits to determine where to find the terminating exchange (TE) that services the called party. A required immediate action is to determine if the dialed number has been ported. This is accomplished by using the services of the transactions capability application part (TCAP) of SS7, which we will discuss later, through a process called a local number portability (LNP) query. The terminating exchange of the call will be identified by the location routing number (LRN) returned by the LNP query.

The basic and often typical network arrangement of SS7 network elements in Figure 3.2 consists of SSPs connected by various means to local or non-local STPs, cross-connected STPs, and a minimum of one SCP. SSPs connect to mated pairs of STPs directly with Access Links (A-Links). Every node is identified in the SS7 network by a separate point code.

The links shown in Figure 3.2 can be of the same facility type. The most common types of links in North America are DS0s, or 56 Kbps circuits, or full T1 facilities. An SSP consists of (among other elements) the voice switch, usually a Class 5 compatible device, and is responsible for mapping signaling received from the subscriber endpoints to SS7 signaling. The signaling protocols of the SS7 network are discussed later in this section. In the PSTN, endpoint signaling is either analog (for example, loop start for basic telephones), or digital (for example, PBX access to the central office, which is PRI ISDN-based).

STPs can be arranged in a hierarchy, or at a single, non-hierarchical level. A hierarchy of STPs may be necessary when some STPs are dedicated to signaling within a portion of the network, such as a region, however loose the definition of a region may be. In that case, a higher level in the hierarchy is

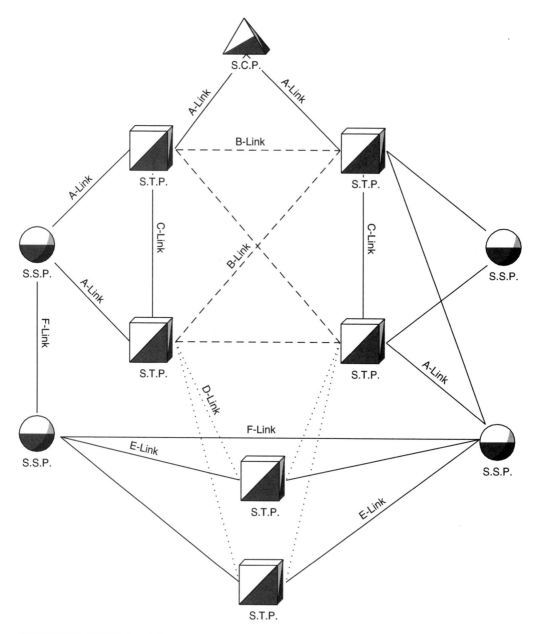

FIGURE 3.2 SS7 Network Topology

required for STPs to signal to other STPs across regional boundaries. In both types of topological arrangement, each service switching point is connected to at least two mated STPs, whose own connectivity in the general case forms a fully meshed graph. A primary objective of the STP topology is to offer robust and redundant router functionality for the signaling protocols of SS7, which in turn translates to reliable telephone service in the public network.

An STP connects to its mated STP using cross links (C-Links). C-Links offer alternative routes to other STPs, in the same or different region in the signaling network, through the mated STP. Signaling across peer STPs of different exchanges or networks is accomplished with bridge links (B-Links). If an STP hierarchy exists, diagonal links (D-Links) are used to signal to STP pairs across levels in the hierarchy. D-links are similar to B-links.

Extended links (E-Links) provide connectivity to STPs not associated with the local exchange, and are used when connectivity between the SSP and its local pair of STPs is lost. Fully associated links (F-Links) connect SSPs directly, but their use is not very common.

STPs connect to service control points (SCP) and possibly multiple local exchanges with A-links.

What are the basic signaling steps necessary to complete a simple telephone call? When a user dials a number, the local exchange (OLE) must find out where the called number is located. From the perspective of the caller, that would be the terminating exchange (TE). If the TE is different that the LE (for example, a long distance call, or a call in the local area to a subscriber served by a difference exchange), the SSP identifies the voice trunk that will be used to connect the call to the adjacent exchange. It then needs to signal its adjacent exchange about its intent to place a call on this trunk, and sends a signal through its local STP using the SS7 protocol. The message is then sent to the adjacent STP over a B- or D-Link. If the adjacent local exchange hosts the called party, it is the terminating exchange and signaling terminates. The call is established as soon the terminating exchange notifies the endpoint (the called party's phone rings) and someone answers the phone. If the immediately adjacent exchange is not the TE, signaling proceeds along through multiple exchanges until it reaches the TE, which is the called party's home exchange. Even so, when the TE is reached, signaling for the call may not be over if the called party has activated any variation of call forwarding features that would take effect when the call request arrives. In that case, signaling will continue until the current home TE is found.

As call signaling proceeds between nodes in the network, each intermediate exchange needs to select an outbound trunk toward its next adjacent exchange, and switch the incoming voice circuit from the inbound trunk to the outbound. For local calls the process is very simple, and the STPs are involved only if multiple local exchanges in the same local area need to be traversed. If a single exchange is both the local and terminating exchange for the call, no SS7 signaling is necessary and the SSP will connect the two subscribers through the voice switch or switches it controls.

The role and importance of the SCP is evident in the support for 800 toll-free number or 900 toll number dialing. Toll-free and 900 numbers are not real telephone numbers—that is, they do not conform to the standard North American Numbering Plan, and the exchange that hosts the number cannot be obtained by simple table lookup. When such a number is dialed, the SSP accesses an SCP using TCAP through its local STP, asking for a translation. The SCP has access to such databases[1] and, once the number is translated, the new routing number is returned to the SSP, along with billing information and other information necessary to complete the call. The local exchange can then proceed to place the call as it would a normal telephone number. Toll-free and toll 900 numbers are normally issued by a carrier, who "owns" the number. It is a regulatory requirement for all carriers to have access to all 800 numbers assigned in the public network, regardless of which one owns them.

Another use of the SCP is with numbers that have been ported to another telephone company. When a number is dialed, it is necessary for the originating exchange to determine if the number has been ported so it can determine how to route it. It initiates an LNP query through the STP to the SCP which accesses its database[2]. The SCP will return a LRN indicating if the number has been ported. The LRN is then used instead of the called party number, as signaling begins to reach the called party. LNP does not necessarily imply a different physical location for the called party.

The SS7 Protocol Stack

SS7 preceded the OSI model in its definition, but there is a loose correspondence between the SS7 protocol stack (shown in Figure 3.3) and the OSI model. The message transfer part (MTP) layer actually consists of three sublayers, the bottom two of which correspond to layers 1 and 2 of the OSI model. MTP1 is the physical signaling data link (SDL), and was originally optimized for 64 Kbps and 56 Kbps digital circuits. At present, network topologies have implementations of full T1 (1.536 Mbps) facilities dedicated to SS7 signaling, and signaling can be also routed over satellite or even ATM trunks.

Layer 2 is MTP2 or signaling link (SL) layer, which is responsible for the error-free, in-sequence delivery of messages to adjacent STPs, the implementation of flow control, retransmission of messages, and selection of alter-

---

1.   The SCP is often synonymous with the database.

2.   The database will be in the SCP or in an integrated STP. If the STP has access to the information, there is no need to access the SCP.

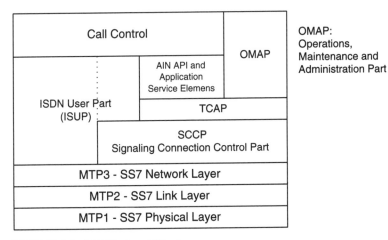

FIGURE 3.3 SS7 Protocol Stack

native links in failover conditions. Error correction is necessary because there is a requirement for a much smaller number of errored messages over the SL than would be allowed under the specified bit-rate of the digital facilities. There are as many MTP2 layers as there are physical links attached to the STP. The messages exchanged by STPs are referred to as signaling units (SU). There are three types of SUs, all of which are delimited with the HDLC flag (X'7E'), and implement bit-stuffing:

1. the message signaling unit (MSU), which contains the signaling message originating at the SSP;

2. the link status signal unit (LSSU), which originates at MTP2 and provides real-time information about the health and status of the links connected to the STP; and

3. the fill-in signaling unit (FISU), which is sent continuously by MTP2 when there is no other signaling information to send.

The use of FISUs in the absence of signaling is different than the normal operation of an HDLC link, which sends flags when the link is idle. The reason for the FISU is to detect immediately a deteriorating link, because a real message employs an FCS sequence for error control and the signaling nodes would get early indication of excessive error rates. The MSU, LSSU, and FISU are shown in Figures 3.4, 3.5, and 3.6, respectively.

MTP3 is at layer 3, which partially corresponds to the network layer of OSI. There is one MTP3 per STP and it provides services to the layer 4 protocols of SS7 and shares joint link management with MTP2. The layer 4 protocols on top of MTP3 are known as *users* or *parts*. The protocol stack in Figure 3.3 shows two such parts, that is, the signaling connection control part

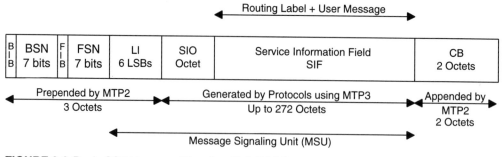

FIGURE 3.4 Basic SS7 Message Signaling Unit (MSU)

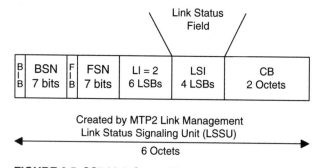

FIGURE 3.5 SS7 Link Status Signal Unit

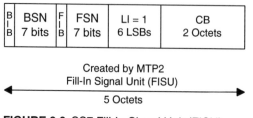

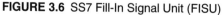

FIGURE 3.6 SS7 Fill-In Signal Unit (FISU)

(SSCP) and ISDN user part (ISUP), both of which are used in North America. Most countries use another part for telephony signaling, the telephone user part (TUP), which is similar to ISUP, and is beyond the scope of this text. TUP is a peer of ISUP in the SS7 protocol stack.

MTP3 is responsible for routing signaling messages between STPs and peer users of MTP, for instance, ISUP or SCCP. This is known as the signaling message handling (SMH) function. MTP3 also maintains signaling flow in cases of network or link malfunction, under the functions of signaling network management (SNM).

ISUP is the protocol used for circuit-switch messaging for the establishment of telephone calls. It is also being augmented to support broadband services offered by the carriers under the name of Broadband ISUP, or B-ISUP. ISUP is used in the wireline and wireless networks to control trunks between exchanges. Much like the ISDN Q.931 signaling protocol, ISUP offers both basic and supplementary services. Basic services control call setup, whereas supplementary services apply to a call after it is in its stable state.

ISUP uses MTP directly for both the basic and supplementary services, but it also offers the capability for end-to-end, call-related signaling between exchanges that are not necessarily adjacent. This type of signaling can be accomplished either directly with MTP using the pass-along method, or indirectly through the use of SCCP in end-to-end signaling mode.

Pass-along, end-to-end user signaling uses the same path taken by the original call setup. Special pass-along messages (PAMs) are generated and relayed by the intermediate STPs until they reach their destinations. On the other hand, the SCCP method uses bypass procedures and signaling is done end-to-end, without regard for the path taken or its relationship to the path used for establishing the call.

Figure 3.7 shows a diagram of pass-along messaging between an SSP with PC = 1 and an SSP with PC = 3. The PAM messages are recognized in all intermediate exchanges and continue to be propagated towards their destination. PAM messages have no associated ISUP parameters.

In contrast, when ISUP uses the services of SCCP, the originating exchange needs to know the point code of the terminating exchange for the signaling message to be routed correctly, as shown in Figure 3.8. Use of the circuit identification code (CIC) in this type of signaling is no longer necessary, as the message may travel over paths unrelated to a call in progress. The use of SCCP by ISUP signaling of this type is the reason that a portion of ISUP is shown on top of SCCP in the SS7 protocol stack.

Description of the Signaling Units of MTP

The FISU, shown in Figure 3.6, is pretty straightforward and is basically a filler when no traffic is present on the signaling link. The length indicator in the packet is LI = 1. The LI occupies the least significant six bits of the third

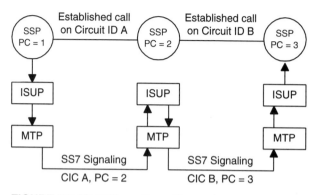

FIGURE 3.7 ISUP Pass-Along Messaging

octet, counting from the left with the BSN octet. The BSN and FSN stand for backward and forward sequence numbers, respectively, and have significance for the receiving party to ensure no out-of-sequence signaling messages are accepted. FISUs can be used to provide acknowledgment to messages. The sequence numbers reflect the last valid sequence numbers of the MSU, and FISUs *do not* get assigned their own sequence numbers.

The LSSU, shown in Figure 3.5, has only local significance and contains status information about the signaling link, per Table 3.1. The LI is set to 1 or 2 depending on whether one or two status octets are included in the message. The status code is right-justified in the least significant four bits of the LSI octet, only three of which are currently used. LSSUs can also be used to pro-

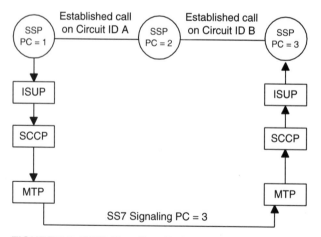

FIGURE 3.8 ISUP Signaling: End-to-End SCCP Method

TABLE 3.1 LSI Coding of LSSU Signaling Unit

LSI CODE	MEANING
000 - SIO	Out of Alignment. The STP sends SIO when the link is first brought up and incoming flags are not detected. Other cases for sending SIO include MSU message length and bit-stuffing violations.
001 – SIN	Normal Alignment. Once flags are received and recognized, the STPs transmit SIN. When both STPs recognize normal alignment, they revert to sending FISUs.
010 – SIE	Emergency Alignment. During SIE and SIN, the STPs do not send MSUs. The STP level 2 invokes the emergency alignment procedure and exits when normal alignment is detected again.
011 – SIOS	Out of Service.
100 – SIPO	Processor Outage. This action also suspends the link from further use until the situation is cleared.
101 – SIB	Busy. MTP3 is requested to stop sending MSUs when this code is received. Used for flow control by MTP2.

vide positive or negative acknowledgment to MSUs via the FSN and BSN fields. LSSUs *do not* get assigned their own sequence numbers. LSSUs and FISUs received in error are not retransmitted.

The context of the LSSU message remains local to MTP2, except to pass information to MTP3 for situations such as busy or processor outage from the far end.

The MSU, shown in Figure 3.4, is the basic signaling information of the MTP3 layer and contains the message received from the user part. The MSU begins with the length indicator (LI) and ends with the inclusion of the check bit field (CB). The LI and CB fields are created and appended by MTP2, whereas the service information field (SIF) is the message received by MTP from the user part layer 4 protocols. The SIF can be up to 272 octets. The service information octet (SIO) is used for MTP to route the message to the appropriate user, and is coded as shown in Table 3.2.

As an example, the pass-along ISUP message will have an SI = 1010 0101, whereas an end-to-end user message using ISUP over SCCP will be coded as SI = 1010 0011.

The routing label (RL) of the SIF is a 56-bit field for the North American ANSI version of SS7 (32-bit field for the ITU-T version), and is divided into three parts.

TABLE 3.2 MSU Service Information Octet (SIO)

SUBSERVICE FIELD SSF (BITS 8, 7, 6, 5)	MEANING	SERVICE INDICATOR SI (BITS 4, 3, 2, 1)	MEANING
0000	International Network	0000	Signaling Network Management
0010	Not Used	0001	Signaling Network Testing and Maintenance
1010	National Network	0010	Not Used
11xx	Reserved	0011	SCCP (TCAP, ISUP), etc.
		0100	TUP
		0101	ISUP

- The first 24 bits (three octets) are the Destination Point Code (DPC) of the end or adjacent signaling point. This code occupies only 14 bits in the ITU version of SS7 (ITU No 7).
- The next 24 bits (three octets) are the Source Point Code (SPC) of the originating signaling point. Similarly, this code occupies only 14 bits in the ITU version of SS7.
- The last 5 bits of the RL field are the Signaling Link Selection code. In the ITU version of SS7, the SLS code is 4 bits.

Load sharing between signaling units is achieved with the signaling link selection (SLS) code in the MSU. The code is derived by balancing the number of voice trunks on the switch vs. the signaling links with a modulo algorithm. A modulo-32 division of the circuit identification code (CIC) produces a code for each trunk, and thus maps 32 trunks per code. The individual bits of the code can then be used by the SSP and the STPs to select an outbound link toward the destination. The SLS in ITU No 7 provides modulo-16 resolution for load balancing.

STPs can alter the signaling link selection algorithm and thus map traffic to other outbound links when congestion or link instability occurs in the network. This process is discussed in the next section.

Flow Control and Error Recovery in SS7

Flow control in SS7 is the responsibility of the MTP2 sublayer. The basic flow control concept is simple and utilizes the LSSU message to throttle a sender when buffers are about to overflow or other processing conditions prevent the STP from catching up with the message flow. In packet telephony, the anticipation is for the lower layers of SS7 to be replaced with IP-based protocols, which will undertake the tasks of MTP in several areas. The exact place of the architectural "cut" for replacement of parts of MTP with IP-based protocol layers is not yet standardized and requires a lot of research in the area of robustness and reliability of the new public network.

MTP2 uses the BUSY indication in the link status indication field in the LSSU to signal its inability to process the rate of arriving messages. When a sender receives the BUSY signal, it holds back the last MSU that has not been acknowledged and all MTP3 messages that were queued up and destined to be sent on the same link. The BUSY signals are retransmitted periodically every 100–120 ms. When message processing returns to normal, the congested MTP2 sublayer sends a positive acknowledgment for the last error-free MSU it received and successfully processed. This signals to the remote MTP2 sublayer that all is back to normal and the transmission of MSUs can resume.

There are potentially serious issues associated with congestion or other malfunctions that cause permanent or semi-permanent BUSY conditions on a link. If the BUSY persists beyond a few (5–6) seconds, the far end may declare the link out of service and proceed to take alternative routes to complete signaling. The process of selecting routes between signaling points involves load sharing as a consideration for the selection. However, once a route to an SSP has been selected, it remains in effect until a reroute is called for by MTP3. The reason for not changing routes in mid-stream is to avoid out-of-sequence messages arriving at their destination. However, once a link has been declared out of service due to instability, unreliability, or congestion, an alternate route will be selected and will remain in force until the status of the failing link returns to normal. A quick method for selecting the route is via the signaling link selector sub-field in the MSU routing label (RL).

The STP makes a decision on which link to select based on the setting of the signaling link selector. This is used both for flow control and load sharing of links in the signaling network topology. Signaling over an unstable link can then be temporarily remapped to another link until the malfunctioning one recovers.

Error control and recovery are implemented in two ways. The basic method detects missing or errored MSUs (bad check bit field) and the receiver requests retransmission. The preventive cyclic retransmission (PCR) method is used on links with large end-to-end delays. The PCR method is simply the retransmission of all unacknowledged MSUs, whether they were received correctly or not (no waiting by the sender), when the sender has no other MSUs to send. We will see more about this method a bit later.

The MTP uses a forward and backward sequence number (FSN and BSN), which are modulo-128 quantities, to implement error control in the MSU. This is a sliding window mechanism similar to the ones found in other packet-switching protocols.

The FSN is set to the sequence number of the MSU currently being transmitted. The BSN from the receiver indicates the last MSU that was correctly received. The flow diagram in Figure 3.9 helps in explaining the basic error method with a good exchange between STPs.

When a message is received error free, the value of the BIB does not change from the value it was set to in the previous message back to the sender. Similarly, for new MSUs, the value of the FIB does not change.

Figure 3.10 shows the basic method of recovery when an MSU is received with errors or MSUs are received out of sequence. Forward MSU number 104 was errored. The sending STP continued to send MSUs, hoping for the best. However, when the receiver got around to it, it returned a BIB = 1 (toggled the bit) and BSN = 103. This indicates that all MSUs after 103 are being discarded or were not received by the far end. The sender then retransmits MSUs 104 and 105, with FIB = 1, to indicate retransmission.

The values of FIB and BIB stay toggled at their new value until another error occurs.

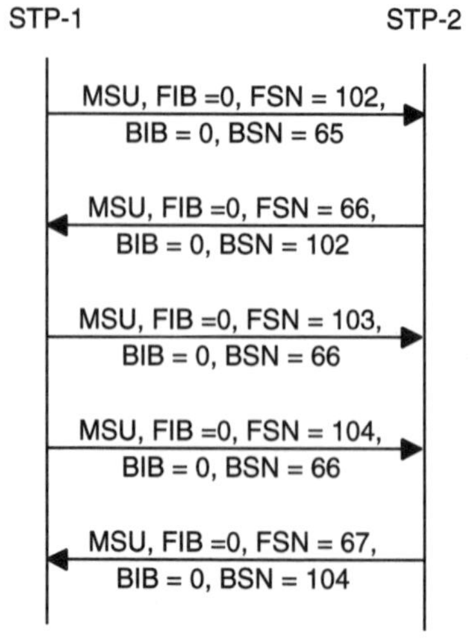

STP-1   STP-2

MSU, FIB =0, FSN = 102,
BIB = 0, BSN = 65

MSU, FIB =0, FSN = 66,
BIB = 0, BSN = 102

MSU, FIB =0, FSN = 103,
BIB = 0, BSN = 66

MSU, FIB =0, FSN = 104,
BIB = 0, BSN = 66

MSU, FIB =0, FSN = 67,
BIB = 0, BSN = 104

FIGURE 3.9 Error-Free MSU Exchange Between STPs

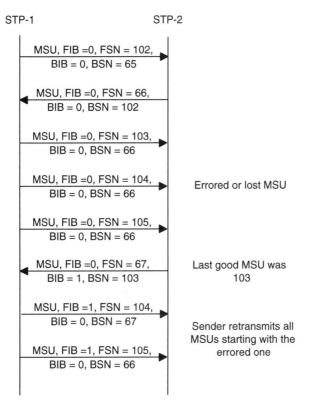

FIGURE 3.10 Errored MSUs Received by the Far End and Recovery

The PCR method is necessary when the one-way delay between STPs is too great, that is, 15–20 ms or more. The idea is for signaling to progress as quickly as possible since it affects call setup time. When there are no new MSUs or LSSUs to send, all the unacknowledged MSUs are retransmitted in cycle. The thinking is that if all unacknowledged messages are being sent to occupy an otherwise idle link, an errored message will be received error-free the second time around. In this method, the use of toggled FIB and BIB bits is not applicable and they are set to 1. Only positive ACKs are returned, and this creates another potential problem. If an MSU is errored and goes undetected for a considerable time due to heavy utilization of the sender, call setup will simply fail or become unacceptably long. It is thus important for the sender to employ either a timer or a MSU sent buffer threshold to stop all new MSU activity and resume sending all the unacknowledged MSUs cyclically, under what is referred to as the forced retransmission procedure.

Routing Methods under Signaling Link Failures

Link congestion is more likely to cause rerouting of signaling messages than hard link outages. Congestion is also more likely to cause temporary instability in the signaling network than a simple link outage. When an event occurs that causes the link to be flagged as out of service, the signaling network management (SNM) functions of MTP3 take action to find alternative routes in the topology. The messages originate with SI = 0 in the service information octet of the MSU to identify signaling network management operations, as shown in Figure 3.11.

The scenario in Figure 3.12 shows actions taken by the MTP when links become unavailable and destinations become unreachable through a particular STP. It depicts the avalanche effect of signaling messages through STP C, when STP D becomes unreachable due to failure of STP B or its links. All signaling end points—that is, exchanges connected to the mated pair of STP A and B—receive transfer prohibited (TFP) from STP B, which causes all signaling to SSP 2 to be routed through STP A.

Depending on the nature of the signaling failure, the number of messages reaching STP C can now overwhelm MTP layer 2 or layer 3, and cause congestion in the link between STP C and SSP 2. This situation will then cause

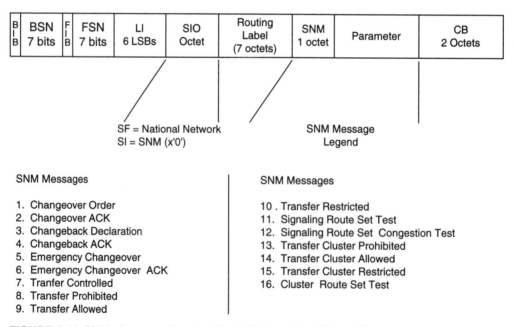

FIGURE 3.11 SNM Messages for Signaling Link Control and Route Management

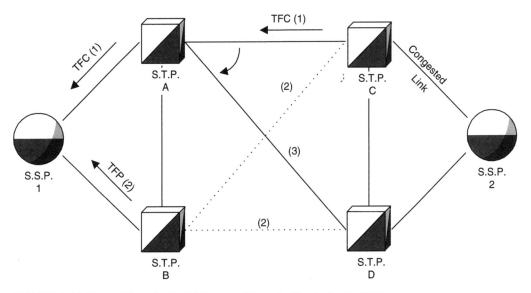

FIGURE 3.12 Use of Transfer Prohibited and Transfer Controlled in SS7

STP C to signal transfer controlled (TFC) back to the MTPs of the originating exchanges. This back-pressure will cause signaling flow to eventually settle at a level where STP C can operate within its limits[3].

A problem arises when SSP 1 tries to reach SSP 2 again through STP B—it continues to see TFPs. STP B has lost connectivity with SSP 2, so it can no longer access STPs C and D. This situation would render exchange SSP 2 unreachable, if it weren't for bridge link (3) between STPs A and D. STP A can reroute messages, whereby all signaling between SSP 1 and SSP 2 will be routed through STPs A and D if congestion persists and affects the quality of service for call setup time. One such method to implement failover is the ChangeOver Order (COO) command. At the judgment of STP C, it can send it to STP A, either on its directly attached B-Link or indirectly through STP D, and instruct STP A to use the B-link connected to STP D. In this case, a specific ChangeBack Order is required from STP C to STP A when the congestion situation ends to resume routing on the direct link between them.

As in all packet-switched networks implementing failover procedures for congested links, care must be taken to avoid link oscillation. This is a tough design problem and involves implementation of hysterysis thresholds in the

---

3.   The reader is referred to the references for more detailed discussions on link congestion management and node congestion status assignment.

buffers triggering the congestion and other conditions that will trigger link failover.

In the simplest case, when no changeover to another route has been ordered, and when the congestion indication between STP C and SSP 2 recedes to acceptable levels, the STP transmits transfer allowed (TFA) messages, indicating to its neighbors it is healthy again and it is permissible to resume signaling on its links.

Basic ISUP Call Setup

Figure 3.13 shows a basic call flow for call setup and termination with an ISDN subscriber and use of basic ISUP messaging on the PSTN. Table 3.3 is a quick guide of the ISDN/Q.931 PRI call processing messages, and similarly

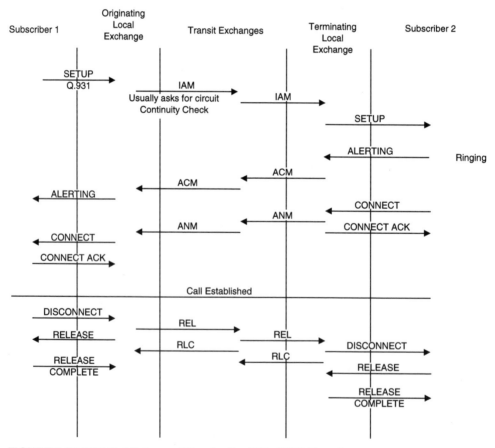

FIGURE 3.13 SS7 Call Setup and Termination With ISDN Signaling

Table 3.4 lists an important subset of the ISUP messages for call control and supervisory functions between exchanges. A major consideration in the design of packet-based telephone networks with service access to the PSTN is providing adequate interworking between the two types of signaling protocols. Later in this chapter we will see scenarios of this type of interworking, and some of the issues that may arise in the reliability of the provided service.

TABLE 3.3 Q.931 Circuit Mode Connection Messages

Q.931 CIRCUIT-MODE MESSAGE CODE	MEANING	NOTES
ALERTING	The called party has been notified of an incoming call. This is a global message originating by the called party and propagating though the network.	Sent by the CCS network to an ISDN endpoint when the ACM message from the far end has been received.
CALL PROCEEDING	The SETUP message has been received and call processing has begun.	This message may be sent when call forwarding is in effect and the call is being redirected. It is of local significance, from the called user to the network.
CONNECT	The connection is set up. This is a global message sent from the called party to the network and back to the calling party.	The user has answered the call.
CONNECT ACKNOWLEDGE	This message acknowledges receipt of the CONNECT message and has local significance. The call is now set up.	Sent from the called party to the network and from the network to the calling user.
PROGRESS	This local message, from the network to the user, indicates whether the call is ISDN end-to-end, or if either endpoint is ISDN equipment. It also indicates the presence of tones in the bearer (B) channel.	This message may optionally convey information as to the reasons why a connection attempt was unsuccessful.

TABLE 3.3 Q.931 Circuit Mode Connection Messages (Continued)

Q.931 CIRCUIT-MODE MESSAGE CODE	MEANING	NOTES
SETUP	Sent from the calling party to the local exchange. Starts the process of call establishment	Sent by the endpoint toward the originating local exchange. Causes the generation of an IAM message toward the terminating exchange. This message has global significance.
SETUP ACKNOWLEDGE	Acknowledges the SETUP message with local significance	Verifies the exchange received the SETUP message but has no other meaning in call processing. It has local significance.
RESUME	Signaled from the user to the exchange to request resumption of a suspended call	This applies to a call that has been previously suspended with a SUSPEND message.
RESUME ACKNOWLEDGE	Locally significant acknowledgment of the RESUME message	The call has been restored. A suspended call is not a terminated call.
RESUME REJECT	The exchange has failed in the resumption of the suspended call.	The call will be terminated.
SUSPEND	The user is requesting temporary suspension of the call by going on-hook for a short time.	These are local messages between the user and the local exchange.
SUSPEND ACKNOWLEDGE	The local exchange has accepted the request to suspend the call.	
SUSPEND REJECT	The local exchange is refusing to suspend the call.	
USER INFORMATION	This message transfers information between two users.	Not pertinent to call setup.

TABLE 3.3   Q.931 Circuit Mode Connection Messages (Continued)

Q.931 CIRCUIT-MODE MESSAGE CODE	MEANING	NOTES
DISCONNECT	Either party in a call can cause this message to be generated by hanging up a call. This message has global significance and is sent by the user to the network or by the network to the user.	The receiving exchange sends RELEASE and the local exchange that sent the DISCONNECT replies with RELEASE COMPLETE, at which point the call is terminated.
RELEASE	Signaled locally in response to receiving DISCONNECT or for any reason that has caused the user or the network to release the circuit.	This message is generated by the network or the user.
RELEASE COMPLETE	Signaled locally in response to receiving RELEASE	
Q.931 Messages		
CONGESTION CONTROL	Generated locally to set or release flow control in USER INFORMATION messages	This message is generated by either the network or the user.
INFORMATION	Sent locally to supply additional information pertaining to the call establishment.	Generated either by the user or the network.
NOTIFY	Conveys information about a call in progress.	This message is generated either by the user or the network.
STATUS	Reply to a STATUS ENQUIRY command	This response message is mandatory when a STATUS ENQUIRY is received.
STATUS ENQUIRY	Locally generated to obtain call status	This message can be generated by either the user or the network.

TABLE 3.4 ISUP SS7 Messages

ISUP MESSAGE CODE	MEANING	NOTES
ACM	Address Complete Message	Sent by the TE when all the IAM requested information has been received. Indicates the far end is processing the call.
ANM	Answer Message	Travels towards the calling party and indicates the called party has answered the call.
BLA	Blocking Acknowledgment	Acknowledges receipt of the BLO message.
BLO	Blocking	Allows an exchange to block calls from appearing on a circuit from the other end.
CCR	Continuity Check Request	Requests a continuity check, and the results are sent forward with the COT message.
CFN	Confusion	The exchange cannot process a received message.
CGB	Circuit Group Blocking	Blocks a range of circuits.
CGBA	Circuit Group Blocking Acknowledgment	Acknowledges a CGB message.
CGU	Circuit Group Unblocking	Unblocks a range of circuits.
CGUA	Circuit Group Unblocking Acknowledgment	Acknowledges a CGU message.
COT	Continuity	Indicates that the continuity check requested by the exchange has either been successful or failed.
CPG	Call Progress	Sent to indicate an event during call processing, such as alerting, forwarding, etc.
CQM	Circuit Query	Sent to a far TE to ask the status of a circuit or a range of circuits.

TABLE 3.4 ISUP SS7 Messages (Continued)

ISUP MESSAGE CODE	MEANING	NOTES
CQR	Circuit Query Response	Response from the far exchange to a CQM message.
CRA	Circuit Reservation Acknowledgment	Acknowledges a CRM message.
CRM	Circuit Reservation	Used to interwork with non-SS7 networks, such as those using MF signaling.
CVR	Circuit Validation Response	Response to a CVT message.
CVT	Circuit Validation Test	Used to verify the ability of two ports to be connected together.
EXM	Exit	Used for interworking with another network. Indicates the IAM has passed to the other network.
FAC	Facility	Requests an action from the exchange, encoded in the service activation parameter.
FOT	Forward Transfer	Sent in the forward direction when operator assistance is required.
GRA	Group Reset Acknowledgment	Acknowledges the GRS command.
GRS	Group Reset	Resets a group of circuits in a similar manner to the RSC command. Takes a range parameter.
IAM	Initial Address Message	Provides the circuit information, carrier ID, and other requirements to complete the call. Used to establish the call.
INF	Information	Provides the information requested by an INR. Provides redirection and billing numbers.

TABLE 3.4 ISUP SS7 Messages (Continued)

ISUP MESSAGE CODE	MEANING	NOTES
INR	Information Request	Sent by an exchange to request additional information about a call in progress. Used for forwarding.
LPA	Loopback Acknowledgment	Acknowledges loopback is being performed as result of a CCR message. The CIC field contains the circuit ID.
PAM	Pass-Along Message	Usually contains another message as parameters.
REL	Release	Indicates the call is being terminated.
RES	Resume	For non-ISDN parties, it indicates a party went on-hook but went back to off-hook quickly and the call should not be terminated. If return to off-hook does not happen in a prespecified time, the SUS message is sent.
RLC	Release Complete	Indicates reception of REL and the circuit can be released and returned to idle.
RSC	Reset Circuit	Places the requested circuit in the reset state. Used when the state of a circuit is not known by the exchange.
SUS	Suspend	When a non-ISDN party hangs up, the SUS is sent first, followed by REL.
UBA	Unblocking Acknowledgment	Acknowledges a UBL message.
UBL	Unblocking	Removes a blocking condition from a circuit.
UCIC	Unequipped Circuit Identification Code	Indicates that the requested CIC is not equipped.

The four fundamental messages for call setup and termination are IAM, ACM, ANM, REL and RLC. Mapping between ISDN and ISUP messages is not very complex, but as the reader already realizes from Table 3.4, a number of ISUP messages relate to control signaling between exchanges, and do not have a direct translation to ISDN messages. We will work through an example of ISUP and MGCP signaling for call setup later in this chapter.

3.2 THE SERVICES OF SSCP AND TCAP

So far we have discussed SS7/ISUP signaling associated with the establishment of a physical circuit between a calling and a called party across the PSTN. As we mentioned earlier, the public network requires services beyond the setup of circuits for voice telephony. Such services include customer information for billing purposes, information lookup for credit card calls, translation of toll-free or 900 numbers to routable numbers, local number portability support, service interworking with the wireless networks, and other advanced network functions and user features. Those types of network services use SS7 messaging that is not directly associated with the voiceband circuit used for a call. The SS7 protocol stack utilizes the signaling service control point (SCCP) layer for non-circuit-associated messaging with other SS7 nodes and back-office systems. The SCCP protocol layer is hosted in the STP.

SSCP occupies the fourth layer in the SS7 protocol stack. The internal architecture of this layer is shown in Figure 3.14. The services offered by the SCCP layer to Application Service Elements (ASEs) are fundamental for the operation of the public telephone network, and it is expected this functionality will be maintained in deployments of public service offerings of IP-based telephony. The design issues are centered around the method of integration of the legacy SS7 protocol stack in IP signaling mechanisms in the public network. The objective is for traditional TDM telephony to interwork with packet networks while continuing to provide support for advanced network features already available on the PSTN. New advanced features introduced in the packet networks must also interoperate with the features of the PSTN. Another aspect of the integration issues facing public deployments of packet–voice telephony is the numerous regulatory requirements that govern the operation of the public network.

SCCP interfaces with TCAP for support of LNP, 800/900 number translation, and the Advanced Intelligent Network Call Model.

SCCP Services

The SCCP layer can be used in one of four classes of service, as shown in Table 3.5. The North American telephone network uses SCCP in connection-

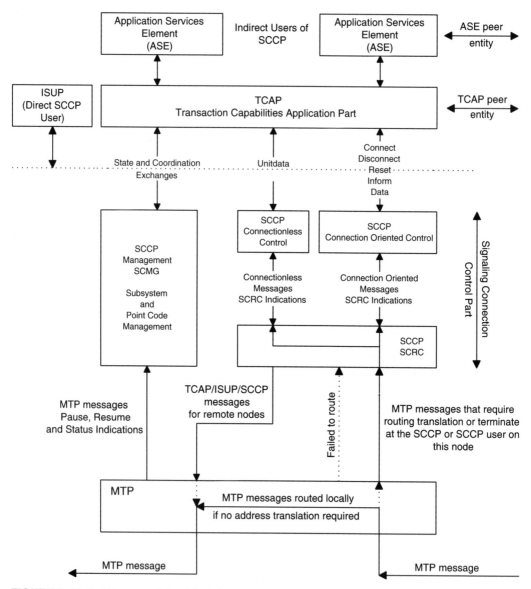

FIGURE 3.14 Architecture of the SCCP Layer

less mode. SCCP provides the subsystem numbers (SSNs) required to address messages to remote applications using its services. As we have seen, the other required element in identifying a remote application is the point code (PC) of the remote node, which is provided by MTP. Global Title Translation of dialed digits is also implemented through SCCP.

TABLE 3.5 SCCP Classes of Service

CLASSIFICATION	TYPE OF SERVICE	NOTES
Class 0	Basic Connectionless Service	Data units from the SCCP users are sent in datagram mode, and units from the same user can be sent out of order.
Class 1	Sequenced Connectionless Service	Data units from the SCCP users are sent in sequence.
Class 2	Basic Connection-Oriented Service	This mode is similar to Class 0, but a connection setup is required for data to flow. No sequencing or flow control is provided.
Class 3	Connection-Oriented Service	This mode establishes a connection and data is sequenced with flow control.

SCCP Messages and Format

The SCCP payload is carried in the SIF field of the MTP message, and the SIO field is coded to indicate SCCP as the service. SCCP messages are constructed in a similar manner to the ISUP messages. Each message contains a fixed mandatory part and a variable mandatory part. The general format of an SCCP message is shown in Figure 3.15.

The caller party address (CDA), calling party address (CGA), subsystem data, and corresponding length fields are optional variable-length parts of the SCCP message. Their content is passed to SCCP from the User Part (TCAP, ISUP), and the SCCP routing function determines the destination point code (DPC) and signaling link selection (SLS) field contents. The DPC is inserted in the CDA field.

The called and calling party address contain the subsystem number (SSN) of the SCCP user. The subsystem numbers defined in the North American network are shown in Table 3.6.

Note that TCAP itself does not have an SSN assigned to it. Instead, the application services utilizing TCAP are explicitly identified and those messages are passed to TCAP by SCCP for ultimate delivery to the application.

For Global Title Translations, the called party address may indicate the presence of a GT, and if it does, the GT itself is included in the CDA field. If GT translation is requested, routing may also be requested, based on the result of the translation. The other option is to request routing based on the destination point code and not perform GT translation. A GT translation

Message Types

1. Connection Request
2. Connection Confirm
3. Connection Refused
4. Data for class 2 (form 1)
5. Data for class 3 (form 2)
6. Release complete
7. Released
8. Unitdata
9. Unitdata Service

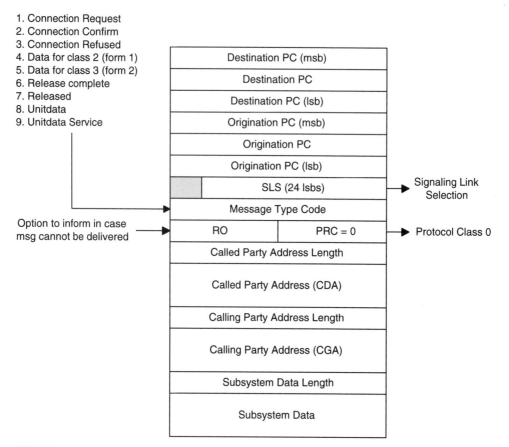

Option to inform in case
msg cannot be delivered

FIGURE 3.15 SCCP Unitdata Message (ANSI)

returns in the PC terminating exchange and the SSN will identify ISUP for call setup.

Subsystem data is passed by SCCP in a transparent manner. It originates and terminates at an SSN using SCCP.

SCCP Interfaces

SCCP connects to MTP below it and TCAP and ISUP above it in the protocol stack. For connectionless service, the messages between the user and SCCP are exchanged with *N-unitdata request*, *N-unitdata indication*, and *N-notice indication* primitives. These primitives define the software interface between the two layers.

TABLE 3.6 Subsystem Numbers in North American SCCP

SUBSYSTEM NUMBER (SSN)	CODE
Not Used	0
SCCP Management Entity	1
ISUP	3
Operations, Maintenance and Administration (OMAP)	4
Mobile Application Part	5
Home Location Register	6
Visitor Location Register	7
Mobile Switching Center	8
Authentication Center	10

SCCP exchanges messages with MTP with basic *MTP-transfer request* and *MTP- transfer indication* primitives, regardless of the type of SCCP service offered to the subsystem above it. MTP Pause, Resume, and Status indication messages are handled by the SCCP management functional block (SCMG) inside SCCP.

SCCP Services in IP Telephony

Packet telephony from service providers will depend on the services and accessibility of the PSTN for a long time to come. Furthermore, the federal regulations governing the PSTN encompass all types of telephony service regardless of the delivery mechanism of the voice data. For example, the use of our basic dialing plan, 800 and 900 numbers, credit card calls, etc., will continue to exist and prosper whether calls originate, terminate, or are transported by the PSTN or any type of packet network.

Some of the issues facing IP-based telephony at the carrier level center on defining transport, routing methodologies, and services similar to those of SCCP. The outcome of these efforts would affect the definition of any new MTP layer (if one is defined), but it is not unlikely that MTP will be replaced with some form of standard IP-based routing in some implementations. If the architectural cut is made in a manner that preserves the interface definition between SCCP and MTP, the pain of migration could be significantly reduced, and major pieces of SS7 code can be reused. This would work to the benefit of IP telephony because it could now signal with the existing stable methodologies, while allowing the new telephone service to deliver benefits in its own areas of merit, such as bandwidth utilization and service integration.

The TCAP Protocol and Services

The Transaction Capabilities Application Part of SS7 (TCAP) facilitates database query and dialog through a relatively simple message set. TCAP allows network operators to access databases and switches for exchanging call-related information that do not relate to the establishment of the voice circuit. It supports end-to-end signaling using the connectionless mode of SCCP, but it also provides a method for reliable end-to-end communication. Functions like LNP query for ported numbers, 800/900 number translation, wireless roaming, and call billing information use TCAP/SCCP in the PSTN. TCAP also allows design and implementation of Advanced Intelligent Network features and call models, some of which may remain relevant in the new integrated packet networks.

Transactions in the SS7 network are specified at two levels. The highest level is application-to-application, whereby applications interface with TCAP through a process and an implementation-dependent interface. The next level is TCAP-to-TCAP.

TCAP Message Types, Formats, and Functions

TCAP messages are divided into three portions: *transaction*, *dialog* and *component*. The first identifies the transaction through the transaction ID, which is used to reference all TCAP messages relating to the transaction. Its significance is local only. The dialog portion is optional in TCAP, and is used for version identification and security in cases where encryption is used. The component portion includes the data received in the operation PDU (protocol data unit) from the application interfacing to TCAP. This is the data that is used by the peer application for initiating local operations, such as a database query.

Figure 3.16 shows the construction of a TCAP message and Table 3.7 shows the TCAP message types. ANSI document T1.114-1996 is the full specification of the protocol.

As an example, the initiation of a database query will be a TCAP message with the Invoke ([last | not last]) Component Type Identifier. If "last" is indicated, it means the remote system has all the information it needs to perform the transaction. If "not last" is indicated, additional components will be arriving in subsequent TCAP messages. A digit translation is a single component message, and the response from the remote system terminates the transaction.

Package Type Identifier
Total TCAP Length
Transaction ID Identifier
Transaction ID Length
Transaction IDs
       Originating ID
       Responding ID
P-Abort Cause Identifier
       (indicates msg abort is present)
P-Abort Cause Length
P-Abort Cause (see text for description)
	TCAP msg Transaction Portion

Dialog Portion Identifier Dialog Portion Length Dialog Portion	

Component Sequence Identifier
Component Sequence Length
Component Type Identifier (one of the following)
       Invoke (last)
       Return Result (last)
       Return Error (operation failure)
       Reject (for protocol errors)
       Invoke (not last)
       Return Result (not last)
Component Length
Component ID Identifier
Component ID Length
Component ID
       Invoke ID (from originator)
       Correlation ID (from response)
Operation Code Identifier
       National
       Private
Operation Code (not examined by TCAP)
Error Code Identifier
Error Code Length
Error Code
Problem Code Identifier
Problem Code Length
Problem Code
Parameter Set or Sequence Identifier
Parameter Set or Sequence Length
Parameter Identifier
Parameter Length
Parameter
	TCAP msg Component Portion

FIGURE 3.16 TCAP Message Construction

TABLE 3.7 TCAP Message Types

TCAP TRANSACTION PORTION – PACKAGE TYPE IDENTIFIER	
Unidirectional	No transaction is required for this type of message. It flows in one direction only. Bi-directional messages require the establishment of a transaction.
Query With Permission	A transaction is initiated with this message, and it can terminated by the receiving node.
Query Without Permission	A transaction is initiated with this message, but it cannot be terminated by the receiving node.
Response	This message ends a TCAP transaction.
Conversation With Permission	Continuation of a TCAP transaction, which is allowed to be terminated by the remote node.
Conversation Without Permission	Continuation of a TCAP transaction, which is not allowed to be terminated by the remote node.
Abort	The sending node is terminating a transaction. Pending components are discarded and will not be sent.

Transaction IDs are required for all transactions, but not for unidirectional messages. Once conversation mode has been entered, all subsequent TCAP messages need to be conversations until one end receives permission to close the transaction. Figure 3.17 illustrates a typical TCAP transaction, whereby the originating application wants to control closing the transaction.

In the PSTN, these messages will be routed by the SCCP and MTP layers at intermediate nodes (not shown in Figure 3.17) and traverse multiple STPs until they reach an SCP that can perform the translation. TCAP does not worry about transport and routing, as SCCP and MTP take care of those details.

Failure Recognition and Signaling in TCAP

TCAP accounts for protocol errors at the message level, as well as component and operation failures. Message failures are indicated in the P-Abort field in the message, with one of the causes listed in Table 3.8. The P-Abort fields are inserted in the transaction portion of the message, following the transaction IDs.

Component level failures are protocol or operation related. Protocol level failures (bad constructs, etc.) are noted with the Reject component type identifier. Operation failures associated with the completion of the requested operation are noted with Return Error in the component type identifier of the message.

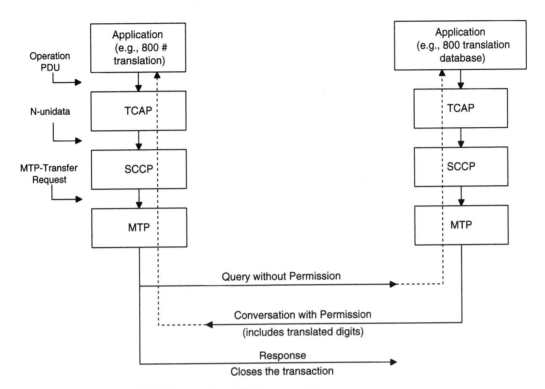

FIGURE 3.17 Typical TCAP Transaction With Conversation

TABLE 3.8 TCAP Message Errors

TCAP MESSAGE ERRORS
Incorrect Transaction Portion—probably a typing error.
Badly Structured Transaction Portion—an issue with the contents of the message.
Unassigned Responding Transaction ID—the ID coming back from the remote system is not recognized as active.
Permission to Release Problem—undefined.
Resource Unavailable—cannot establish the transaction.
Unrecognized Dialog Portion ID.
Badly Structured Dialog Portion.
Missing Dialog Portion—if the dialog portion is mandatory and not present.
Inconsistent Dialog Portion.

3.2.1 TCAP in the Advanced Intelligent Network

The Advanced Intelligent Network (AIN) is a service control and network architecture that allows local exchange carriers to migrate call control functions from the local switch to a programmable device. This approach has become very important in the quest to realize expedient implementation of new services. Decades of design and deployment of services in the monolithic architectures of traditional Class 5 switches have created an unacceptably high cost and delay structure for the offering of even a single new service. Carriers have experimented with proprietary architectures, such as CORBA-based distributed computing and service creation environments, but the AIN basic call model appears to be winning as the preferred method for service creation. This is true for both the PSTN and packet-based telephony. The AIN relies on SS7 for its functions and the role of TCAP is fundamental to the realization of the advanced intelligent basic call model.

The basic call model of the AIN is simple, and consists of two half-call models, the *originating* and the *terminating*. Call processing is partitioned into stages, and each is identified and designated as a point in call (PIC). This can be thought of simply as a state in the life of a call. For all or some of the PICs, the SSP may query the SCP or other device implementing telephony features, to receive instructions on how to handle the call at this stage. The basic call model query uses SS7/TCAP messaging. SSP queries and the device(s) providing the responses in effect "pace" the SSP through the stages of the call processing, thus allowing the SSP to become "mindless" of the type of services being offered. Figures 3.18 and 3.19 show a combined simplified call model of the AIN for the originating and terminating endpoints. There are two types of events that cause call processing to be suspended, namely triggers and requested events. Each type of event has a corresponding detection point (DP). Triggers are provisioned on a per-line or multiple line basis and trigger detection points (TDP) in the SSP suspend call processing. Event detection points (EDP), on the other hand, are encountered while processing a call. If a PIC state has been designated a detection point and if the SSP wishes to be paced by the SCP, the state transition causes a side trip to be taken through the SCP or other device for obtaining additional information.

The advantages of the AIN basic call model are in great cost savings and the timeliness of new service offerings. Public packet networks for voice telephony will benefit from the AIN call model because equipment for service creation in the PSTN is reusable in any topology that maintains the SS7 signaling capabilities, at least at the TCAP level. Service design and deployment then become expedient and cost-effective and all the attention can be focused on fine-tuning the new elements of the packet networks, such as the call processing signaling and media transport mechanisms and topologies.

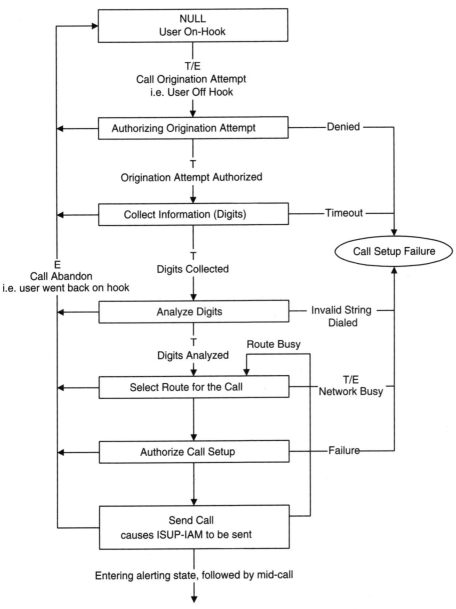

FIGURE 3.18 Simplified AIN Basic Call Model (Originating Endpoint)

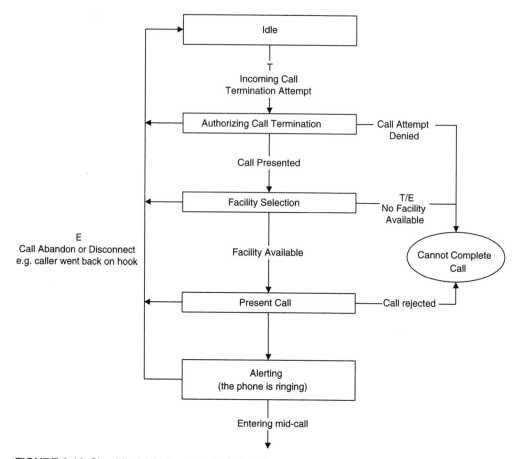

FIGURE 3.19 Simplified AIN Basic Call Model (Terminating Endpoint)

3.2.2 SS7 in IP Telephony and Closing Thoughts on PSTN Signaling

Even a casual look at the TCAP/SCCP specification documents is enough to convince us that the value added by TCAP to PSTN telephony is too significant to be discounted by any new packet network deployments. In the case of enterprise private networks or IP telephony over the Internet, it is not required to perform Global Title Translations, credit card data lookup, LNP queries, etc., but once such a network wishes to interwork with the PSTN, things change immediately.

It is most likely that TCAP functionality will exist in the new voice telephone network as is, at least in the short term. This means TCAP will either continue to use SCCP in some implementations or be placed somewhere in the fourth layer of the IP protocol stack and transported end-to-end via TCP or other reliable transport mechanism.

Another item for serious consideration is that two of the original reasons for engineering out-of-band signaling in the PSTN in the first place were robustness and reliability. Any attempt to convert from the SS7 protocol to an IP-based scheme would invariably require the same thinking regarding service availability. Therefore, such an endeavor would require either a slow conversion of SS7 links to IP-based links or the simultaneous deployment of a parallel out-of-band IP-based signaling network between carriers.

The direction of the solution of this issue will involve much more work in the standards groups, so in the meantime the TCAP/SCCP/MTP protocol layers will continue to exist in the current incarnation of SS7, and continue to provide services for initial rollouts of IP telephony from the IXCs and LECs of all kinds. And this direction is bound to be good enough for a long time to come.

3.3 CALL CONTROL IN PACKET NETWORKS

In this section we look at the fundamentals of the basic IP-based call models. We begin by looking at a call flow involving two parties involved in a call and the activity at their respective endpoints. A basic call flow is a set of signaling exchanges between the MGCs and the endpoints at the media gateways, to establish and terminate a call, as well as to collect billing information, performance, and other vital statistics. Call models can become very complex when the most common consumer telephony features are accommodated, or when one or both parties is attached to a PBX on the other side of a media gateway.

Basic call setup consists of creating a connection between two endpoints and selection of the media type. Path selection and routing issues may or may not be part of call processing in each network implementation. There are two call processing cases that must be examined from the perspective of signaling and media transport: call with endpoints in homogeneous networks and call with endpoints in heterogeneous networks.

Homogeneous Networks. In this case, the endpoints reside in administrative domains that use the same signaling protocol for call setup, and no interworking translation of signaling exchanges is necessary across administrative or network boundaries. The media is sent end-to-end on the same transport protocol. Notice that it is not necessary to support the same media format within a homogeneous network. In other words, media transcoding is a possibility, and depends on the capabilities of the endpoints involved in the connection.

The reader should not be surprised to hear that the PSTN itself is not a homogeneous signaling network. For example, subscriber signaling uses a diverse set of hardware and software protocols (loop start, ground start, PRI or CAS for PBXs, etc.), and trunk signaling can be SS7-based with ISUP messaging, or use multifrequency (MF) signaling (emergency 911 services, etc.). International networks use TUP as the signaling protocol. Similarly, an enterprise LAN can contain multiple logical homogeneous topologies, but as whole be a heterogeneous network from a signaling perspective. For example, one set of endpoints may be using H.323 signaling with dedicated gate-keepers, while other sets may be using SIP or MGCP. For those endpoints to place calls between them, signaling protocol interworking functionality will be necessary.

In general, it is unlikely we will encounter a homogeneous call setup across the public network when VoIP services begin to be deployed, except perhaps for calls originating and terminating within the administrative domain of a single service provider.

Heterogeneous Networks. These networks include segments or elements implementing different signaling protocols and the challenge is to create interoperability for call setup between the endpoints. Distributed IP-based enterprise networks, with PSTN hops to attach to remote segments, are the latest incarnations of heterogeneous networks. In those networks, media transcoding for voice telephony may or may not be necessary. For example, consider two LAN segments connected over an IP network (shown in our reference topologies in Chapter 1), whereby one segment uses S/MGCP signaling and the other one uses H.323. Signaling requires translation at the boundaries of the two networks, but if the endpoints support the same media coding capabilities, no media translation is necessary. Any packet network connected to the PSTN will require media transcoding, except when G.711 is the end-to-end selected media format.

We will proceed to review basic flows of the three major IP-based signaling protocols that dominate the new networks, which will need to interoperate across the administrative boundaries of service providers. This is necessary for ubiquitous telephony access in the new public network. We analyze the following scenarios in this section:

- S/MGCP signaling in the domain of each media gateway controller, media gateway, and endpoint.
- SS7/ISUP to S/MGCP signaling, for call setup across the PSTN.

- SIP to S/MGCP call setup and termination.
- S/MGCP to H.323 call setup across the PSTN.

In the first example we analyze call setup in a homogeneous network, with only two MGCs, and later we will see how signaling interworking in more complex scenarios is achieved.

3.3.1 Basic Call Flow with S/MGCP

The two steps in basic call setup begin with signaling from the endpoint that wants to place a call. This can be a basic analog phone (as in this example), or a PC phone, or a PBX of TDM or IP technology. Figures 3.20 and 3.21 are generic call models for S/MGCP call establishment and termination based on the procedures and protocol constructs we discussed in Chapter 1.

3.3.2 Signaling in a Homogeneous End-to-End Network

Signaling for call setup affects performance in two major areas. The first area is the time it takes to complete the call setup. In voice telephony, this is referred to as post dial delay (PDD) and is the time between the last digit dialed by the user and the beginning of ringing at the remote end. The second area affects the number of calls per second that the network can accept at its access points. The more computationally intensive the call processing, the fewer the calls that can be accepted by the service nodes and the more equipment required to meet load requirements—thus, the desire for a simple call processing model and signaling protocol in the next-generation IP telephony services. Simplicity of call setup may be a utopia, if a call spans administrative domains of heterogeneous networks. The complexities of such call setups will be determined primarily by the ease with which signaling protocol mapping can be realized, as well as platform design issues related to billing, configurations, user mobility, performance, diagnosability and other parameters.

A homogeneous signaling layer offers distinct advantages, regardless of the type of the network technologies used to implement the various network segments. Call setup requires a single protocol end-to-end, and no intermediate protocol translations and interworking functions are necessary. An opposite example is signaling between an IP network and telephone users POTS service. In such cases, there is a mandatory extra interworking step at the ingress and egress to and from the PSTN that affects performance both in the calls-per-second area and in the QoS of the delivered speech. On the other hand, the drawback of a completely homogeneous network is the possible lack of flexibility in choosing equipment types, which may have economic ramifications.

In general, integrated packet networks are expected to be heterogeneous because of the strong support for each of the dominant signaling protocols.

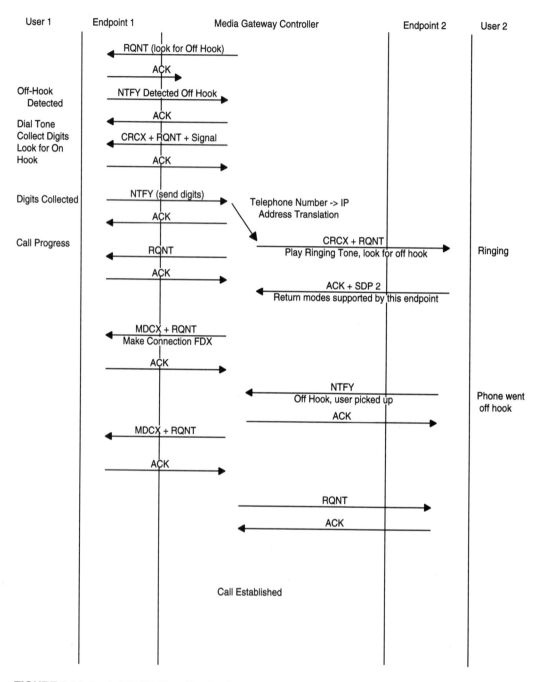

FIGURE 3.20 Basic MGCP Signaling for Call Establishment, Single MGC

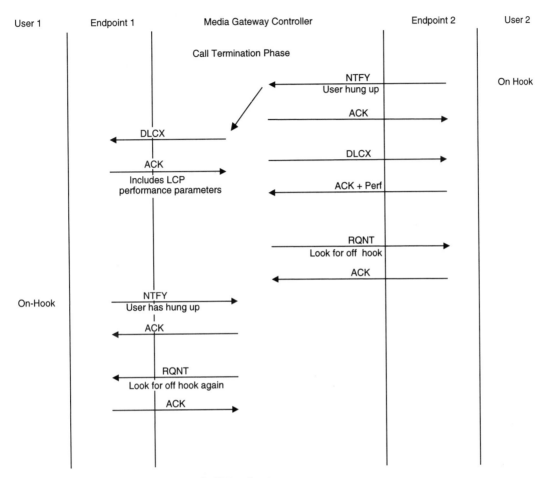

FIGURE 3.21 MGCP Signaling for Call Termination

The most prominent paradigm in the industry is the Packet–PSTN–Packet model. Within this context, various second-level signaling mechanisms are significant. Residential MGs perform signaling for voice, voiceband and data calls, with video not too far away. Voice support is in the sense of support and emulation of POTS service for black phones.[4] Voiceband is for modems and fax, while support for video seems to be perpetually assigned to the famous Future Consideration status in the standards groups.

---

4.   The industry term *black phone* indicates generic telephone service, with some or all of the offered Class 5 features. Delivery of the Class 5 feature set to black phones is beyond the scope of this text.

In a homogeneous IP network, calls can terminate at an endpoint served by the same MGC or a remote endpoint served by a different MGC.[5] In the latter case, we need MGC synchronization for call setup, codec and bandwidth negotiation, as well as QoS guarantees, performance monitoring, and usage data gathering for billing purposes. The subject of MGC synchronization is pretty much open, with various proposals floating in the industry. The main design issue is support for telephony features not accommodated by the common set of ISUP messages.

We begin with a call between endpoints terminating at the same MGC. This is the *on-net* case and is shown in Figures 3.20 and 3.21. Table 3.9 walks through the commands and responses with annotations relating to diagnostic issues and possible handling of signaling exchange malfunctions in the process.

TABLE 3.9 Call Flow Example for Basic Voice Call Setup

COMMAND/ RESPONSE	PARAMETERS	SYNTAX EXPLANATION
RQNT (message from the MGC to endpoint) (1)	56 aaln/1 @yourfavorite.net MGCP 0.1	NotificationRequest, TransactionID number is 56, endpoint name, Protocol MGCP version 0.1
	N: mgc@ yourfavorite.net:5678	Send your notifications to mgc@ yourfavorite.net on UDP port 5678. The endpoint must be able to resolve the domain name to an IP address via DNS lookup or other means. Otherwise an IP address must be supplied.
	X: ABCD56	RequestID
	R: hd	Notify the MGC upon observing Off Hook
ACK (response from the endpoint) (2)	200 56 OK	The NotificationRequest was accepted by the endpoint.

---

5.   In the most general cases, the originating and terminating MGCs could belong to different service providers. This aspect has no bearing on the flows we examine.

TABLE 3.9 Call Flow Example for Basic Voice Call Setup (Continued)

COMMAND/ RESPONSE	PARAMETERS	SYNTAX EXPLANATION
NTFY (message from the calling endpoint to the MGC) (3)	503 aaln/1@yourfavorite.net MGCP 0.1	Notify, TransactionID 503, endpoint name, Protocol MGCP version 0.1 (we will not repeat the protocol description)
	N: mgc@ yourfavorite.net:5678	The NotifiedEntity is the same
	X: ABCD56	RequestID
	O: hd	Observed Event: Off Hook
ACK (from the MGC to the calling endpoint) (4)	200 503 OK	Notification accepted by the MGC
CRCX (message from the MGC to the calling endpoint) (5)	58 aaln/1@ec1.yourcarrier.net MGCP 0.1	CreateConnection, TransactionID 1401, endpoint_name@domain.net, Protocol Version
	C: ABCD3	CallID
	L: p:10, a:PCMU	LocalConnectionOptions: packetization period = 10 ms, audio type = PCM μLaw
	M: recvonly	ConnectionMode: Receive Only (half duplex)
	N: mgc@yourfavorite.net:5678	NotifiedEntity
	X: ABCD57	RequestID
	R: hd, [0-9#*T] (D)	Off Hook, digit match for requested events. This is a combination command because it asks for a CreateConnection and also contains a Notification Request. (This is allowed in the MGCP specification.)
	D: (0T | 00T | [2-9]xxxxxx | 1[2-9]xxxxxxxxx | 011xx.T)	Digit Map for the dial plan

TABLE 3.9 Call Flow Example for Basic Voice Call Setup (Continued)

COMMAND/ RESPONSE	PARAMETERS	SYNTAX EXPLANATION
	S: dl	Signal: **Play Dial Tone**
ACK (from the Calling Endpoint to the MGC) (6)	200 58 OK I: 00053C v=0 c=IN IP4 10.1.70.15 m=audio 3456 RTP/AVP 0	Notification accepted by the MGC, with I = ConnectionID. The SDP parameters are: Protocol version = 0, network type = IN, protocol IPv4, IP address is 10.1.70.15 mode = audio, RTP port = 3456, audio profile 0 (PCM μLaw)
Notice that the SDP string with the media capabilities of the originating endpoint is returned with the ACK response to the CRCX command. The CRCX did not send an SDP.		
NTFY (message from the calling endpoint to the MGC) (7)	578 aaln/1@yourfavorite.net MGCP 0.1	Notify, TransactionID 578, endpoint name,
	N: mgc@ yourfavorite.net:5678	The NotifiedEntity is still mgc@ yourfavorite.net:5678
	X: ABCD57	RequestID matches the value in the CRCX command.
	O: 1, 7, 0, 3, 5, 5, 5, 1, 2, 1, 2	Observed event: A digit sequence that matches a generic digit map in the dial plan
At this point, the call processor needs to translate the E.164 digit string (the telephone number dialed), and convert it to an endpoint and domain name, or IP address.		
ACK (from the MGC to the calling endpoint) (8)	200 578 OK	Notification accepted by the MGC, matching transaction ID

TABLE 3.9 Call Flow Example for Basic Voice Call Setup (Continued)

COMMAND/ RESPONSE	PARAMETERS	SYNTAX EXPLANATION
RQNT (message from the MGC to the calling endpoint) (9)	60 aaln/1 @yourfavorite.net MGCP 0.1	NotificationRequest, TransactionID 60, far endpoint name.
	X: ABCD58	RequestID
	R: hu	Stop collecting digits, look for On Hook. Notice there is no memory of previous notification requests from the MGC to the MG
ACK (from the calling endpoint to the MGC) (10)	200 60 OK	NotificationRequest accepted by the endpoint.
CRCX (message from the MGC to the called endpoint) (11)	62 aaln/1@yourfavorite2.net MGCP 0.1	The MGC now needs to create a connection at the called endpoint. The endpoint identifier points toward the outgoing circuit.
	C: ABCD3	CallID is the same at both ends
	L: p:10, a:PCMU	LocalConnectionOptions: packetization period = 10 ms, audio type = PCM μLaw, must be the same at both ends
	M: sendrecv	ConnectionMode is full duplex. The SDP is present and this can be done.
	N: mgc@ yourfavorite2.net:5678	NotifiedEntity, for the domain of the called party.
	X: ABCD58	RequestID
	R: hd	Look for Off Hook.
	S: rg	Signal: Ring the phone. When the phone goes Off Hook the ringing will stop.

TABLE 3.9 Call Flow Example for Basic Voice Call Setup (Continued)

COMMAND/ RESPONSE	PARAMETERS	SYNTAX EXPLANATION
	v=0 c=IN IP4 10.1.70.15 m=audio 3456 RTP/AVP 0	This is the SDP of the connection, and must be the same at both ends.
Notice that the second endpoint receives the media encoding capability of the originator with the SDP in the CRCX command. The ACK that follows indicates the media format is not supported by the called endpoint; a negotiation has to take place between the endpoints through the MGC call processor. Endpoints are allowed to specify all the media encodings they support in the SDP, and the MGC will select one that exists in both ends.		
ACK (from the called endpoint to the MGC) (12)	200 62 OK I: 01054D v=0 c=IN IP4 10.1.70.17 m=audio 1297 RTP/AVP 0	ConnectionID selected by called endpoint The called endpoint returns its own SDP, such as endpoint IP address, UDP port, media type and mode of the connection.
MDCX (message from the MGC to the calling endpoint) (13)	64 aaln/1@yourfavorite.net MGCP 0.1	The MGC now needs to modify the connection at the calling endpoint and finish the setup of the transport address.
	C: ABCD3	CallID is the same at both ends
	M: sendrecv	ConnectionMode is full duplex. The SDP is present and this can be done.
	X: ABCD60	RequestID
	R: hu	Look for On Hook.
	S: rt	Signal: Play local ringback
	v=0 c=IN IP4 10.1.70.17 m=audio 1297 RTP/AVP 0	This is the SDP of the remote connection.

TABLE 3.9 Call Flow Example for Basic Voice Call Setup (Continued)

COMMAND/RESPONSE	PARAMETERS	SYNTAX EXPLANATION
ACK (from the calling endpoint to the MGC) (14)	200 64 OK	NotificationRequest Accepted by the endpoint
The MGC has now established a half-duplex path between the two endpoints. The calling endpoint is still in receive mode, for the purpose of avoiding potential fraud. The phone at the far end is ringing and the local end is playing a locally generated ringback. In the PSTN, for domestic calls, ringback is generated by the terminating exchange.		
NTFY (message from the called endpoint to the MGC) (15)	100 aaln/1@yourfavorite2.net MGCP 0.1	Notify, TransactionID 3001, endpoint name.
	N: mgc@ yourfavorite2.net:5678	The NotifiedEntity is still the same for the called endpoint too.
	X: ABCD58	RequestID
	O: hd	Observed event: The phone went off hook. Somebody answered.
ACK (from the called endpoint to the MGC) (16)	200 100 OK	Notification accepted.
MDCX (message from the MGC to the calling endpoint) (17)	66 aaln/1@yourfavorite.net MGCP 0.1	The MGC now needs to modify the connection at the calling end, place it in full duplex and look for On Hook. This is another combination request.
	C: ABCD3	CallID is the same at both ends.
	M: sendrecv	ConnectionMode is full duplex. The SDP is present and this can be done.
	I: 00053C	ConnectionID
	R: hu	Look for On Hook.

TABLE 3.9 Call Flow Example for Basic Voice Call Setup (Continued)

COMMAND/ RESPONSE	PARAMETERS	SYNTAX EXPLANATION
	X: ABCD66	RequestID
ACK (from the calling endpoint to the MGC) (18)	200 66 OK	Notification accepted by the endpoint
RQNT (message from the MGC to the called endpoint) (19)	102 aaln/1@yourfavorite2.net MGCP 0.1	The MGC needs to ask the far endpoint to also look for On Hook
	X: ABCD68	RequestID
	R: hu	Look for On Hook.
ACK (from the EC1 to the MGC) (20)	200 102 OK	NotificationRequest accepted
The call is now established and the two parties can talk to and hear each other. At this point, the MGC is not performing any signaling functions with either endpoint for the duration of the call (until either party hangs up).		
NTFY (message from the called endpoint to the MGC) (21)	104 aaln/1@yourfavorite2.net MGCP 0.1	Notify, TransactionID 2003, endpoint name, Protocol Version
	X: ABCD68	RequestID
	O: hu	Observed Event: The far end (called party) hung up

TABLE 3.9 Call Flow Example for Basic Voice Call Setup (Continued)

COMMAND/ RESPONSE	PARAMETERS	SYNTAX EXPLANATION
ACK (from the Called Endpoint to the MGC) (22)	200 104 OK	Notification accepted
The MGC now needs to delete the connection at both endpoints. It needs to send two DLCX commands, one to each endpoint.		
DLCX (message from the MGC to calling endpoint) (24)	106 aaln/1@yourfavorite.net MGCP 0.1	Notify, TransactionID 106, endpoint name,
	C: ABCD3	CallID
	I: 00053C	ConnectionID of the deleted connection at the calling endpoint
DLCX (message from the MGC to the Called Endpoint) (25)	108 aaln/1@yourfavorite2.net MGCP 0.1	Notify, TransactionID 108, endpoint name, Protocol Version
	C: ABCD3	CallID
	I: 01054D	ConnectionID of the deleted connection at the called endpoint
ACK (from the calling endpoint to the MGC) (26)	250 106 OK P: PS=1245, OS=62345, PR=780, OR=45123, PL=10, JI=27	Includes performance data

TABLE 3.9 Call Flow Example for Basic Voice Call Setup (Continued)

COMMAND/ RESPONSE	PARAMETERS	SYNTAX EXPLANATION
ACK (from the called endpoint to the MGC) (27)	250 108 OK P: PS=790, OS=45700, PR=1230, OR=61875, PL=15, JI=27	Includes performance data
RQNT (message from the MGC to called endpoint) (28)	110 aaln/1@yourfavorite2.net MGCP 0.1	The MGC needs to ask the far endpoint to also look for On Hook
	X: ABCD4	RequestID
	R: hd	Look for Off Hook.
ACK (from the called endpoint to the MGC) (29)	200 110 OK	Simple ACK
NTFY (message from the calling endpoint to the MGC) (30)	220 aaln/1@yourfavorite.net MGCP 0.1	Notify, TransactionID 2003, endpoint name
	X: ABCD66	RequestID, same as in step 17
	O: hu	Observed event: The calling end has also hung up
ACK (from the calling endpoint) (31)	200 220 OK	Simple ACK

TABLE 3.9 Call Flow Example for Basic Voice Call Setup (Continued)

COMMAND/ RESPONSE	PARAMETERS	SYNTAX EXPLANATION
RQNT (message from the MGC to the calling endpoint) (32)	112 aaln/1@yourfavorite.net MGCP 0.1	The MGC needs to ask the far endpoint to also look for On Hook
	X: 0123456789B3	RequestID
	R: hd	Look for Off Hook.
ACK (from the calling endpoint to the MGC) (33)	200 112 OK	Simple ACK
At this point both parties are ready to make and receive other calls. There is no additional cleanup required by the two endpoints. But the call flow in this example is uncomplicated to the point of being simplistic for some of the more sophisticated features supported even by today's SS7-based telephony. This issue will be discussed further in this text.		

The example call flow should not paint an incorrect picture of the complexities involved in actually providing telephone service. Call flows implementing telephony features will be very complex. Even if we assume—in our wildest dreams—that the PSTN went away, we will still need to replace the feature set supported by the present telephone network. Included in this concern is the 99.999% reliability of the network we have enjoyed up to now. This is a hard act to follow, but viable VoIP and integrated services will not become ubiquitous until reliability and dependability have been demonstrated.

Primary line telephone service is a service regulated by the federal government. If a carrier wants to sell local telephone service, they must adhere to the regulatory requirements without exception. Some examples of regulatory requirements include operator services, 911 emergency calls, wiretapping by law enforcement, allowed network downtime, etc. The PSTN also includes the rest of the world, and any new method of signaling will have to interwork with signaling in international networks, which are also regulated by their local governments. When we add to this picture the future requirements of intelligent networks (IN), the preceding call flow is only a very fundamental and basic example of numerous complex call flows that come up when the pen hits the paper in a platform design process.

3.4 HETEROGENEOUS CALL SETUP—MAPPING SS7 TO IP-BASED CALL CONTROL

Call setup for calls across the PSTN involves mapping of the IP-based signaling stack to the SS7/ISUP protocol. In the example call flow,[6] shown in Figure 3.22, a customer device capable of issuing PRI commands (for instance, a PBX), is serving a user who is placing a call to an endpoint managed by a an IP-based media gateway controller. The case study shows only the most basic ISUP messages IAM, ACM, and ANM for the setup portion of the call. It is possible that in the course of placing and managing a call, the signaling network will use a larger set of the suite of ISUP messages between the local exchange of the originating party and the terminating calling agent. It is thus anticipated that signaling platform implementations will support the entire collection of ISUP messages for both ANSI-based and international networks.

Table 3.10 is a walk-through of the transactions shown in the call flow of Figure 3.22.

When either of the parties hangs up, procedures for call termination will be invoked. In this example we assume the party on the VoIP end of the call went on-hook first (the called party). The call termination actions are shown in Figure 3.23 on page 214 and a discussion of the signaling steps follow.

When the called party hangs up, a NTFY command is issued by the media gateway to the MGC, notifying it of the event. Command syntax is similar to the example we analyzed in basic MGCP call termination of Figure 3.21. The first business at hand for the MGC is to delete the connection between the MG and the PSTN gateway and clean up the call context. The DLCX command is issued and is acknowledged by the PSTN Gateway and the MG with a positive ACK along with performance parameters. At the same time, the MGC sends the ISUP REL command to the originating exchange to release the call. At the OLE, the REL command causes a DISCONNECT command to be sent to the call originator. Signaling completes with an exchange of the RELEASE and RELEASE COMPLETE messages, at which time the context of the call is considered cleared.

Accounting and billing information is stopped when the REL command is sent on the SS7 network. Following all the cleanup work, the calling agent

---

6. Adapted from an example by Huitema, Andreasen, Arango and Prakash.

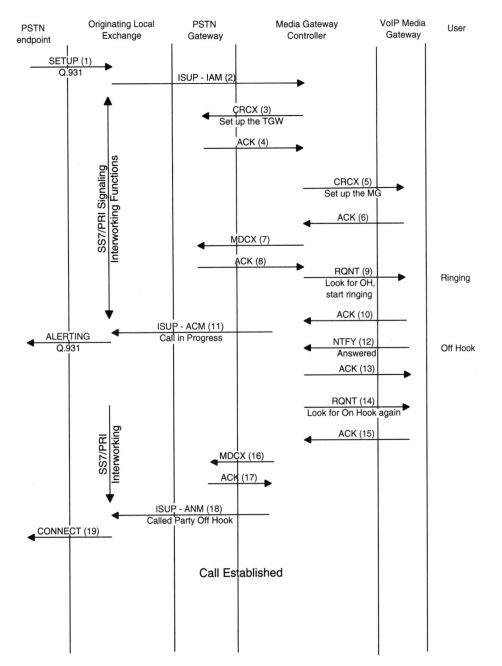

FIGURE 3.22 ISUP to S/MGCP Call Setup Through a PSTN Gateway

TABLE 3.10 PSTN to RGW Signaling for Call Setup

TRANSACTIONS	PARAMETERS	NOTES AND EXPLANATION
SETUP (PRI message from the PSTN subscriber to the local exchange) (1)	This Q.931 message initiates call establishment. At a minimum it carries information about the type of circuit requested for the call.	Upon receiving the SETUP message, the originating local exchange (OLE) will first do an LNP query (not shown) and then proceed to initiate SS7 signaling.
In case of CAS signaling, the OLE would signal to the CPE to collect digits. This call flow applies after the digits have been analyzed by the OLE and it is ready to send the ISUP initial address message (IAM).		
IAM (SS7 message from the OLE to the adjacent exchange) (2)	The IAM carries the forward circuit information, carrier identification code, called party number, and optional parameters, such as a request for circuit continuity test and possibly calling party number.	This is the most comprehensive and complex message in the ISUP suite. In this example it is shown traversing a single hop from the OLE to the exchange hosting the VoIP media gateway controller. In general, there can be multiple hops before the terminating exchange is reached.
Steps 3 through 10 in the call flow represent a basic MGCP call setup like the example we saw in Figure 3.20. The MGC simply sets up a connection between the called endpoint and the endpoint on the PSTN gateway that maps to the circuit on which the incoming call is received. If any media transcoding is required, it will be performed by the gateway. After the message requesting the MG to ring the called party's phone (the endpoint) has been acknowledged, the MGC will send the ISUP address complete message (ACM) in step 11 to the exchange which sent the IAM (the OLE in this example). The ACM indicates the IAM was delivered successfully and, if all is working well, the phone is now ringing. We are now waiting for someone to answer the phone. Once the OLE receives the ACM, it sends the Q.931 ALERTING message to the originator of the call. At that point, the caller hears audible ringing.		
NTFY (from the called endpoint to the MGC) (12)	This message carries the indication that the phone has gone off-hook, which means someone answered the phone. The message is acknowledged by the MGC in step 13.	

TABLE 3.10 PSTN to RGW Signaling for Call Setup (Continued)

TRANSACTIONS	PARAMETERS	NOTES AND EXPLANATION
RQNT (from the MGC to the called endpoint) (14)	The MGC needs to sensitize the endpoint to detect the hang-up condition (phone went back on-hook). The MG acknowledges this message in step 15.	
MDCX (from the MGC to the PSTN gateway) (16)	This message completes the call setup by making the connection between the endpoint and the gateway full duplex. It is acknowledged by the gateway in step 17.	
ANM (18)	This ISUP message is sent by the MGC as soon it completes the call setup in its domain with steps 16 and 17. Upon receiving the message, the OLE sends the Q.931 CONNECT message to the call originator, and the call is now considered to be stable. Call accounting information for billing purposes is also initiated at this point.	

notifies the endpoint on the MG to be on the lookout for a new off-hook event, to accept new call attempts. This completes the call termination procedure.

Call Setup between SIP and RGW Clients across the PSTN

In this scenario, construction of the media gateway controller supports call setup between a SIP client and an endpoint on the MG controlled by the MGCP protocol. A basic call flow signaling would start with an INVITE from the SIP call agent to the MGC, which would be mapped to a CRCX command and sent to the media gateway controlling the called endpoint. Signaling would proceed as shown in Figure 3.24.

As soon as the INVITE message is seen by the MGC, the called endpoint must be located. Location services may be necessary at this point if the MGC is not immediately aware of the location of the called party. This could be as simple as performing a simple DNS lookup to translate a URL, or other more complex services may be implemented as part of the service design to support user mobility. The SIP "trying" informational code will be returned to the originating endpoint as soon as the endpoint has been identified and the CRCX has been sent indicating the desire to set up a call. When the endpoint

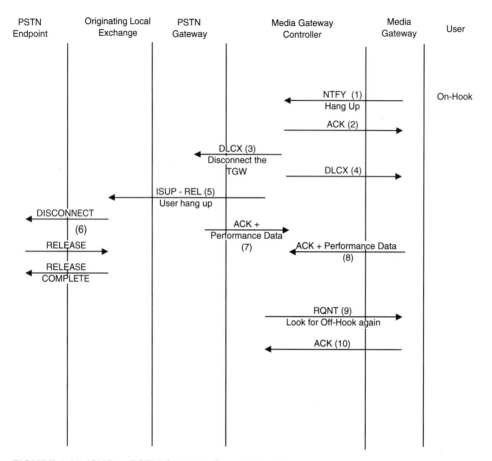

FIGURE 3.23 ISUP to PSTN Gateway Call Termination

replies with ACK, the MGC will request for the phone to ring and request notification of the off-hook condition. At the same time, a SIP "ringing" informational code will be sent to the originating endpoint.

As soon as the called party picks up the phone and the NTFY is received by the MGC, a success code (code 200) will be sent to the SIP endpoint. The SIP ACK will complete the call setup and media will start flowing between the endpoints. The call has been set up!

This is a simple example, but it demonstrates the message types that would be used in the setup of a call. For VoIP telephony over the public network there are numerous other considerations that enter the picture and must be accounted for in the call setup. One of those is, of course, possible media type negotiation between the endpoints. The SIP ACK message would carry

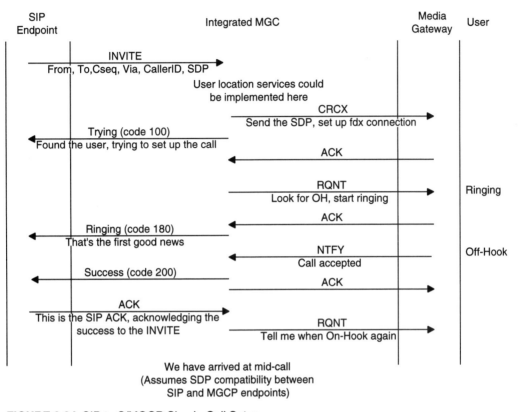

SIP
Endpoint

Integrated MGC

Media
Gateway   User

INVITE
From, To,Cseq, Via, CallerID, SDP

User location services could
be implemented here

CRCX
Send the SDP, set up fdx connection

Trying (code 100)
Found the user, trying to set up the call

ACK

RQNT
Look for OH, start ringing

Ringing

ACK

Ringing (code 180)
That's the first good news

NTFY
Call accepted

Off-Hook

Success (code 200)

ACK

ACK
This is the SIP ACK, acknowledging the
success to the INVITE

RQNT
Tell me when On-Hook again

We have arrived at mid-call
(Assumes SDP compatibility between
SIP and MGCP endpoints)

FIGURE 3.24 SIP to S/MGCP Simple Call Setup

the accepted SDP by the SIP endpoint and this information would be conveyed to the MGC for possible modification of the SDP at the called endpoint.

Some other design considerations would involve billing and user authentication. Implementation of these and other service-oriented capabilities are platform design dependent and will vary among systems. These functions would be critical if the SIP to S/MGCP signaling involved a PSTN hop, regardless of the nature of the remote endpoint. The SIP INVITE message has a simple mapping to the ISUP IAM, which could generate an immediate backward "trying" SIP message. The ACM indicates the remote phone is ringing, and would generate "ringing" by the MGC towards the SIP endpoint. When the called party answers the phone and an ANM is received by the MGC, it would report a "success 200" to the SIP endpoint. The ACK from the endpoint would initiate media cut-through and the two parties would be able to hear each other.

Continuity testing in the various segments of the call path is one of the numerous other implementation details facing the platform designers of an integrated service MGC.

Call Setup Between H.323 and S/MGCP Endpoints Through the PSTN

In Chapter 1, we discussed a mixed topology with H.323 and S/MGCP endpoints that did not involve a PSTN hop. If there is packet network connectivity between the two types of users without venturing into the PSTN, things will remain relatively simple. The call flows in this section, shown in Figures 3.25 and 3.26, demonstrate the interactions between the H.323 PSTN gateway and a RGW gateway signaled with S/MGCP and the SS7 network over ISUP.

The endpoint on the S/MGCP media gateway is originating the call in this example.

Up to and including step number 8, the signaling flow is the basic S/MGCP call setup. The MGC asks for notification on off-hook and when it gets it, it asks for a valid digit string and requests that the endpoint play a dial tone. The digit map is either pre-existing, or is downloaded with the RQNT command in step 5. Once digits have been collected, the MGC determines that the called party is across the PSTN and needs to set up the call with its own PSTN gateway. The process begins by sending a CRCX to the gateway and asking for an IAM (ISUP) message to be sent across the SS7 network. The gateway will seize an outbound circuit and initiate signaling to set up a TDM circuit across all the intermediate exchange hops between itself and terminating exchange.

The TE signals to the H.323 gateway/gatekeeper, indicating an incoming call. The GW/GK opens a TCP connection, with the call flow we analyzed in Chapter 1, and then sends the H.225.0 SETUP message to the called endpoint with the H.245 fastStart option. This action opens a logical channel for the media stream and sets the capabilities for the connection (we assume the called endpoint supports the fastStart option, as we have discussed earlier; otherwise formal H.245 signaling procedures are necessary). The called endpoint returns ALERTING, indicating the "virtual phone" is ringing. This action causes the ISUP ACM message to be sent back towards the originating exchange. When it arrives at the MGC, it causes an RQNT message to be sent to the calling endpoint, asking it to play ringback. Ringback can also be played from the terminating exchange, or the H.323 gateway, depending on the network design.

When the called party answers the incoming call, its own CONNECT+ fastStart message is sent to the H.323 GW/GK. This action generates the ISUP ANM message and it is propagated to the MGC of the calling party. This in turn causes the ringback tone to be removed and the connection to the

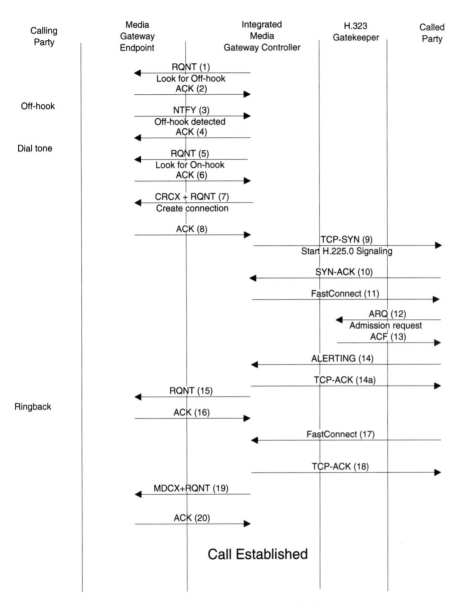

FIGURE 3.25 S/MGCP to H.323 Call Setup Over the PSTN

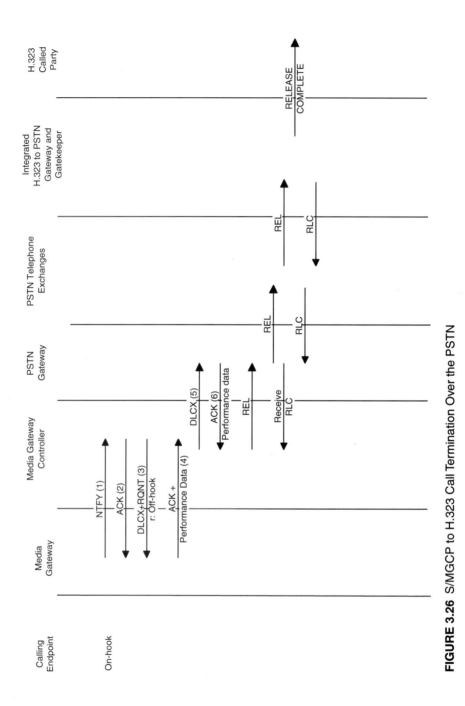

FIGURE 3.26 S/MGCP to H.323 Call Termination Over the PSTN

calling party to be converted to full duplex. The MGC is also asking for on-hook notification from the calling party with the RQNT command, to detect when the calling party has hung up. At this time we have arrived in mid-call and the two parties can hear each other.

Call termination is shown in Figure 3.26. The calling party hangs up first.

The calling party places the phone-on hook and a notification is sent to the MGC. The MGC then sends a DLCX to both the MG endpoint and the PSTN gateway. It also notifies the endpoint to look for off-hook again. The acknowledgments of the DLCX commands as usual will contain the performance data for the connection.

The MGC then proceeds to issue the ISUP REL (RELEASE) towards the terminating exchange. The arrival of the REL at the H.323 gateway results in a RELEASE COMPLETE H.225.0 message to be sent to the called endpoint. The H.323 Gateway then returns RLC towards the PSTN gateway, which effectively signals the termination of the call.

Some things to remember: The H.225.0 message set does not support DISCONNECT. If the H.323 endpoint had hung up first, the ISUP message exchange on the PSTN would have been identical. Also, the design of the H.323 network and signaling endpoints would determine the exact nature of the RAS exchanges between the endpoints and the H.323 gateway and gatekeeper. For example, the endpoint may have desired to remain registered, or requested disengagement. In the case of H.323 hang-up, the MGC would have deleted the connection to the MG endpoint, starting with step 3 of the call flow.

Parameter Conversion Between SS7, Q.931, and H.323 Signaling

It becomes immediately obvious that mapping of messages and parameters between the various signaling protocols is a tedious task that must be executed carefully. In Table 3.11, we show a basic mapping between SS7 signaling parameters and the Q.931 and H.225.0 signaling protocols, with annotations to help the reader understand the basics. More complex mappings are likely in actual implementations, especially in media gateways that support multi-party conferencing among subscribers across dissimilar signaling domains.

Table 3.12 shows a typical mapping between the ISUP IAM message and Q.931 SETUP. Although most of the information can be mapped and carried across the network, the two signaling protocols do not have an exact correspondence of information elements, due to their different nature, origins, and signaling purpose. This is presented as a simple illustration of the issues associated with protocol mapping and interworking. As the VoIP signaling protocols mature to address primary service telephony across the public network, protocol interworking in service platforms will continue to represent a major development investment on the part of the service providers.

TABLE 3.11 Basic Information Element Mapping Between ISUP, Q.931, and H.225.0

H.225 ELEMENT	Q.931 INFORMATION ELEMENT	SS7 ISUP PARAMETER
Bearer Capability	Bearer Capability	User Service Information
Called Party Number	Called Party Number	Called Party Number
Called Party Subaddress	Called Party Subaddress	Access Transport
Calling Party Number	Calling Party Number	Calling Party Number
Calling Party Subaddress	Calling Party Subaddress	Access Transport
Cause	Cause	Cause Indicators
Date/Time	Date/time	(no mapping)
Display	Display	(no mapping)
Extended Facility IE	Extended Facility IE (no ANSI)	(no mapping)
(not used)	Higher Layer Compatibility	Access Transport
Keypad Facility	Keypad Facility	Called Party Number
(not used)	Lower Layer Compatibility	Access Transport
(not used)	More Data	(no mapping)
(not used)	Network-Specific Facilities	(no mapping)
Notification Indicator	Notification Indicator	Notification Indicator
Progress Indicator	Progress Indicator	Access Transport/Progress Indicator Broadband ISUP
(not used)	Repeat Indicator	(no mapping)
(not used)	Restart Indicator	(no mapping)

TABLE 3.11 Basic Information Element Mapping Between ISUP, Q.931, and H.225.0 (Continued)

H.225 ELEMENT	Q.931 INFORMATION ELEMENT	SS7 ISUP PARAMETER
(not used)	Segmented Message	(BISUP only)
Sending Complete	Sending Complete	(no mapping)
Signal	Signal	(no mapping)
(not used)	Transit Network Selection	Transit Network Selection
User-to-User	User-to-User	(no mapping, BISUP only)

TABLE 3.12 Illustrative H.323 (SETUP) to SS7-ISUP (IAM) Parameter Mapping

Q.931 CALLING PARTY (SETUP)	SS7 ISUP (IAM)
Bearer Capability	User Service Information
Keypad (called party number in reverse direction)	Called Party Number
Calling Party Number	Calling Party Number and/or Generic Address
Calling Party Subaddress	Access Transport
Called Party Number	Called Party Number
Called Party Subaddress	Access Transport
Transit Network Selection	Transit Network Selection
Low Layer Compatibility	Access Transport
High Layer Compatibility	Access Transport
Progress Indicator	Access Transport

3.5 CLOSING THOUGHTS ON MIXED NETWORK VOICE TELEPHONY

The simple examples we worked through in this section represent the tip of the iceberg in the complexities involved when signaling protocol interworking is designed for prime time. VoIP needs to work with the PSTN in a transparent manner in order to maintain the "look and feel" of high quality telephone service we have been accustomed to. The services of SS7 are too numerous to expect any VoIP deployment in the public network will displace SS7 signaling in the short term. The best and most sure-footed approach for the quick acceptance of VoIP in the consumer market is leverage of the existing capabilities of the PSTN in areas where invention is not required.

CHAPTER 4

Metrics for Voice Quality

As we move beyond signaling and transport mechanisms for delivering pack-etized voice across IP-based networks, an immediate concern becomes the quality of the delivered speech and whether there are means to measure it objectively. We are now ready to start looking at objective voice quality mea-surement methodologies, which have been researched and developed in the past few years. However, in order to understand the measurement objectives and methods, we must first understand the quantities being measured and the environment variables under which they are being observed. We have seen already that IP networks present several challenges to the designer of inte-grated services due to the drastic departure from conventional techniques used to deliver media as compared to the simplicity of the TDM network. As we go along we will see some of those challenges, and we will revisit the voice qual-ity subject in Chapter 5 with a simple case study in measurement methodology.

4.1 VOICE QUALITY IN CONVERGING TDM AND IP NETWORKS[1]

Traditional telephony networks are built to provide an optimal service for time-sensitive voice applications requiring low delay, low jitter, and constant

---

1.   The author wishes to thank Stefan Pracht of Hewlett-Packard, Network Systems Test Division, for his contribution to this section.

but low bandwidth. IP networks on the other hand have been built to support non-real-time data applications such as file transfer or email. These applications are characterized by bursty traffic, with occasional peaks in demand for high bandwidth, but are not sensitive to delay. Quality of Service (QoS) in IP networks remains a subject of research, but the common target centers around the minimization of packet loss due to impairments and traffic management issues. As hard as it may be sometimes, QoS can be brought under control in private pure IP networks, especially in the enterprise. In the last few years, however, the Internet has served as proving ground for integrated services technologies, and voice transport in particular, on a network that does not guarantee quality of service. A lot of things have been learned, and technology refinements from this experience have been instrumental in enabling telephone service providers to construct IP-based voice telephone networks for delivery of toll service. All indications are the carriers will provide IP-basic voice telephony service as a first step, and integrated interactive multimedia applications as the technology matures and gains wide consumer acceptance.

The desire to combine telephony and data networks into a single packet-based network capable of carrying integrated services requires that the new public network be equipped with mechanisms that ensure reasonable and predictable quality of service (QoS) for all applications. This is especially important considering that users of the PSTN are accustomed to a high service and toll-quality voice quality standard. Providing comparable quality and service offerings as in the PSTN will drive the initial acceptance and success of VoIP services.

We list some of the critical factors that affect our overall user experience with telephone service in Table 4.1.

In this chapter, we focus on the primary aspects and critical parameters that affect voice quality. By voice quality we mean the fidelity of the reproduced speech and its intelligibility—the ability to extract the information out of a conversation. These two attributes appear similar at first glance, but are not necessarily dependent on each other. We will proceed in the following sections to explain and understand the factors influencing the delivery of high voice quality in the presence of ideal service and network conditions. The impact of network impairments on voice quality are presented in Chapter 5.

4.1.1 Clarity

Clarity is closely related to speech intelligibility, the latter being a subjective measure of how much information can be extracted from a conversation. Speech clarity depends on a variety of factors and only a few are well understood. For instance, certain frequency bands in the audio spectrum are more

TABLE 4.1 Influencing Factors in Quality Perception

SERVICE QUALITY FACTORS	VOICE QUALITY FACTORS	
PSTN and VoIP Networks	Common to PSTN and VoIP Networks	Additional Parameters for IP Networks

Telephone Services—for example, Calling Card, 800/900 services, Call Forwarding, Voicemail, etc.
Availability—down time, network busy indications
Reliability—dropped calls, wrong numbers, calls not completed
Post-Dial Delay
Price
	Loudness
	Delay
	Echo
	Clarity:
	  Intelligibility
	  Noise
	  Fading
	  Cross talk
		Delay-Jitter
		Clarity:
		  Packet Loss
		  Bandwidth
		  Compression

important for speech intelligibility than others. As an example, the 250–800Hz audio band is less important for speech intelligibility than the frequency content between 1000–1200Hz. We will discuss the importance of measurable parameters in sub-bands of the audio spectrum, for maximizing the perceived speech quality.

What are the influencing factors for clarity in an IP telephone network with PSTN interworking? Let's look at some of the elements contributing to speech clarity, using a simple, high-level packet topology shown in Figure 4.1.

The network components in the end-to-end path of a call all have some impact on the voice clarity:

- The basic telephone devices on both sides of the call affect the voice clarity through the quality of the loudspeaker and microphone and possibly the uncompensated acoustic echo generated between the speaker and microphone. This is a parameter not related to the type of network used to transport voice, but impairments add to degradation of voice quality and all contributors must be considered. This issue is very important in wireless communications.
- The PSTN network uses digital voice transmission between exchange offices. Digitization has a minor impact on clarity through minimally increased signal-to-noise ratio, but not enough to cause significant and perceived degradation of quality.
- The VoIP Gateway of our previous discussions attaches to the PSTN and converts the digital voice samples on the TDM trunks to packet

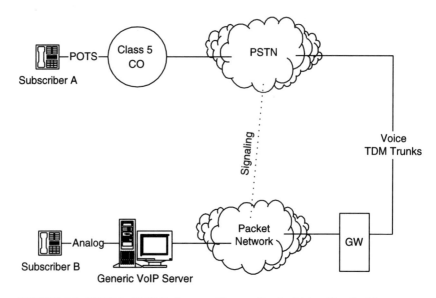

FIGURE 4.1 POTS to VoIP Reference Connection for Voice Quality Measurement

form of the same or different encoding. If transcoding from PCM (G.711) to compressed voice takes place, this is one of the places where it could happen. The gateway components affecting clarity are the gateway's speech codec, possible silence suppression mechanisms, the comfort noise generator, and the type of transcoding that may be necessary for the call.

- In addition, the IP network may affect the delivered speech quality if there is no guaranteed QoS, and this results in excessive jitter and packet loss. The PSTN, as we mentioned already, may be inefficient but it rarely drops bits or digitized voice samples.

- The Generic VoIP Media Gateways of our reference topologies also affect the clarity through their own speech codecs and possible silence suppression and Voice Activity Detection mechanism.

4.1.2 Packet Loss

Packet loss is not uncommon in IP data networks. Can we live without control of this parameter in a packet voice network? When the path of a packet stream carrying voice experiences congestion, routers may start discarding packets. Regardless of the algorithm used to determine which call is being affected, some calls will be affected more than others. Especially in cases where multiplexing and aggregation of traffic streams are implemented for classes of service, packet loss can cause serious problems in the quality of plain old telephone service.

Packet loss does not necessarily mean packets never arrived at their destination. For voice telephony, a packet that arrives too late to be useful is equivalent to a lost packet and is discarded by the receiver. The net effect for the call that experienced late packets is that of packet loss. However, statistics kept at endpoints may specifically classify and identify late packets.

The PSTN does not suffer from these ailments. Bits are switched between trunks with bandwidth reserved and maintained for the duration of the call.

For non-real-time applications such as file transfers, packet loss is undesirable but not critical—the protocols allow retransmission to recover dropped packages. However, in the case of real-time voice, information has to arrive in a certain time window to be useful in reconstruction of the voice signal. Retransmission would add an extensive delay to the reconstruction and is not practical.

To avoid packet loss, traffic management mechanisms are required in the IP network. Flow control and traffic prioritization algorithms are necessary to ensure the integrity of signaling and media transport. Modern routers may be designed to implement a variety of such schemes, and we already saw one of those in the RSVP protocol in Chapter 2. Other techniques involve bundling of funneled traffic with Multi-Protocol Label Switching (MPLS), and traffic classification with IP Differentiated Services. In general, the reader will find there may be caveats placed on the media streams that enter traffic management algorithms. Furthermore, the algorithms may not be flexible or quick enough to account for real-time network parameter reconfiguration or sudden changes in traffic flow.

Regardless of which methods are used, a deeper problem remains. Quality of Service for speech and other applications is defined on an *end-to-end* basis and therefore requires that sufficient network resources be provided throughout the *entire* network path. So, one may ask, can a connectionless protocol such as IP be treated as *truly connectionless* when the time comes to make the design decision? Do the necessary traffic classification and path selection schemes really make it more connection oriented, in the sense that media path selection must be predictable? Path selection predictability may not be an overwhelming issue for an enterprise network or single ISP environment where all resources can be administered through one network manager. However, it is almost impossible to administer networks across multiple administrative domains with the current state of IP telephony. When we make a simple long distance call across different pure IP-based carrier services, for example one from the local carrier and one on the IXC network, the first leg of the call goes to the Local Exchange, which in turn routes the call to our favorite IXC. Managing this simple scenario in the new packet-based public network is an enormous task that has not yet been conquered in VoIP telephony.

Achieving predictable and manageable QoS in a network requires that all network elements (i.e., routers and switches) in the path of a call are equally capable of identifying voice traffic and *allocating the required resources* for the duration of the call. This is still the exception rather than the rule in today's IP networks because interoperable implementations are lagging behind the standardization process of the specifications.

4.1.3 Speech Codecs

A speech codec transforms analog voice into digital bit-streams and vice versa. In addition, some speech codecs use compression techniques, removing redundant or less important information to reduce the transmission bandwidth required. Compression in particular is a balancing act between voice quality, local computation power, delay, and network bandwidth requirements. Compressing voice signals is computation-intensive. The greater the bandwidth reduction, the higher the computational cost of the codec for a given level of perceived clarity. In addition, greater bandwidth savings generally cost a higher end-to-end delay. The network planner must make an informed tradeoff between bandwidth and voice quality.

Furthermore, low-bit-rate speech codecs such as G.729 and G.723.1 try to reproduce the subjective sound of the signal rather than the shape of the speech waveform. This means any lost or severely delayed information can have a much more noticeable effect on the clarity than with a higher bit-rate speech codec or the G.711 method of compression.

4.1.4 Silence Suppression

A Voice Activity Detector (VAD) is a speech gate. When the caller is talking, the VAD gate opens and voice packets are transmitted. When the caller is silent, the gate is closed and no packets are sent. Since human conversations are essentially half-duplex in the long term, the use of VAD can realize reduction in bandwidth requirement in the area of 40–50%, over an aggregation of channels. Figure 4.2 shows the behavior of a VAD and its associated parameters.

4.1.5 Comfort Noise Generation

A Comfort Noise Generator (CNG) is a receive-side device which is a complementary function to the VAD. Its operation is simple. During periods of transmit silence, when no packets are sent, the receiver has a choice of what to play out to the listener. Muting the channel—that is, playing absolutely

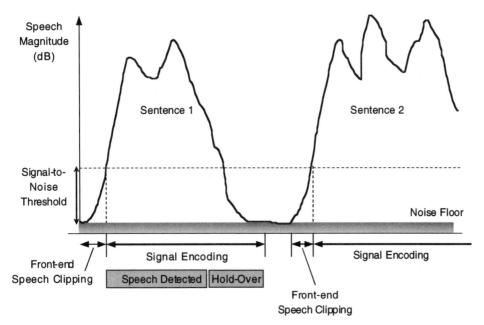

FIGURE 4.2 Voice Activity Detector (VAD) Behavior

nothing—gives the listener the unpleasant impression that the channel has gone dead (the dead-air syndrome). A CNG capability at the receiver generates locally low-level noise signal for presentation to the listener during transmit silence periods, with parameters specified by the transmitting end. The match between the locally generated noise and the "true" background noise present at the source determines the quality of the CNG.

4.1.6 End-to-End Delay

Delay is the time required for a signal to traverse the network. In the telephony context, end-to-end delay is the time required for a signal generated at the talker's mouth to reach the listener's ear. The end-to-end delay is the sum of the delays across all the network devices and links traversed by the media streams. Here are some contributing factors for different types of networks and elements:

1. The PSTN delay is determined primarily by the transmission delay on long-distance trunks. Delays through network switching equipment, such as DACS, is minimal. Transmission delay becomes especially high when one (or more) satellite links are involved in the path of a call; a geostationary satellite link has a transmission delay of about 250

milliseconds (ms). The TDM public network is well tuned to deliver low delay, and in that regard it is a hard act to follow.

2. Packet delay is primarily determined by the buffering, queuing, and switching or routing delay of the IP routers.

   • Packet capture delay is the time required to receive the entire packet before processing and forwarding it through the router. This delay is determined by the packet length, link layer operating parameters, and transmission speed. Using short packets over high-speed trunks can easily shorten the delay. VoIP networks use packetization rates that seek to strike a balance between connection bandwidth efficiency and packet delay.

   • Switching or routing delay is the time it takes a network element to forward a packet. This time is used to analyze the packet headers directly or derive indirect information from state information kept in the network elements, check the routing table, and finally forward the packet to an output port. The switching time of a network element is based on its architecture and optimized implementations of its routing tables. New IP switches can significantly speed up the routing process by making routing decisions and forwarding the traffic in hardware devices instead of software. Multi-Protocol Label Switching also holds significant promise in achieving an optimum operating point of forwarding speed and predictable quality of service.

   • Queuing time—due to the statistical multiplexing nature of IP networks and the asynchronous nature of packet arrivals, some queuing, thus delay, is required at the input and output ports of a packet switch. This delay is a result of the traffic load, the length of the packets and perhaps even the statistical distribution of traffic over the switch ports. Over-provisioning router and link capacities can reduce but not completely eliminate this delay. Estimating the queuing size at the endpoints can be complicated by the presence of large variances in jitter.

3. VoIP gateways and VoIP terminals also contribute significantly to the delay.

   • Voice signal processing at the sending and the receiving sides, which includes the time required to encode or decode the voice signal from analog or digital form into the voice-coding scheme selected for the call and vice versa, adds to the delay. Some codecs are also compressing the voice signal, which further increases the delay due to the necessary computations. The higher the compression, the more voice bits that need to be buffered, and the more complex the processing required, the longer this component of the delay.

- On the receive side, voice packets have to be delayed to compensate for variation in packet interarrival times. Packets generated with constant spacing in time (constant intervals) will generally arrive at the receiver with spacing randomly distributed. The measure of the interarrival variance is the jitter. This effect is due to the different buffering and queuing times a packet experiences inside the network elements on its path from one endpoint to the other(s) in a call. Jitter smoothing is required because the speech codec requires a constant flow of data without gaps between. This component of the delay can be reduced by designing a network with a lower delay jitter at each node and with as few nodes as possible, but for wide area telephony this cannot be guaranteed when the call path spans carrier domains. Using mechanisms that prioritize voice traffic over other traffic in the network can also reduce the jitter significantly. Jitter is minimum in the public TDM network because digital voice samples traverse nodes that are synchronized, and the minimum speech sample quantity is one octet (byte).

- On the transmit side, packetization delay is another factor that must be entered into the calculations. The packetization delay is the time it takes to fill a packet with data. The larger the packet size, the more time required. Using shorter packet sizes can shorten this delay but will increase the overhead because more packets have to be sent, all containing similar information in the header. Striking a balance between voice quality, packetization delay, and bandwidth utilization efficiency is of paramount importance to service providers.

How much delay is too much? Delay does not affect the speech intelligibility but rather the character of a conversation, up to the point where no conversation is possible at all. Below 100 ms, most users will not realize the delay. Between 100 ms and 300 ms, users will realize a slight hesitation in the partner's response. Interruptions are more frequent and the conversation can get out of "beat" as the delay increases. Beyond 300 ms, the delay is obvious to users and they will frequently have to back off to prevent interruptions and "talk-over". Delay above 300 ms is not suitable for toll telephony, and the challenge is to keep it under 100 ms, for "best" overall quality.

The rule of thumb in voice engineering is *the shorter the end-to-end delay, the better the perceived quality and overall user experience.*

4.1.7 Echo

Echo is the reflection of a signal through the network, with enough delay to become perceptible to the listener. Echo with a typical delay of 16–20 ms is called *sidetone* and is even desirable. It is reassuring during a conversation to hear a sidetone of our voice. However, echo with a delay in excess of about 32 ms can be annoying to the speaker. Let's see the origins of echo in the public network and what is being done to combat this natural phenomenon.

In POTS service, the 2-wire local loop is connected to a 4-wire trunk at the local telephone exchange, using a device called a *hybrid*. The hybrid separates the send and receive paths in order to carry them on separate pairs of wires. Because this separation of send and receive path is not perfect, some of the receive signal leaks onto the send path and generates an echo. Another source of echo is the handset of a phone and the hands-free set of a phone or PC terminal. They can cause *acoustic* echo, which is the result of poor voice coupling between the microphone and the loudspeaker or earpiece.

Echo cancellers are devices that are deployed in voice networks to reduce or eliminate echo. They monitor speech from the far end at their observation point on the receive path and use this information to compute an estimate of the echo that is then subtracted from the send path at the same observation point. Echo cancellers are deployed as close to the source of the echo as possible, such as the local loop, that is, the tail end, or the handset. However, echo cancellation can be designed at any point in the network, including placing observation points looking into the direction of the network.

The quality of echo cancellers can be determined with a few key parameters:

- *Convergence time*—the time required for the echo canceller to adapt to the monitored circuit and provide adequate echo reduction.
- *Cancellation depth*—the reduction in echo strength achieved, measured in dB.
- *Double-talk robustness*—the echo canceller does not lose its cancellation ability under conditions of simultaneous talking from both ends of the connection.

We see a more detailed discussion of echo control later in this chapter.

4.2 AUDITORY PERCEPTION AND TESTING METHODOLOGIES

As consumers we have enjoyed the clarity and overall quality of the public network for many years, but things are changing rapidly. Slowly but surely *toll-quality* voice is taking another meaning, and it is being replaced by terms such as *carrier-quality*, with which the average consumer is still not very familiar. Toll-quality in the TDM world of the PSTN is synonymous with faithful waveform reproduction across the 300–3400 Hz spectrum. Carrier-quality is quantified through different means, which is the subject of this section.

Speech contains a non-uniform distribution of signal amplitudes and frequencies. Two coding methods that have been used in the public network to accomplish the traditional toll-quality speech reproduction are Pulse Code Modulation (PCM) and Adaptive Differential Pulse Code Modulation (ADPCM). Simply stated, PCM is a simple and memoryless sampling of the speech waveform at 8KHz rate and medium step resolution (12 bits or better), followed by coding of the samples with a word length of 8 bits. Bit reduction is accomplished though logarithmic segmentation of the dynamic range, to achieve acceptable and fairly constant signal-to-noise distortion ratio. North American PCM systems use a *companding*[2] process that divides the input signal into 16 non-uniform segments. Within each segment, coding is allocated the same granularity (steps), but the segments are more densely packed in the low-levels signal to offer better resolution. The resulting PCM voice sample consists of a single bit to indicate whether the value is negative or positive, three bits that identify the segment and the last four bits that code the level within the segment.[3]

PCM coding takes on the entire audio spectrum at once and achieves a very good reproduction of the original waveform, at the relatively high cost of 64 Kbps transmission bandwidth. On the other hand, ADPCM uses knowledge derived from the signal to create an anticipated next sample value and thus code less redundant information about the signal. The basic idea of ADPCM is to receive PCM input, create a prediction of what the next sample would be, and code the difference between the predicted and actual sample values. Reductions to 48, 32, 24 and 16 Kbps are achievable, as described in ITU-T Recommendation G.726. In simple terms, the expected value of the next sample is created by an *adaptive predictor*, which sums previous weighted values of the reconstructed signal and weighted previous values of the quantized difference signal. Speech waveforms are fairly predictable in the short term, which results in pretty good estimations. The key to the success of the ADPCM algorithm is the accuracy with which a speaker's vocal attributes are modeled. There are no perceptual coding characteristics utilized in PCM and ADPCM, and the reduced signal-to-noise ratio of ADPCM is still insignificant from a perceptual standpoint. ADPCM coding as low as 32 Kbps qualifies as toll-quality voice.

Both the PCM and ADPCM speech coding formats are conveniently accommodated in the digital signal hierarchy of the public network. The 8 bits of a PCM sample occupy a DS-0 timeslot inside a DS-1 signal, whereas two 32 Kbps ADPCM samples can be placed in the same timeslot. However, the rudimentary 2-to-1 efficiency of the ADPCM algorithm has long been

---

2.   A composite word constructed from the terms *comp*ressing and exp*anding*.

3.   The reader is referred to ITU-T G.711 specification for a full description of the segmentation process and sample coding scheme for A-Law and u-Law PCM signal representation (Tables 1 and 2 of the G.711 document).

recognized as inadequate to accommodate the explosive growth rate of the telephone network and still maintain toll-quality service. The number of circuits required to carry today's massive telephony volume is growing at an enormous rate, and telephony carriers have sought drastic methods to make efficient use of transmission facilities. They have been looking for alternatives that will allow them to add value by offering service integration and interactive multimedia over the same physical links. To complicate matters more, the desire to combine voice, video, and data on the same medium has put a lot of pressure on technologists to find ways to make room for more voice channel capacity on physical links.

The first dimension to the voice telephony puzzle is the discovery of an optimum method to further compress a digitized speech waveform in a manner that increases the voice channel capacity, without reducing the voice quality perceived by the consumer. Clearly this was impossible to achieve using TDM techniques of fixed-bandwidth channelization, because once a call has been established, the circuits are set up and remain fixed until the call is terminated. There are known methods to achieve sub-rate multiplexing in the Digital Signal hierarchy within a DS-0, but they were deemed early on to be too complex to manage and did not offer the ability to control and allocate the bandwidth on demand in a flexible and speedy manner upon call establishment. In other words, the methods available to manage subrate circuits within a B-Channel in ISDN-PRI are so complex that effective bandwidth utilization by integrated voice and data applications became close to being a nightmare. So, the idea of using TDM techniques to accomplish dynamic bandwidth allocation of compressed voice channels with data applications was abandoned.

At first it was not easy to convince the carriers that the TDM infrastructure of the PSTN had reached its scalability limits, and not everybody is convinced the current PSTN will become obsolete any time soon, at least for voice. However, the need to manage bandwidth in the backbone and accomplish better network scalability vs. cost was starting to be recognized and discussed seriously by the carriers in the mid-1980s. ATM has its roots in finding better mechanisms to manage the bandwidth in the backbone network than is achievable with TDM techniques. Once we were all convinced of the recurring costs to match a non-scalable network with the demands of the consumer appetite for integrated voice and data services, the task became a little easier for the proponents of packet technology as the transport infrastructure for the new services. The Internet itself has played a big role in this quest, not only as the educational Information Superhighway, but also as a proving ground for voice compression technologies and media delivery mechanisms, which are now being seriously implemented and are on their way to our homes as basic telephone service over controlled public carrier networks. The lack of adequate bandwidth in the local loop from the local central office to our home, coupled with the strong consumer demand for integrated voice and data services, has paved the road for technological breakthroughs in voice coding and transport.

Figure 4.3 shows a road-map to voice coding technology either in use or under serious consideration for packet-based voice services and voice telephony in private networks. Basic waveform coding techniques deliver excel-

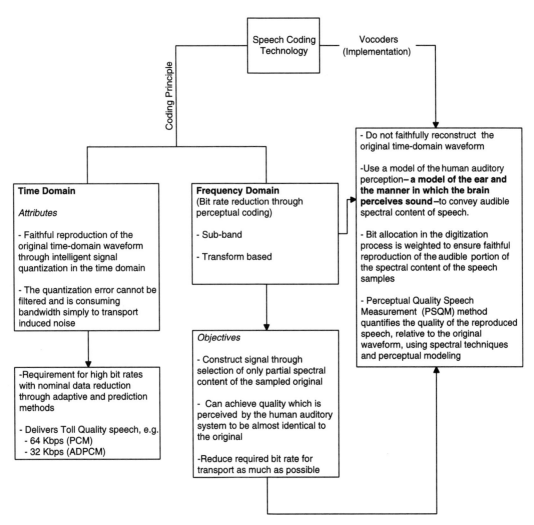

FIGURE 4.3 Voice Coding Technology

lent quality with rates down to about 16 Kbps. ADPCM is of slightly lesser quality than PCM, but the imperfections of the telephone handset mask the imperfections caused by the speech coding, and thus they are not perceivable by the human ear. Below the 16 Kbps barrier, the quality of speech delivered from a reconstructed waveform is so seriously affected as to be considered unacceptable for toll telephone service. The research in speech coding technology focused its emphasis on compressing voice in a manner that does not affect the perceived speech quality, rather than the degree to which the reproduced speech waveform is a faithful replica of the source signal. To this goal, engineering has used knowledge obtained from medicine, and in particular the field of acoustics. Studies in the propagation of sound from the external environment through the stages of the ear to its interpretation by the brain has taught us that precise waveform reproduction is *not* necessary to convey all the audible information contained in speech. The science that studies our perception of sound and the manner in which we extract and retain information from acoustical signals is called *psychoacoustics*.

Use of a perceptual model of our auditory system in a voice coder implementation allows it to code information in a manner such that inaudible sounds need not be coded and transported. The task of the coder is to identify the part of the audible spectrum of the digitized speech that would not be perceived by the human brain if reproduced. Classification of spectral content as inaudible is a dynamic process that requires knowledge of the frequency response of the ear, and an accurate representation of the auditory perception function in the coding process. Coders that use perceptual models of the auditory system are called *vocoders*, and operate in the frequency domain. In the current state-of-the-art, models of the auditory system used for speech compression are imperfect and research in this field is continuing, but the present coding schemes have achieved significant data reduction with high quality in speech encoding.

4.2.1 Definitions and Basic Principles

Central to the discussion of perceptual coding is the frequency response of the human ear. The ear converts sound wave pressures into stimuli which are transmitted to the brain. It is in effect an extremely sophisticated transducer, characterized by a set of frequency response curves across the audio spectrum. The loudness curves of Figure 4.4 demonstrate clearly that the ear does not perceive sounds in a linear manner, and it exhibits its greatest sensitivity in the 1 KHz region of the audio spectrum. The most important curve is the Threshold of Hearing curve, which defines the barrier between audible and inaudible sounds…well, almost.

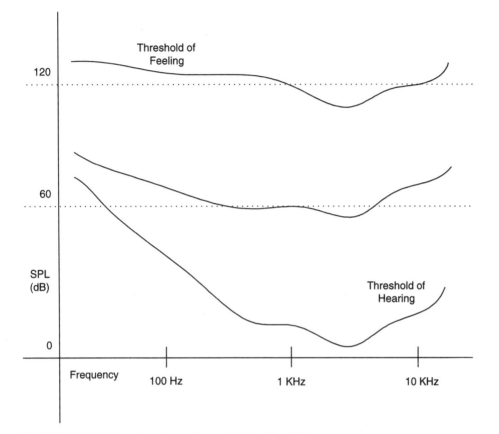

FIGURE 4.4 Auditory Loudness Curves Using Sine Waves

A significant concept used in perceptual coding is the principle of *sound masking*, which is the effect of a tone or narrow-band noise of enough loudness to make other tones or sounds within a narrow spectral band inaudible. Masked sounds would be audible, according to the loudness curves, if there was no masking sound present. As an example, consider the effect of turning up the volume in your car stereo to mask the sound of the engine. The sound of the engine does not go away, but the sound of the stereo creates the perception that it has. The importance of sound masking is that by removing frequencies that will not be audible when the speech is reproduced at the other end, the required bit rate to code the signal can be reduced. By completely ignoring the masked sound in the coding process we ignore any perceptual impact the masked sound would have on the coded signal. This is not critical to the delivered quality of the coded speech for simple conversational voice.

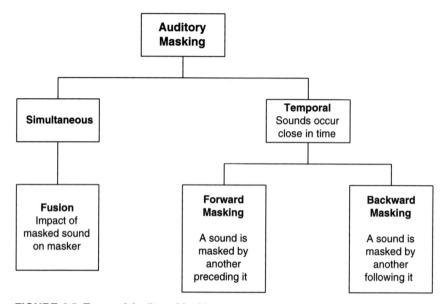

FIGURE 4.5 Types of Auditory Masking

This is the simple explanation of masking, and its variants are shown in Figure 4.5. There is another concept in auditory perception known as *fusion*, which is not used in the perceptual coding methods used in vocoders. Fusion refers to the impact a masked signal has on the masking signal. In simple terms, just because the car stereo masked the engine sound and the engine sound is not perceived, it doesn't mean that it has no impact on the stereo sound (music, etc.). However, this type of reverse impact is not of major perceptual importance for telephone conversations.

The concept of masking helps us understand another measure in auditory perception, that of the *critical band*. The ear has been modeled with the use of a set of critical bands covering the audio spectrum. These bands are narrower in the lower frequencies and become wider as we move to the higher frequencies. The Bark Scale in Physhoacoustics is such a set of critical bands used in perceptual speech quality measurements with help from frequency warping. The process of *frequency warping* defines a mapping of the *linear* spectrum into a *perceptual* spectrum. We will see this process when we discuss the Perceptual Speech Quality measurement (PSQM) method later in this chapter.

Pohlman has produced an excellent reference on the principles of digital audio. In this section we will concentrate on coding schemes for voice telephony, and proceed to analyze the PSQM industry standard algorithm that measures and quantifies the quality of coded speech in an objective manner. To this effect we need to define some terms before we proceed with further analysis.

A fundamental physical quantity in auditory perception is the *Sound Pressure Level* (SPL) produced by an acoustic signal. This is the ratio of the power contained in the signal to the reference point power contained in a *barely audible* sound, expressed in decibels. Barely audible sound levels are points on the threshold of hearing curve. The use of the decibels is necessary to account for the full dynamic range of the ear, from the barely audible sound to the discomfort level of pain. The threshold of hearing is neither constant nor linear across the audio spectrum, but the value obtained by a 1 Khz tone is used as the reference level because this is the point of maximum sensitivity of the ear. The formula that expresses the threshold of hearing is as follows:

$$Threshold\ of\ hearing\ =\ 10^{-12}\frac{W}{m^2}$$

The Sound Pressure Level is expressed as SPL = $10\log_{10}$(P$_{sound}$/P$_{threshold\ of\ hearing}$). The threshold of hearing is the thus the 0 dB level in the scale.

At the other extreme we establish the Threshold of Feeling (or pain), which is the power of 1 W/m^2. Simple substitution in the SPL formula sets the upper extreme at 120 dB.

$$Threshold\ of\ feeling\ =\ 10 \cdot \log_{10}\left[\frac{1\frac{W}{m^2}}{10^{-12}\frac{W}{m^2}}\right] = 120dB$$

SPL values beyond the comfort limit are also audible, but painful, and can damage the ear. For example, the sound of a jet engine can exceed 150 dB in close proximity. The sound produced by modern rock bands is sometimes beyond the upper threshold as well.

Pitch is the attribute of our auditory perception that allows us to order sounds on a musical scale. Pitch is often confused with frequency, but it is only proportional to the logarithm of frequency, except at the low and high extremes of the audio spectrum. Sounds with periodic content have pitch, for example, a note played on the piano. *Noise does not have pitch*. It is key to note that loudness tends to distort the auditory perception of pitch. It is difficult, for example, to tune an electric guitar with headphones, because the headphones produce higher SPL and the perception of pitch by the ear is shifted.

Faithful reproduction of pitch is very important in speech quality.

Timbre is a sound quality attribute that allows us to identify sounds of the same pitch, intensity and duration. For example, timbre is used by the auditory perception system to identify instruments playing the same note, that is, the difference between the same note played on the piano and on the violin.

Timbre may be one of the first victims of perceptual coding for voice telephony.

4.2.2 Perceptual Coders

The two primary types of perceptual speech frequency domain coders are *sub-band coders* (SBC) and *adaptive transform coders* (ATC). Sub-band coders try to match the frequency response of the critical bands of the auditory system. The idea of sub-band coding is fairly simple, but the implementation is not. The input signal is decimated by passing it through a parallel set of steep cutoff bandpass filters, each of which performs its own independent quantization of the output signal. The original signal can be synthesized in the reverse manner at the receiver by passing the quantized samples through a synthesis filter bank. Sub-band coding has good time delay characteristics, but it offers coarse frequency resolution.

Transform coding improves the resolution in the frequency domain at the expense of time delay. This type of coding uses Discrete or Fast Fourier transform, of Modified Cosine Transform, and groups the resulting coefficients in a manner that emulates the critical bands of the auditory model. The Dolby AC-2, the Lucent PAC, and the SONY ATRAC, which is used in the MiniCD, are examples of transform coders.

Codecs use either *source* or *hybrid* coding schemes. The road map for the two types of coding schemes is shown in Figure 4.6. A source coder—a vocoder—discards the original waveform after it develops a model of how the speech was generated. The model parameters are saved and transmitted to the receiving end, but the synthesized speech is of low quality. Very low bit rates are achievable with source coding, but they have difficulty re-synthesizing speech from multiple simultaneous speakers.

Hybrid coders are more complex and the most important ones utilize AbS, the Analysis by Synthesis method. This is the method used in CELP

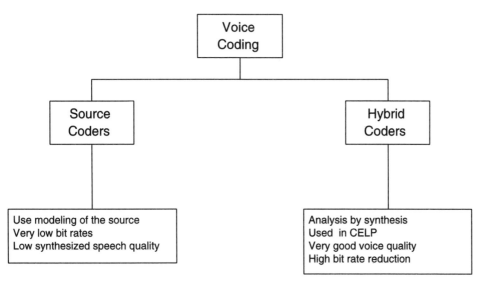

FIGURE 4.6 Primary Methods of Voice Coding

speech coding. Hybrid coders offer voice quality between that achieved with source coders and waveform coders, with sufficient bit reduction to make them a suitable choice for producing high-quality voice for packet networks.

4.2.3 Establishing the Metrics for Voice Quality

There are only a few universally accepted performance metrics defined for voice and voiceband telephony. Even the most-discussed metrics on application performance shed very little light on the behavior of the application when network impairments do occur. Packet voice telephony is impacted by combinations of parameters and network behavior. The critical issues in delivering robust voice service can be summarized as follows.

1. Cell or packet loss through the network
   - Bit error rate resulting in cell loss
   - Traffic management issues in the access or the backbone
2. User-perceived performance degradation due to coding schemes
3. Packet delay due to encoding, packetization, and network performance
4. Attributes perceived by the human senses
   - Echo, speech and video clarity, voice delay, background noise
5. Jitter, which may be aggravated as a result of service integration through the backbone.
6. Reliable vs. unreliable methods to connect endpoints in a call

7. Impact of integrating multicast and unicast applications through the same backbone.
   - Live testing methodologies to quickly distinguish the contributing sources of impairments and quickly bypass or remedy the causes to resume robust service

Can a network designed for voice transport handle integrated and interactive multimedia as an extension of its capabilities? If we employ an end-to-end design for voice, does the same design scale to support video and data? Do we get back to square one when the standards groups figure out how to support service for general topologies in the wide area? The downside of taking this risk is that one or more overlay network(s) could end up materializing, although the users will still perceive service integration. The result would be greater cost for the provider of the service and operator of the network.

It is not known at this time how video will be tested in a manner consistent with the model described in P.861. Certainly data QoS, that is, low throughput, large delay, etc. has immediate quantitative impact on the user and the application. But a new model may be necessary to mimic the perception of visual quality by the human senses in real-life situations. The good news is that there are far fewer methods to process a video signal than the maze of codecs developed for audio processing. So, however complex the perceptual processing of video, at least the permutations of supported capabilities at integrated endpoints will be far fewer than their audio counterparts.

4.3 PERCEPTUAL SPEECH QUALITY MEASUREMENT

ITU-T Recommendation P.861 specifies a model to map actual audio signals to their representations inside the head of a human. Before one raises an eyebrow about the methodology, one should also consider that there are psychophysical equivalent representations of audio frequency and intensity in the brain. This is how we hear and perceive sounds. The basic idea of the modeling approach is to take a measurement of processed (compressed, encoded, etc.) signals, perform an objective analysis between the original and the processed version, and offer an "opinion" as to the "goodness" of the signal processing functions that operated on the original signal. The result is an absolute number, not a relative comparison between the two signals.

The high-level reference model shown in Figure 4.7 whose purpose is two-fold. The first step results in an objective but relative measure of the speech quality. The second step maps objective data to opinion scores to offer a correlation with previously accepted techniques to characterize voice quality. Here we present a brief explanation of the detailed construction of the PSQM

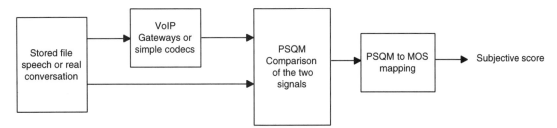

FIGURE 4.7 Perceptual Speech Quality Measurement Model

model for informational purposes. The challenges of measuring voice quality in real-life situations are a little more complex, and more data is often necessary, than derived in recommendation P.861. We must account for the presence of multiple codecs in the path of a call and a sophisticated network between the various endpoints of a multiparty call. We often require the ability to tap into various parts of the topology to perform a measurement with respect to the origin of the audio source. Such extensions are necessary for assessing the impact of individual voice processing points along the path of call. This is useful for obtaining intermediate readings of network behavior, with traceability to the source of impairments that cause voice quality degradation.

With the use of distributed test instrumentation, the input and output signals can be modeled at the endpoints of the voice call. First, let's look at the basics of the PSQM algorithm.

4.3.1 PSQM – Perceptual Speech Quality Measurement

Voice quality consists of a mix of objective and subjective parts, and varies widely among the different coding schemes and the types of network topologies used for transport.

In assessing the suitability of a network to support toll telephony service, it is necessary to take objective measurements of the voice quality in real networks with appreciably large geographies that may be subject to impairments. Such networks include sophisticated intranets, private carrier networks, and inter-carrier topologies which can span the entire country. We must account for error rates that are expected to be relatively small, but not zero. Error rates in the packet-based domains manifest themselves mostly as packets with bit errors, packets dropped or misrouted. The PSQM algorithm offers the voice engineer a tool to derive simple objective bottom-line numbers that map complex network parameters to the quality of service being delivered.

PSQM analysis uses several steps in processing the input and output signals. The steps correlate the intermediate values and end with a cognitive measure to produce the final result. Figure 4.8 shows the sequence of processing steps for both the input and output signals.

Before measurements can be taken, we need to calibrate the measurement instrument. System calibration is performed using the assumption that the optimum listening loudness is at –26dBov.[4] The calibration signal used is a 1KHz sine wave at a level of –64dBov. This tone should not be filtered, and noise should not be added as it is passed through the system.

There are two steps in the calibration process. The first step is to scale the maximum value of the *pitch power* to the value of 10,000.

$$S_p = \frac{10000}{\text{max (pitch power of output tone)}}$$

This results in a calibration factor of $S_p = 6.4661e^{-06}$.

The second calibration is made for loudness. The value $S_l = 240.05$ is obtained when the scaling calibration is done properly.

After calibration is complete, we can start feeding input and output signals into the instrument executing the PSQM algorithm. But there is a catch—PSQM requires *time-aligned* input and output stream samples. This simple requirement may not always be easy to achieve, especially in distributed testing, if the time lag between input and output cannot be easily obtained. Alternatively, an acceptable way to achieve near-time-alignment is to obtain the time lag that results in the maximum value of the cross-correlation between samples. The first and last active samples in a sequence are those for which the border sample, plus the four immediate samples outside the sample range, have a total magnitude of 200 or more.

The time-aligned output sequence needs to be scaled to account for the of the system. The scaling factor is defined as follows:

$$S_{global} = \sqrt{\frac{range^{\Sigma(x[n])^2}}{range^{\Sigma(y[n])^2}}}$$

---

4.   The quantity *dBov* represents the number of decibels relative to the overload point of the digital system.

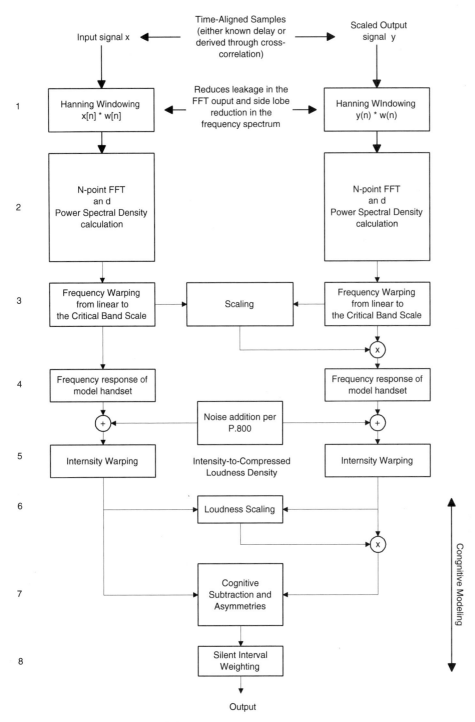

FIGURE 4.8 Basics of the PSQM Algorithm

The output signal is then multiplied by S_{global} to give $y'(n) = S_{global} *$ $y(n)$, which is then used as the input to the process.

Once the system has been calibrated and the scaling factors have been obtained, the time sequence is mapped to the frequency domain via an FFT. The first step of the process is windowing using the Hanning window. Windowing is necessary in order to minimize frequency leakage. The Hanning window is given by the following equation:

$$w[n] = \frac{1}{2} * \left[1 - \cos \left[\frac{2\pi n}{N-1} \right] \right]$$

With $0 \le n \le N - 1$, where N is the number of samples in the sequence.

In step 2 the windowed sequence is fed into the FFT. This is a good point to calculate Power Spectral Density (PSD) of the signal sample. Step 3 is the mapping of the PSD from the straightforward frequency spectrum to the critical band scale (Bark Scale). Research on the subject of sound perception has shown a clear relationship between the two perceptual attributes known as *pitch* and *loudness*. We discussed pitch earlier in this section and the simple definition of loudness is as follows:

Loudness is the attribute which allows the brain to order sounds from soft to loud.

Other bin sizes and resolutions have also been used to perform the frequency warping step in auditory perception coding, but the frequency band allocations for the PSQM algorithm, based on 16 KHz sampling rate, are shown in Table 4.2.

At the end of step 3 we have obtained a representation of the input and output sound samples in the auditory frequency spectrum, and from then on the algorithm operates in the "internal"— that is, human subject—domain.

At this point in the algorithm, a scaling of the frequencies of the output sample is necessary. This scaling is performed on a per-band basis in the critical bands. The multiplier of each band is the ratio of the power of the warped input over the warped output.

Step 4 passes the sound samples through a filter with the attributes of a telephone handset. The ITU has also determined a handset's transfer function, and that analysis appears in Recommendation P.830. Also, at this step external noise (Hoth noise) is added to simulate the environment.

Step 5 performs intensity level warping to an auditory scale and steps 6, 7, and 8 constitute the cognitive modeling process, which is where the processed streams meet for the first time. Cognitive modeling requires elements from both sets of signals.

Loudness scaling is performed with respect to the input signal. In step 6 we obtain the sampled noise disturbance density, which is little more than the absolute value of the input loudness minus the scaled output loudness, plus a small adjustment factor to account for internal cognitive noise. Simply stated, if the result of the subtraction of the output scaled spectrum on a per-band basis from the input spectrum is not zero, then the value represents the spectral density of noise in the processed output.

TABLE 4.2 Critical Band Frequency Allocations for PSQM Analysis

BAND INDEX	UPPER FREQUENCY [IN HZ]	FIRST FFT BIN IN THIS BAND	LAST FFT BIN IN THIS BAND	BAND INDEX	UPPER FREQUENCY [IN HZ]	FIRST FFT BIN IN THIS BAND	LAST FFT BIN IN THIS BAND
0	15.6	0	0	18	590.8	18	18
1	46.9	1	1	19	631.2	19	20
2	78.1	2	2	20	672.9	21	21
3	109.4	3	3	21	716.6	22	22
4	140.6	4	4	22	760.4	23	24
5	171.9	5	5	23	804.6	25	25
6	203.1	6	6	24	851.4	26	27
7	234.4	7	7	25	898.3	28	28
8	265.6	8	8	26	947.0	29	30
9	296.9	9	9	27	997.0	31	31
10	328.1	10	10	28	1051.0	32	33
11	359.4	11	11	29	1108.0	34	35
12	390.6	12	12	30	1168.0	36	37
13	421.9	13	13	31	1231.0	38	39
14	453.1	14	14	32	1297.0	40	41
15	484.8	15	15	33	1366.0	42	43
16	519.2	16	16	34	1437.0	44	45
17	553.6	17	17	35	1509.0	46	48

Asymmetries are introduced when time-frequency components are either added or left out of the speech processors. The most common reason for the introduction of asymmetries between the two signals is noise suppression. Step 7 computes a noise factor to account for asymmetry effects, which is the sum across all the bands of the product of the noise disturbance density of the previous step, times the asymmetry factor, times the bandwidth of a critical band.

The last step calculates the average loudness of the noise during silent frames and active frames, for voice encoding. This value, which is also the PSQM value for the sample trace, is the weighted average of the noise factor over the active frames plus the weighted average of the noise factor over silent frames. The weighting modifies the influence of silent intervals in the quality measurement.

The objective for high quality speech reproduction is to keep the PSQM number as low as possible. The recommended maximum value for a PSQM measurement is 6.5, although higher values can occur. However, above the 6.5 value, the delivered speech is not intelligible and is unsuitable for toll telephony.

4.4 VOICE QUALITY TEST INSTRUMENTATION

One simple approach to testing voice quality is to use traditional telephony network techniques to determine the quality of a voice call. These techniques include comparing waveforms on a screen, doing Signal-to-Noise Ratio (SNR), Total Harmonic Distortion (THD) measurements, and others. However, traditional voice quality measurement techniques are neither applicable nor meaningful in VoIP networks, due to the use low bit-rate codecs, and new techniques to measure voice clarity had to be created. The advent of the PSQM algorithm and the effect of packetization of voiceband data made it necessary to introduce sophisticated instrumentation for test and measurement of the delivered quality across packet networks. The ingredients of "quality," as we have discussed already, can then be measured and their values can be used as a quantitative measure of the VoIP service from a high-level, user perspective.

In this section we provide an overview of testing end-to-end voice quality using Hewlett Packard's Telegra Voice Quality Tester (VQT). The importance of this measurement, in the simple reference diagram of Figure 4.9, is that the result is a form of quantification of the user experience. It can be used to compare VoIP networks to traditional voice networks by using the same measures. The comparison to the traditional phone networks is the ultimate quality check VoIP networks have to pass to be accepted by a larger audience.

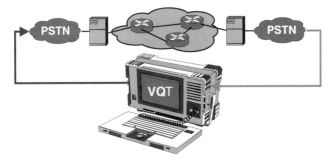

FIGURE 4.9 HP Telegra Voice Quality Tester (VQT)

The following measurements are necessary to characterize the quality of the user experience in a network topology.

1. Clarity. Clarity is the amount of information that can be extracted from a conversation. Speech quality can be measured using the PSQM method discussed earlier.
2. End-to-end delay. Delay is the time it takes for speech to traverse the network. Delay can have an impact on how we perceive the tone of conversations and can lead to constant interruptions if not controlled.
3. Voice Activation Detection analysis. VAD is used to save bandwidth by sending packets only when speech is present. The effectiveness of the voice activity detector can be determined by measuring the following:

   • Silence suppression - front end clipping (FEC) and holdover time (HOT)
   • Comfort noise generation
4. DTMF Tone Analysis. DTMF tones are not properly reproduced when carried across voice networks using low-bitrate voice codecs. Analysis of DTMF tone degradation is required for these networks to ensure the proper functionality of such systems as voice mail and calling cards. The important distortion parameters include amplitude and frequency shift.

Let's take a look at some typical key measurements that will be necessary across packet networks.

4.4.1 Delay Measurement

The end-to-end delay is the sum of the delays at the different network devices and across the network links that the voice traffic passes through, including traditional and VoIP networks. Delay does not affect the intelligibility but rather the character of a conversation.

A single delay measurement through a VoIP network is of limited use and multiple samples need to be taken. Delay in VoIP networks can vary over time for many reasons. Especially in topologies where IP packets are allowed to take different routes, it is important to know if alternate routing decisions are allowed during busy periods in the network. If the dynamics of a particular time period cause alternate routes to be selected, voice quality could be affected due to network configuration issues, alternate routing algorithms through dissimilar administrative domains, and other reasons which can cause paths to be selected using different criteria during certain times. In addition, gateways in the path of a call could be dynamically adjusting their jitter buffers, which would have a further impact on delay. Delay trend analysis allows us to determine the average delay through a network, as well as characterizing the minimum and maximum delays experienced. This can be useful in characterizing network behavior under varying traffic loads. Figure 4.10 provides an example of a delay trend analysis.

Measuring delay in both directions independently is also important, because the path across a network can be different for each direction.

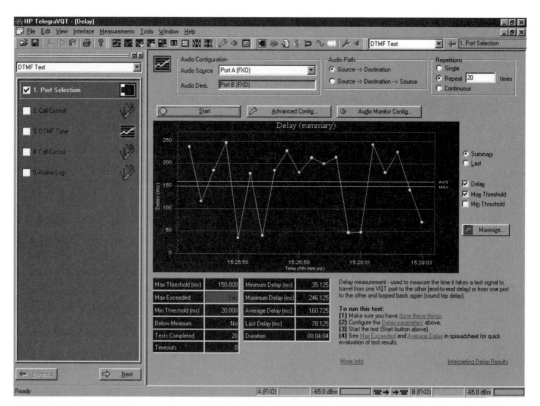

FIGURE 4.10 Delay Measurement in Trend Mode (Courtesy HP-Telegra VQT)

Clarity analysis provides a delay measurement together with the PSQM score, but the accuracy achieved is of limited use. Remember, this particular delay calculation may be the result of a cross-correlation to time-align the signal samples, and as such is an approximation. Delay measurement accuracy can be significantly enhanced via measurement of the impulse response of the network.

4.4.2 Clarity Measurements

The PSQM algorithm was initially designed for measuring the speech quality produced by voice codecs, and does not take into account network related impairments such as severe distortions and time clipping effects, which can be generated through packet loss. Accurate measurement requires the use of an enhanced version of PSQM, called PSQM+ which takes these types of impairments into account.

The use of speech samples in VoIP networks for clarity measurements is more important than pure tones or noise. Low bitrate codecs used in VoIP networks try to re-create the hearing experience of the human end-user and are not tuned to re-create tones or noise signals, thus giving a false impression of the speech quality the network could provide.

Clarity testing is performed between the two ends of a voice stream across a network. To measure clarity in a repeatable manner, the application must transmit a known speech sample and compare it with the received signal. The received signal is either the voice sample looped back to the originating instrument or processed at the far end.

Figure 4.11 shows an example of a clarity measurement using PSQM+. In addition to the average PSQM score, the send and received analog speech signals are graphed with the correlated PSQM score over time. This gives us more data to further analyze poor speech quality results because the PSQM score correlated with the two analog signals allows us to identify packet loss, jitter, or the effects of other impairments more easily.

The PSQM number of a signal quality measurement can exceed the maximum recommended figure of 6.5 in real-life situations, however, such a high number is usually rendered unacceptable for normal conversational use, and is not suitable for telephone service.

4.4.3 Voice Activity Measurements

Measurements of voice signal activity show that as much as 40–50% of the time there is no speech content in one direction of the channel. The effect of VAD is reduction of the effective bandwidth of a voice call. For example, if the voice packetization function produces 80 bytes of digitized and compressed voice every 10 ms, this would consume 8 Kbps of bandwidth, not

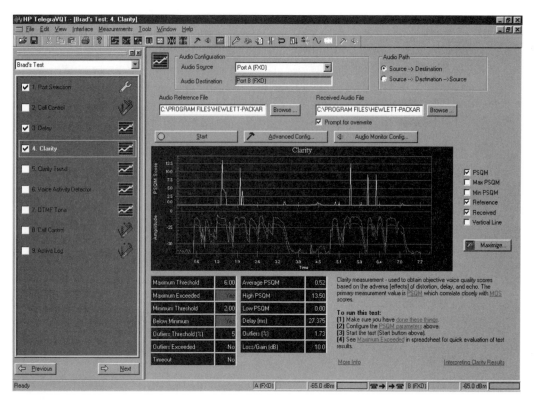

FIGURE 4.11 Clarity Measurement

counting transport and link layer protocol overheads. With silence suppression, this figure can be reduced to about 5 Kbps, either by not sending bits during silence periods, or sending lower-rate encodings of background noise. In either case, the receiving end is required to play out background noise during periods of silence at the far end to avoid the perception that the line is dead. However, it is also necessary for the receiver to start playing out real speech packets when they start arriving again, without introducing front-end clipping.

Whether or not effective bandwidth reduction based on VAD can be reliably implemented when engineering the capacity of a trunk is a subject of intense research, but VAD measurements are necessary to assess and learn more about this subject as packet voice technology matures.

Figure 4.12 shows a VAD measurement with front-end clipping of the signal and holdover time, where only background noise is being sent.

Another important measurement in this context is the relationship between received background noise and the comfort noise because changes in the background noise can also be annoying. The correlation between the

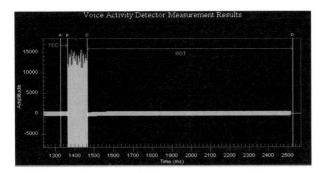

FIGURE 4.12 Voice Activity Detection Measurement

two types of noise can be achieved through a frequency domain comparison of background vs. comfort noise.

4.5 ECHO MEASUREMENT AND CONTROL

This type of measurement quantifies the effect of echo in the network. Echo is ubiquitous in the public telephone network and can be either useful or annoying if left uncontrolled. The difference between the two experiences is the one-way delay in the network. If the one-way delay can be kept under 16–20 ms, echo actually adds a nice sidetone to the conversation and gives the feeling that the telephone line is alive. Some echo can be tolerable in the high 20s (ms) range, but at those values and above, it is time to think about controlling the echo. The TDM version of the existing PSTN can barely manage to keep delays under this value, partly because of the inevitable delay due to the distance between talker and listener. Mobile telephones, which use various compression schemes and experience other delays, always require echo cancellation. The same is true for telephone calls routed through a satellite hop.

There are two types of echo. Electrical echo (Figure 4.13) occurs in the PSTN at the central office, where the 4-wire interface is converted to a 2-wire interface en route to the ultimate endpoint in the subscriber's domain. The conversion point is a hybrid circuit, which causes part of the energy to be reflected back to the sender. It then traverses the reverse path to the originating endpoint. If the energy loss in the hybrid is high—for instance, 20 dB or more—the reflected signal does not contain enough energy to create unacceptable echo for moderate one-way delays. If the hybrid loss is low to moderate, the reflected signal does result in audible echo and must be eliminated.

This problem was originally tackled with a process called Via Net Loss (VNL) and echo suppressors. VNL is a simple scheme that adds series atten-

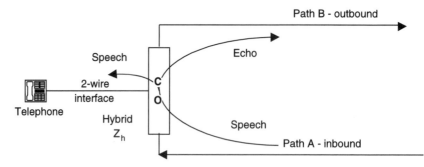

FIGURE 4.13 Electrical Echo Generation

uation in the receive and send paths in the 4-wire section. The echo is attenuated twice as much as the voice signal, but the voice signal does suffer from this scheme. This is because many VNL paths can be traversed in an end-to-end call and the resulting attenuation makes the voice signal too weak. Echo suppression is also an early form of controlling echo, and is a little more effective in maintaining speech quality than VNL.

Figure 4.14 shows the basic idea of an echo suppressor, in a block diagram form.

The idea behind echo suppression is to create a high loss return path when there is significant energy on the forward path. The forward path is the one with the currently active speaker. Once a signal is detected, the detector causes loss on the return path at 35 dB or more, thus eliminating any echo and just about everything else on the return. The effect is that of a switch that opens when the far end speaker is talking and closes when the near speaker takes his or her turn. Echo suppression can be annoying because it has the effect of clipping the other party and giving a strange effect to the conversa-

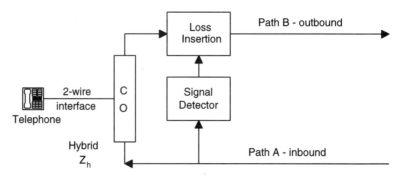

FIGURE 4.14 Echo Suppression

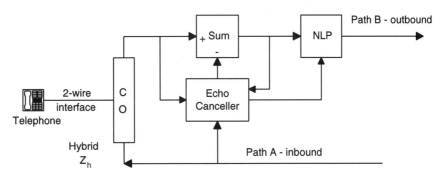

FIGURE 4.15 The Process of Echo Cancellation

tion. The obvious requirement is for speakers to be polite and not interrupt others in mid-sentence. However, this is the only good attribute of this approach to control echo.

Echo suppression, if used, must be present at both ends for echo to be suppressed in both directions. It can be an analog or digital implementation.

Facsimile equipment is intolerant of the reverse channel "choking" imposed by echo suppression. Echo suppressors must be equipped with tone disabling capability to turn off suppression when a facsimile Answer tone is detected.

Echo cancellation is a better and much more sophisticated scheme to reduce or eliminate echoes. Figure 4.15 shows the basic block diagram of echo cancellation.

Echo cancellers are normally placed on the digital part of the network, and are implemented using microcoded algorithms running on DSPs. Some more sophisticated echo cancellers have been implemented in ASICs to allow for handling more one-way delay in the network. Like suppressors, cancellers need to be at each far end for elimination or at least adequate reduction of echo.

The idea behind echo cancellation is to create a device that can "learn" from the transmitted signal and then create an attenuated version of that signal and subtract it from the return path after some delay. The net effect is reduction or complete elimination of the echo content on the return signal. Echo cancellers are, therefore, very intelligent and complex devices, but even they can present some problems in telephony applications, as we will see. A key performance differentiator between cancellation and suppression is that echo cancellation does not attenuate the return circuit and thus avoids annoying side effects in a conversation.

4.5.1 Impulse Response Measurement

Perhaps the most fundamental function of the echo canceller is the modeling of the impulse response of the hybrid with terminal paths A and B.[5] The impulse response of a circuit fully characterizes its frequency response as well. The transfer function of the circuit is simply the Fourier Transform of its impulse response. When the input signal and the impulse response become known to the echo canceller, the echo is computed as the convolution of the two series. The result is fed into the algebraic summer which removes the computed quantity from the signal, thus effectively removing the echo, but not completely at first. Figure 4.16 shows an impulse response measurement using the HP-Telegra VQT.

For speech analysis, note that the transfer function is useful when a linear codec is in use, but in situations where a nonlinear codec is used, the results need careful interpretation to be useful. Non-linear codecs carry state information and the transfer function is influenced by previous activity on the network.

4.5.2 Echo Cancellation Parameters

The output of the algebraic summer of Figure 4.15 is used by the canceller function as an error input, which helps reduce the echo further. The continuous "learning" of the impulse response of the hybrid in real time is referred to as filter *adaptation*.

The condition known as "double talk" is of importance in measuring the effectiveness of an echo canceller, because when both speakers are speaking adaptation must be stopped but cancellation will continue. It begins again when the canceller detects no energy on the near end. Speech quality should be maintained during periods of double talk. Delivering speech clarity, without inadvertent clipping of either party's beginning syllables, is paramount for effective operation of the echo canceller.

There are some important parameters one needs to examine before choosing an echo canceller. One of them is its convergence time. This is the time it takes the device to start performing cancellation at its specified rating, that is, the time it takes to minimize the error feedback back into the echo canceller. Minimization of the error means the device has "found" the echo signal and is "locked" on to it. The shorter the convergence time, the better

---

5.   Impulse response measurement will be done toward the network if the echo canceller has been deployed looking in the other direction.

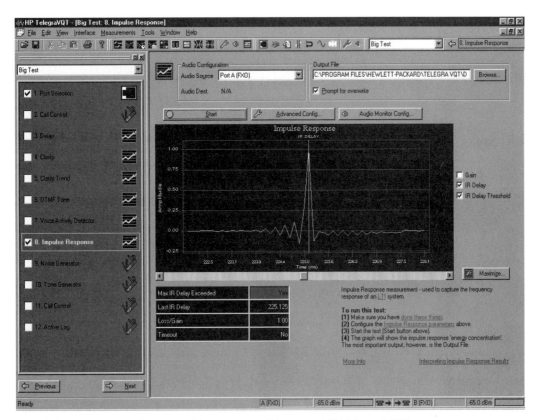

FIGURE 4.16 Impulse Response Measurement (Courtesy HP-Telegra VQT)

the device. When large delays are encountered in the network, this becomes a critical parameter.

Acceptable echo canceller convergence time ≈ 50–60 ms

The maximum echo tail needs to be commensurate with the delay in the network. The longer the tail, the more delay can be handled by the echo canceller. As we will see elsewhere, the most recent standardization activities classify as acceptable delays that were unheard of in voice telephony until a couple of years ago. It is therefore imperative for long tails to match closely the one-way delay experienced in packet voice telephony. One drawback of

DSP-based echo cancellation is the length of the tail, which tends to be in the area of 128 ms, but not much more. ASIC solutions are required for cancellation beyond 128 ms. When 150 ms is classified as "acceptable" delay by packet voice working groups, the issue is clear. Furthermore, acoustic echo is not sufficiently reduced or eliminated by plain DSP implementations.

Maximum echo tail for packet voice $\leq$ 128 ms

The parameter that determines the effectiveness of this cancellation process is the Echo Return Loss (ERL). The greater the ERL, the better the echo canceller. Good ERL is in the 6 dB range. Enhancements to ERL can improve loss (introduce more echo loss) in the 30–35 dB range. One basic requirement for proper operation of an echo canceller is that the echo path is linear and time-invariant to ensure correct and timely convergence.

The echo canceller block feeds into the Non-Linear Processor block (NLP), whose function is to adaptively account for non-linearities present in the echo signal. These are basically due to noise factors from real noise or quantization effects. The goal of the NLP is to eliminate non-linear echo components.

Facsimile transmission is the type of voiceband data that is particularly intolerant to echoes in the network. The ITU-T has specified a series of tests in the newer recommendation G.168, which offers better reference measurements and criteria than recommendation G.165 for digital echo cancellation.

In G.168, Composite Source Signals (CSS) are used at both ends of a fax connection to measure the effectiveness and performance of echo cancellation. The composite signals mimic the power spectral density of speech, which is a major factor in the convergence agility of most echo cancellers. Like suppressors, echo cancellers must be equipped with the ability to detect the 2100Hz tone with phase reversals to turn themselves off. New echo cancellers must converge quickly and eliminate echo in the handshakes sequences in Phase A of the T.30 protocol. (We discuss the T.30 protocol in Chapter 6.)

4.5.3 Echo Measurements

When measuring echo across VoIP networks using low bitrate codecs, traditional echo measurements with tones or noise are no longer applicable. A more sophisticated method is to use real speech to determine the functionality of an echo canceller. Correlating the received echo with the PSQM score allows us to analyze how annoying the received echo was to end-users.

There are two fundamental measurements when analyzing echo cancellers:

- Reflected echo with one party talking
- Signal degradation when two or more parties are talking

In the case of one party talking, we measure the reflected echo coming back. Following are important parameters that need to be quantified:

- *Echo in Speech*: This specifies the maximum relative echo-to-speech signal level. When the echo in speech is large it will be noticed, and will also be reflected in distortion and degradation in the PSQM number, that is, its value will become higher. This parameter allows the user to correlate the human perception of echo with the overall speech quality.
- *Echo in Silence*: Specifies the echo-in-silence signal level. Echo in silence is much more perceptible to the user. Echo that might not be perceptible when talking becomes apparent in silence, even at moderate levels.
- *Echo-Free Speech Percentage*: This shows how much of the conversation was actually distorted by echo and can be used to determine the overall user experience during the call.

Figure 4.17 shows an example of echo measurement.

In a related measurement, we determine the behavior of the echo canceller under conditions of double talk. Double talk occurs when both parties are talking simultaneously, and the challenge for the echo canceller is to detect it and stop canceling the incoming signal.

It is important to measure the far end signal and assess the degradation caused by the echo canceller during double talk. For this measurement we use real speech and measure the perceptible degradation of the second party's voice via a PSQM score.

4.5.4 DTMF Signal Quality Measurement

Signal quality degradation can affect DTMF tone recognition. DTMF tone transport is extremely important in voice networks because the networks carry not only the dialed number of the called party, but are also used to activate basic telephony features, such as voice mail, credit card calls, etc. Distorted DTMF tones could render one's telephone service inoperable.

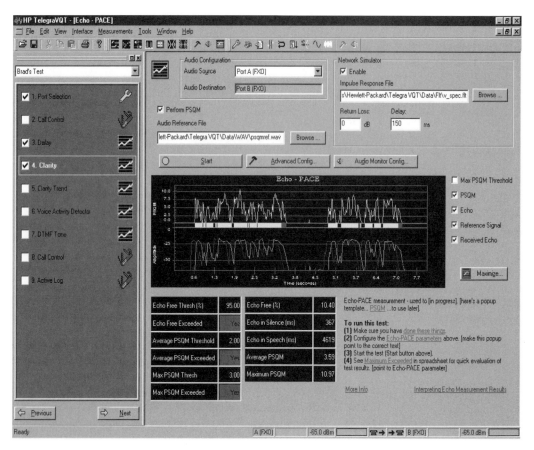

FIGURE 4.17 Echo Measurement (Courtesy HP-Telegra VQT)

DTMF tones are generated by the phone keypad using two distinct high and low frequencies with equal amplitude. Low-bitrate codecs in voice networks have difficulties transmitting DTMF tones and reproducing them with high fidelity. Tuned for speech rather than sine-wave signals, they alter frequency and amplitude of the two tones to the point that they can no longer be recognized.

DTMF tone measurement can help investigate problems with tone degradation on a network by measuring the distortion parameters. Testing for DTMF signal quality presents a few minor challenges. DTMF tones are used in systems for end-to-end user signaling. As such they must be carried faithfully by the network in analog form, not degraded by echo suppressors and cancellers, and must be accurately produced in digital form for DSPs to process them in real time in the network.

The important parameters when measuring DTMF tones are the frequency shift of the two frequencies and the DTMF twist. DTMF twist is measured in dBm and shows the difference in the amplitude levels of the two frequencies.

A typical DTMF tone measurement is shown in Figure 4.18. The important aspect of tone measurement is to analyze the distortion introduced to each of the frequencies in amplitude and shift.

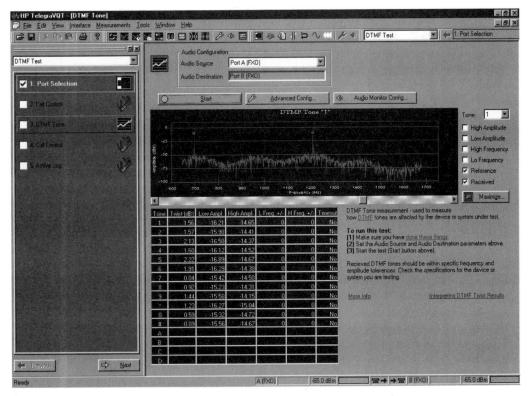

FIGURE 4.18 DTMF Tone Measurement (Courtesy HP-Telegra VQT)

4.6 SUMMARY

We have seen an effective and objective method to quantify voice quality in any type of network. There is a large number of possible impairments in the end-to-end path of a call in the wide area that can affect speech quality to a degree that it becomes unacceptable for telephone service. A solid defense against such undesirable situations is to engineer the new packet networks in a manner such that bandwidth efficiencies are not gained at the expense of the reliability of transport. It is too soon to make inferences as to how speech patterns will affect parameters like bandwidth utilization during periods of silence suppression. This is true especially if the intent is to cross-allocate bandwidth among unrelated subscribers, solely on the basis of VAD bandwidth savings from each call. In the short term, it is more likely that data and voice that share the same facilities will continue to be treated unequally, with the net effect of the available data bandwidth expanding and contracting to accommodate voice traffic which will carry the highest QoS rating, especially in the wide area.

CHAPTER 5

A Simple Case Study in Measurements

5.1 OBJECTIVES

We have arrived at the point where we can look at voice quality from an objective measurement standpoint. Several texts have been written in the past few years on the subject of QoS in the context of packet delivery, but little has been written about the impact of packet loss on specific applications. It is nice to know what the packet loss rate in the network really is, but what does it really mean to the application?

The impact of packet loss[1] on data applications running over TCP has been explored to a larger degree than its impact on voice quality. The reason appears to be two-fold. First, packet networks for voice telephony with appreciable network complexity have not yet been deployed in large scale. Thus, reference networks for benchmarking voice quality have been only extrapolations of experimental setups, measuring mostly delay and possibly jitter, but without enough specifics on what the user *hears* on the phone. Second, up to very recently, voice quality measurements in packet networks have been *subjective*, rather than *objective*. Again, the reason appears to be two-fold. First, an objective clarity measure—such as PSQM—was not available for a long time. Second, test equipment implementations of the PSQM algorithm that

---

1.   The term packet loss is used generically here. It means any packet that either did not arrive at its destination, or arrived in a manner that made it unusable, for example, a very late packet for voice playback, which may just be discarded by the application.

offer a detailed time-based analysis of voice clarity in a repeatable manner have only recently become available. The ability to repeat test measurements is necessary for ensuring the consistency and correctness of the results.

In this first effort to tie packet QoS to effective impact on voice quality, we take steps to create a representative environment for taking measurements. Although it is not yet possible to take large samples across real distributed packet networks, test equipment can be configured to simulate large topologies with varying reliability and packet-level QoS. We must first construct a reference topology that would be representative of a network whose behavior parameters we want to understand, and proceed methodically to construct the test scenarios. The objective of the test is to assess the result of network impairments on a stored voice sample, such as those played by typical announcement servers. But before we enter the lab, we need to take a step back and look at the big picture of telephone service in the wide area.

5.2 FROM THE BIG PICTURE TO THE LAB

When we put it all together as a single picture at the highest level, the creation of reference points in the complete topology for measuring key system and network parameters appears to be an intimidating task. Indeed, by looking at Figure 5.1, it is easy to place the necessary observation points for network characterization, but this is not easy to accomplish in a real-life situation. The main problem we are facing is the distance separation between observation points to conduct tests that require timing synchronization among the instruments. Let's look at some general purpose reference points and see what we can expect to see and gain from our observation.

The media gateway that is installed in the customer premises will send and receive multiplexed media and signaling streams for all the endpoints it serves. This is safe to say, because in all the technologies under consideration for VoIP services there is a single physical link, which carries multiplexed information streams. In the case of VoIP networks, signaling and media will have dedicated transport addresses, that is, either separate IP addresses or the same IP address with different transport layer port (UDP or TCP). We place our reference point inside the customer premise, which is where the call will be originating.

As a first step in the characterization process, we need to baseline as many measurements as can be made within the customer premise, without venturing into the network. This is extremely useful information for understanding the impact of network elements on voice quality. Delay and network impairments can take their toll on the delivered quality of service and overall user experience. Network impairments refer to any factor that will cause loss

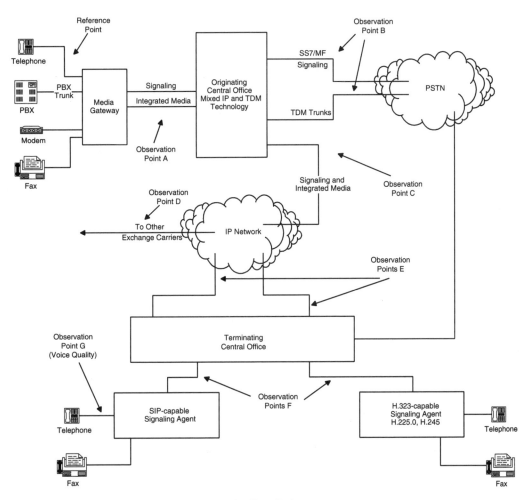

FIGURE 5.1 High Level Network Topology for Test References

of voice samples in transit, in the form of packet loss. These can be due to physical link impairments or router and concentrator traffic management configurations and malfunctions along the way. The facilities that will be used to transport VoIP services are of the same quality as the facilities used today to carry TDM voice. Therefore, simple bit error rates are not going to affect the voice quality substantially. However, traffic management issues will have a bigger impact on the overall quality of service, and it is important to have a basis for comparisons.

High on the agenda for quality and performance characterization is the data which can be gathered at observation point A. This is the place where we can observe what the media gateway does to the service, without interference from other network elements. Baseline measurements for codec delay and jitter introduced by the packetization and coding processes are done at this point. A comparison with the self-contained measurements within the customer premise will give us an understanding of the operating characteristics of the media gateway. Observation point A can be either at the customer premise on the network side of the MG, or at the CO looking toward the MG. In the latter case, constant values to adjust for delay caused by the distance between the MG and the CO must be accounted for in the calculations.

We treat the Central Office as a black box for general purpose measurements. The implementation of platforms that will provide the VoIP services could vary greatly among providers, and no standards exist on reference architectures for service platforms. This leaves us with the observation points B and C, for a service that ties directly to the PSTN and also has external links to an IP packet network. The purpose of referencing observation point B is to understand the impact of the CO itself on the quality of telephone service. At point B we can detect the effect of any possible transcoding from compressed voice, as it would appear at point B, to G.711 as it would be placed on TDM trunks. However, this type of data gathering and comparison is not so easy to accomplish. Voice samples exist in packet form at point B, whereas they are G.711 PCM samples at point C, for calls directed towards the PSTN. Establishing an absolute reference point for measuring delay is difficult due to the different transport formats, but not impossible if we measure the delay with an instrument like the VQT. To this effect the need arises to create a "voice tap" into the TDM stream, playing a stored voice sample and comparing the clarity and delay with the TDM version by playing it through a device such as a PBX. As we see later, standard PBXs feature very low internal latencies and their behavior and parameters can be characterized relatively easily.

Observation point C lends itself a little more easily to characterization, because voice samples are still in packet format. Absolute delay through the CO can be measured with standard techniques, if we know IP transport addresses and link layer parameters. Simultaneous measurements with point A are easier to achieve if both points are tapped into at the CO.

Points E and D are at the other side of the cloud, and they are useful in characterizing the cloud itself, in conjunction with what was learned at point C. The parameters we will learn are mostly the existence of any physical impairments, jitter, and delay through the core network. It is important to keep in mind that in most cases a very large statistical sample of measurement data must be gathered before inferences can be made about the operating characteristics of the core IP network. One must be very careful to note that traffic-related congestion issues cannot be invoked easily as part of making a simple measurement on one call. Such impairments can be inserted, but their construction is complex and beyond the scope of this text.

There are specific and very important ramifications for proper characterization of point D. Eventually all carriers will interconnect via VoIP networks for pure integrated IP-based services, and this is one area where there is insufficient knowledge at this point about the signaling protocols, failure recovery mechanisms, and all the other considerations that have gone into the comparable LEC-IXC or IXC-IXC interface in the current PSTN. As VoIP services proliferate and the technology gains acceptance, this reference point will receive increased attention by the standards groups for its specification.

We anticipate a degree of symmetry in service topologies, in that there will be an originating and a terminating Central Office (Carrier Exchange) in the path of a call. Point E is therefore equivalent to point C, as is point A to points F. Comparisons of data gathered between one set of points and the previous set characterizes the part of the topology between them. Points F are important because in the worst case there will be two transcodings between three different formats on the path of a call across the PSTN. Point A has codec A, the PSTN is at G.711, and the terminating CO may be using yet a third coding format toward the remote subscriber at point G. The core IP network may or may not be using the same coding format as either of the endpoints in the call. All this transformation of the voice sample, plus the potential impairments in the network, will impact the voice quality.

We have arrived at our final destination, point G. This is the other end of the call, and this is where we want to measure clarity, delay and the other parameters of voice quality. But there is a small caveat in our endeavor. In the best of cases, the physical distance between the originating reference point and point G will be measured in tens of miles, or even in the hundreds of miles. It is thus impossible to expect that a single measurement instrument can be attached at both endpoints in a general topology, and this makes parameter characterization in the lab very important.

In the following paragraphs we will setup a simple reference network topology to evaluate parameters in a lab environment. One big benefit of a simulated environment is that we can enter impairments *when we want*. It is not easy to create a simulated Central Office, but it is possible to define the bounds by which a Central Office must live, in order to provide acceptable telephone service with respect to the overall user experience in a conversation.

5.3 EQUIPMENT SETUP AND CONFIGURATION

Before we design the simulated topology and begin with equipment setup, it is important to note the baseline acceptable delay in a packet network. Delay in voice telephony will continue to be the subject of debate until the consumer market has voted (in the way the consumer market typically votes) whether the higher delays of packet networks are acceptable for basic telephone service. But what *is* acceptable delay in any case? The simplest explanation one can give is for delay not to have an impact on the overall user experience in a telephone conversation. How is that possible to measure? It is indeed very subjective, and lends itself to debate and interpretation. The reason for the debate is the fundamental observation that packet networks add delay which is greater than that of ye olde PSTN. But it is important to note that the added delay it is not necessarily the by-product of packet network technology only. Voice coding technology and transcoding across network segment hops share a big portion of the responsibility in this area. Opinions abound in the engineering community as to what amount of end to end delay would be acceptable, partially because large deployments of telephone service are still in the planning stage. The ETSI TIPHON project, for example, reports quality is "best" with one-way delays up to 150 ms. Furthermore, 3 classifications of "goodness" are proposed as "best," "high," and "medium," plus one additional classification for "best effort" service.

Regardless of the delay values that will become acceptable, delay needs to be fully characterized in the public network, such that high-quality primary telephone service can be offered by the carriers. One key factor in delay calculations is whether PSTN hops between packet networks will be present in the path of a call. This is important to understand, particularly if transcoding is necessary at the hop boundaries. Each IXC generally deploys private network topologies, which may or may not use TDM techniques to transport voice and voiceband data. We will concentrate on developing methodology that is useful in measuring delay in the general case of network technology used for VoIP transport. The major choices currently available for this task are, of course, TDM, ATM, and variants of SONET.

In the lab we set up a simple network, which has reference measurement points corresponding to the architecture of Figure 5.1, and consists of a three-level hierarchy. This test network is shown in Figure 5.2. The first reference point in the hierarchy is a simple PBX, which can be either CAS or PRI-based. The presence of the PBX is not necessary, but if one is available it ensures we can take a baseline measurement of delay and clarity in extension-to-extension calls using plain G.711 coding. A local call through the PBX is effectively a loopback of a voice circuit for purposes of clarity and delay measurement. This first step helps us baseline clarity and delay, and also get a sanity check of the instrumentation setup. This step can be omitted if voice quality parameters for G.711 coding are known, and baseline characterization of voice quality and delay are deemed not necessary for the purposes of the test.

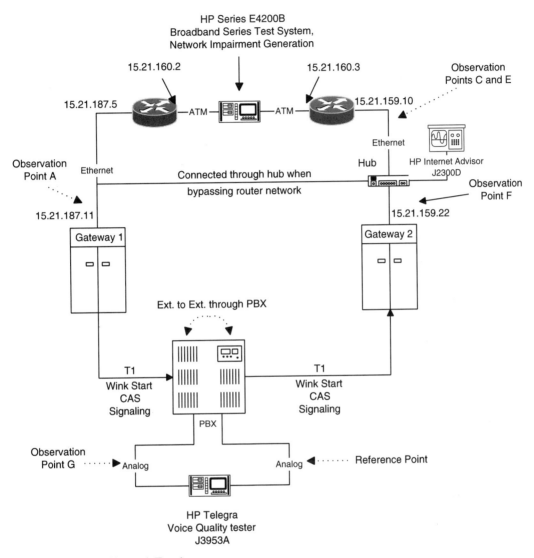

FIGURE 5.2 Test Network Topology

The details of the second reference point in the network will vary, depending on the type of platform being tested. A generic view of a VoIP "gateway" is shown in our case, for purposes of illustration, with media flowing through each of two gateways. Consistent with our previous discussions on reference architectures, the generic gateway can be thought of as a Customer Premise Equipment (CPE) media gateway (MG) serving a PBX, or a

CO-based MG terminating a PBX CAS or PRI line. We are interested in this case in the VoIP stream that comes out of the gateway, which in its most basic operation uses G.711 as the basic IP payload, without transcoding. It can, however also perform transcoding between the G.711 format on the PBX side, to whatever codec format has been negotiated with the remote endpoint across the IP network.

As the reader will recall from our protocol discussions, some protocols and architectures allow media paths to be routed through the gateway, in addition to the server performing the basic call signaling functions. We use two gateways in this configuration, which do not need to be identical, but require support for a common signaling protocol to set up calls between their endpoints.

When the VoIP gateways are placed on the same IP subnet, the gateways' contributions to clarity, delay, jitter, and other parameters can be independently characterized in this basic configuration. The dashed line between gateway 1 and either the hub or the router indicates the connection between gateways is either direct on the same subnet, or goes through an IP network "cloud." (ç careful with the IP addresses and subnet masks in the lab to avoid routing loops and ensure end-to-end equipment reachability! As a first test, try using a traceroute command from either gateway to the other, to see if signaling and media packets will flow in the manner shown in the reference network diagram.) By connecting to the first router we create a flexible topology that can be enhanced to emulate a wide area network with the use of additional test equipment.

A minimum of two routers is necessary in this test configuration, and they are connected to a network impairment simulator via an ATM interface. The network simulator device used for this purpose is the Hewlett-Packard E4200B Broadband Series Test System. It functions as a "bad guy" in the network, exacerbating the jitter that exists in a typical wide area network and creating fixed, variable, and sometimes unacceptable delays for ATM cells carrying the voice samples for our test purposes. The process of impairment insertion in the cell stream is shown in block form in Figure 5.3.

The network impairment simulator is transparent to the IP network, that is, it is not addressable at the IP level. It can simply be thought of as the network "cloud" whose characteristics we want to simulate, such that we can collect relevant data at the observation points.

The cells carrying VoIP packets are filtered based on the value of the VPI/VCI, such that impairments are inserted only on the stream of interest. Variable delay is the first stop, and the cell delay values are taken from mathematical distributions offered in the user choices. For most measurements the use of variable delays is acceptable, if the precise relationship of the delay to the application is not the focus of the test.

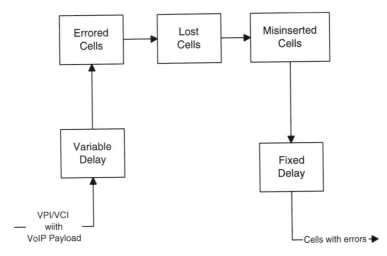

FIGURE 5.3 Insertion of Network Impairments in the Cell Stream

Errored cell and lost cell occurrences can also be made to conform to a user selectable distribution, and can be independently filtered on the VPI/VPI, such that different cell streams can experience different impairments. The net effect of either and both of these impairments is to create unusable cells. Again, care must be exercised in correlating the impact of actual impairments to the effect on the application, because protocols may have built-in self-defenses against moderate impairments. One such self-defense may be the sending of duplicate packets, compressed in another format, with the hope of reconstructing at least a major portion of the original voice information if impairments occur in transit.

Robust implementations will mostly be immune to misinserted cells, because packet headers will appear with unexpected and unrecognized values. If the implementation discards misinserted cells, the effect is *none at all*. The cells did not carry useful information in the first place, and nobody will miss them when they are discarded.

The ability to insert fixed delay is actually very useful in voice measurements. We can vary this important network parameter immediately while holding a conversation and determine the limits of perceived quality of service, from the perspective of the user experience. In other words, we can try out the proposed delay parameters for "goodness" of service and see if we are in agreement.

In our configuration, two analog PBX ports are attached to the voice quality measurement instrument, the VQT. The VQT can play stored voice samples into extension 2001, and receive them back, also in analog form, in extension

2002. This simple setup is all we need to take clarity measurements in the reference network, but things do get a little more complicated in the wide area. The PBX has been programmed with a dialing plan that permits off-premise calls to be made by dialing a control digit before the actual number. This is similar to dialing "9" from your office or hotel room to get an outside line. Without outside line access, all calls are port-to-port and consist of a 4-digit string. The VQT can perform the outside line access automatically as well.

The Broadband Series Test System has been configured as a network impairment simulator and shows us parameters that cannot be seen with voice quality measurements. These include ATM cell jitter (which translates to cumulative packet jitter at the endpoints), OAM cell activity, other ATM traffic such as signaling for call processing, and the bandwidth consumed by the voice call. Of course, one of the major uses for this instrument is to insert the impairments whose effects we are measuring.

With all this great information in hand, we are ready to start taking some measurements!

5.4 BASELINE MEASUREMENTS

By simply dialing the number 2002 from the keypad of extension 2001, the PBX is smart enough to know this is a port-to-port call and does not signal on the trunk to the gateway. Once the call is made, the voice sample is played out at the calling port and received at extension 2002. The top trace of the lower part of the graph in Figure 5.4 is the original voice waveform, while the bottom one represents the received version. The top part of the graph in Figure 5.4 shows the computed PSQM scores for the trace. We see very good and faithful reproduction of the speech, with very little delay. The TDM delay incurred by looping PCM voice samples through the PBX is about 1 ms, or less. The PSQM score averages at about 1, with a low in the 0.25 range, and the high score in a range very close to a score of 2. This is a very normal range of values for TDM transport of PCM voice samples.

One of the difficulties associated with PSQM testing is establishing the relative time delay between the input voice signal and the output signal, as we said in Chapter 4. Without a precise time reference for the input signal, a PSQM measurement will yield incorrect results. When the same instrument is at the controls at both ends, this is a fairly simple thing to do. The origin is known in advance.

A natural question to ask is "How do I take such a measurement in end-to-end mode, when the T_0 origin is either not known or cannot be conveyed to the far end?" This is a tough problem, and the recommendation made in the P.861 specification is for a cross-correlation to be computed between the two signals, and accept the delay that maximizes its value. The Δt that results in the largest value of the cross-correlation is a good approximation of the rela-

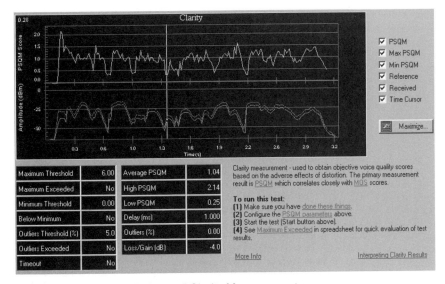

FIGURE 5.4 Baseline Delay and Clarity Measurement

tive time delay between the two signals, and as close as we can get some-times in the general case of distributed networks.

It is always a good idea to run a test several times to ensure its repeatability. In this simple case, the values of Table 5.1 were obtained, and they are consistent with each other and our expectations.

TABLE 5.1 PBX Voice Clarity Measurements

PBX INTERNAL CALLS			
	Test 1	Test 2	Test 3
Average PSQM	1.04	1.04	1.03
High PSQM	2.14	2.14	1.95
Low PSQM	0.25	0.21	0.21
Delay	1.00	1.00	1.00

5.5 TESTING WITH CONNECTED GATEWAYS

There are two major connectivity modes we can use to take live measurements in our reference network. In the first case, the gateways become members of the same IP subnet, bypassing the router and network cloud. In the second case, a fully simulated network topology is used, whereby calls are generated and quality is measured in the same manner as in a real network.

5.5.1 Directly Connected Gateways

The two gateways can attach to the same subnet, but all IP addresses and masks must be set to consistent values. In the configuration of Figure 5.5, the IP addressing scheme is classless, with a mask of 255.255.255.0. Both gateways connect directly to the Ethernet hub. If all addressing has been set up properly, we can place an off-premise call though the PBX and the gateways. The PBX requires dialing an access code for off-premise calls (for example, "9"), and after a second dial tone is played, we can proceed to dial the outside number, which is the number of the line connected to the other port of the VQT.

We introduce the HP-Internet Advisor in this picture, placed on the same subnet as the gateways, which will help us with performance and signaling protocol measurements not related to voice quality. There are a few performance measurements that can be made at this point:

1. Call rate capacity characterization of the Gateways
2. Call setup time for basic calls
3. Jitter and packet loss weighted QoS measurements.

Call rate capacity measurement requires knowledge of the maximum call rate of the gateway in calls per second, and any parameters that may be affecting the capacity specification. It is also necessary that we can generate call arrivals to bring the call load to the maximum level and exceed it enough to cause the system to invoke fault recovery procedures due to the excessive call load. The challenge in this task is to make the measurement precisely at the point of system malfunction. Capacity performance testing is beyond the scope of this text, as it could easily occupy a textbook of its own!

Call setup time is a little more difficult to measure in a live distributed system. This is the time from the last digit dialed to the time the phone rings at the far end, and is usually referred to as Post-Dial Delay (PDD). The simplest form of measuring post-dial delay in our setup is to capture the protocol messages with the Internet advisor, and subtract the times of capture.

1. For the SIP protocol, the PDD measurement points are shown in Figure 1.27. The start of time (T_0) is the stimulus that caused the origination of the INVITE message (for example, digit dialing, or pressing an icon on a terminal), and T_{final} is when the "ringing" packet is sent by endpoint B.
2. For the H.323 protocol, Figure 1.12 shows the relevant measurement points. T_0 is the stimulus that caused the H.225.0 SETUP message at the

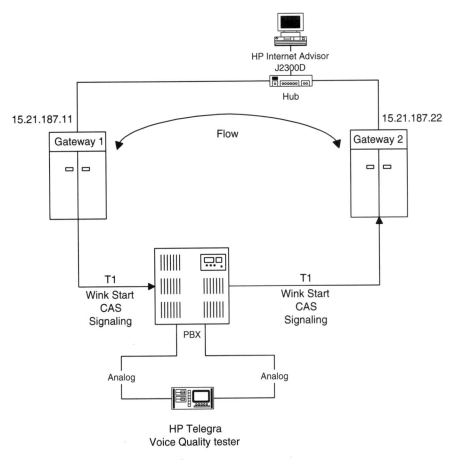

FIGURE 5.5 Direct Connected Gateways

station of party A, and T_{final} is when the ALERTING message is sent by the station at party B.

3. In MGCP-based protocols, T_0 is the NTFY message carrying a valid digit string, and T_{final} is any MGCP message that indicates "ring" as a signal in the payload (Signal S: rg - ring).

The reader should note that these measurement points will not produce data on processing time at the endpoints, just before the stimulus message is sent to originate the call to the far end, and just after the packet to ring the phone is received. This resolution may be acceptable, because post dial delay is measured in the hundreds of milliseconds, whereas processing of a packet is in the microsecond, or low millisecond range.

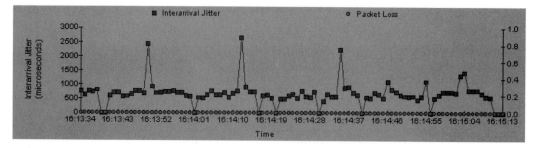

FIGURE 5.6 Packet Interarrival Jitter and Loss in the Time Domain

Jitter and packet loss measurements can be taken for reference at this point as well. With the use of the RTP QoS Monitor (RQM) feature of the Internet Advisor, we can capture the nominal jitter caused by the gateways themselves. Since there is no network present at this point, the values for jitter can be subtracted from the values we obtain when we test the entire network topology. If you decide to do the jitter evaluation at this stage, it is recommended you take several readings and ensure there is no appreciable variance in the measurements. Wide variances at this stage would point to implementation idiosyncrasies with the gateways, which the network designer must include in the calculations for the other network parameters.

The jitter measurement example shown in Figures 5.6 and 5.7, was obtained with the RQM application of the Internet Advisor. Figure 5.6 shows the time domain jitter of a real time packetized media trace, whereas Figure 5.7 is the distribution of jitter values for the trace. The latter graph is important for assessing the variance of jitter in calculating the depth of receive buffers. Notice that due to the discrete nature of jitter distributions, the average jitter value may never occur in the measurements.

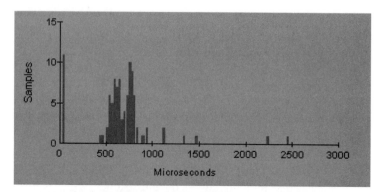

FIGURE 5.7 Distribution of Packet Jitter from Trace

5.5.2 Routed Calls

At this stage we are well equipped with reference data from the PBX and the gateways when they are connected directly through a hub. As in the previous stage, we want to measure voice clarity first without impairments, to baseline the complete simulated topology. The clarity results we expect in this test will depend on whether G.711 coding format was used, or whether another codec format was selected during call setup. A quick measure with G.711 reveals no loss in clarity, but additional delay added by the packetization process and the router network. G.711 packetization involves simple transport of the PCM samples in IP packets, with no processing expended to convert the coding of the signal.

Our reference network in this case is shown in Figure 5.8. The Internet Advisor will capture signaling and media packet streams, whereas the Broadband Series Test System is modifying operating parameters such as delay and packet loss.

The results start to become more interesting when we select transcoding through the gateways. This would be equivalent to the case of a PBX connected to a CO via an TDM interface, and a customer dials a number served by a VoIP domain. In some media gateway along the path of the call the media format will be converted, and this impacts the delay as well as the clarity.

The reader should note that absolute characterizations of codecs and service platforms are not possible with a single test network setup, unless critical design parameters of the platform can be introduced in the test topology. The reason is that implementations vary among equipment manufacturers, and designs of gateways at the premise and the CO affect the results. The following discussion is illustrative on some of the methods used to achieve characterization in a typical configuration.

For voice clarity measurement, our observer is placed in point G, and the VQT setup does not change when we introduce the complete network. The observer is the VQT instrument, which is receiving the voice sample it is playing out at the reference point.

Table 5.2 shows a sampling of some results taken by playing the same voice sample without network impairments. Clarity has degraded with the addition of the transcoding from G.711 (PBX) to the new compression scheme. The result is high quality speech reproduction at the receiving end (PSQM average of less the 3.0), even though the High PSQM has exceeded 4.5 and 5.0 in one of the measurements. The morphology of the PSQM trace indicates we did not have prolonged intervals of unacceptable. The test was run several times with very consistent results and waveforms. Because the numbers were obtained in a robust network without packet losses, the voice quality impact we are seeing end-to-end is primarily the result of the transcod-

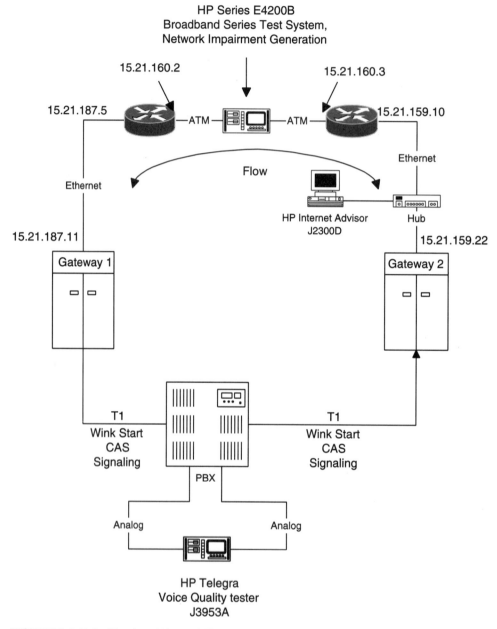

FIGURE 5.8 Fully Simulated Network Topology

TABLE 5.2 Clarity Measurement Results, Routed Calls

CLARITY MEASUREMENT RESULTS— ROUTED CALLS			
Average PSQM	2.56	2.53	2.51
High PSQM	4.71	4.73	5.32
Low PSQM	0.58	0.65	0.53
Delay	136.5	136.5	136.5

ing from G.711 to compressed format at gateway 2 (ingress to the network), and back to G.711 at gateway 1 (egress point, and ingress to the VQT).

There are close similarities between the PSQM graph of Figure 5.4 and Figure 5.9. Even though the clarity has obviously degraded, the morphology of the two PSQM curves, especially the time occurrences of the highs and lows, bear similarities. We will see how this deviates as we start introducing impairments in the path of the call.

Figure 5.10 shows the clarity measurement result obtained when we started introducing packet loss with the Broadband Series Test System, during the playing of the speech sample. At the bottom half of the VQT screen,

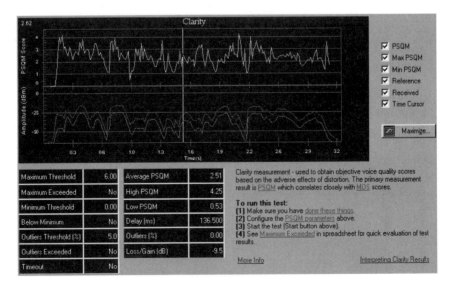

FIGURE 5.9 Clarity Measurement Through "Cloud," No Impairments

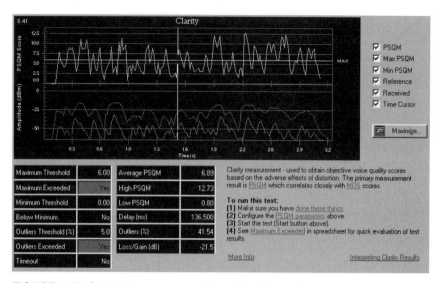

FIGURE 5.10 Clarity Measurement, Errored and Lost Packets

the original sample. Similarly, the PSQM trace bears no similarity to the trace in Figure 5.4 and Figure 5.9. We also see the delay has not changed, although this will be true is most cases of low to moderate network impairments, depending on the implementation. If the endpoints need to increase the depth of the jitter buffer, this value could be increased by a few frames, thus deteriorating the user experience even further.

The packet loss we inserted was artificially high to make sure we simulated the effect of network congestion, whereby packets in transit arrive at a congested point and are discarded until traffic flow equilibrium is reached. The most severe packet loss occurred in the last half of the trace, after the 2.2 sec time mark. The resulting PSQM values indicate the resulting speech was unintelligible.

Things can actually get worse when we introduce high variance in the delay through the network to render some of the arriving packets unusable. Figure 5.11 shows a trace of multiple impairments, with PSQM spikes well above the maximum recommended by the ITU for intelligible speech. The delay observed by the VQT was still the same for all the measurements, but the resulting clarity measure was indeed that of unusable speech quality. The results from three runs of this test are shown in Table 5.3.

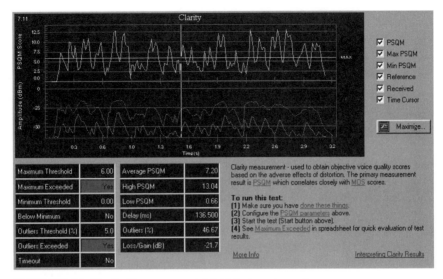

FIGURE 5.11 Clarity Measurement, Multiple Impairments

TABLE 5.3 Routed Calls, Multiple Impairments

CLARITY MEASUREMENT RESULTS— ROUTED CALLS, MULTIPLE IMPAIRMENTS			
Average PSQM	7.20	6.89	7.11
High PSQM	13.04	12.73	13.19
Low PSQM	0.66	0.80	0.62
Delay	136.5	136.5	136.5

5.6 OBSERVATIONS AND CONCLUSIONS

Quality of Service in terms of simple measures of packet loss is not quite meaningful in assessing the quality of delivered speech in VoIP networks. Clever techniques are already being implemented in coding algorithms and transport mechanisms to account for network impairments unlike those we have seen on the PSTN. Therefore, it is important to use a tool that delivers an objective measure of the speech quality, and then, if possible, try to map packet delivery problems to exact impact on speech quality. One of the big problems we will face is reproduction of speech quality problems in live networks. When things go wrong, common sense will call for the creation of reproducible test procedures in the live network, but by that time the reasons for the impairments may be gone. This simple observation is why the more incremental statistics and snapshots of traffic conditions that are kept in the core network, the better.

The best defense against packet network impairments due to traffic flow issues is to engineer them such that the probability of congestion at any point is as close to zero as possible. This may affect the bandwidth gain we can realize from packet technology and voice coding techniques, but this issue remains one of the valid tradeoffs in network design. The manner in which Voice Activity Detection is used, and whether any bandwidth savings can be realized from VAD in terms of oversubscribing trunks and equipment, is still the subject of debate for IP networks. Impairments due to network congestion can have large a impact on speech quality, very quickly and on many connections at once. The result will be not one, but many active connections suffering degradation of service. As additional services are beginning to be integrated, the issue of delivered QoS will loom even larger.

More work is needed in the area of engineering the new VoIP networks, and it appears certain we will be visiting this issue again as we move closer to interworking at the packet level across carrier domain boundaries.

CHAPTER 6

Voiceband Call Considerations— A Detailed Look at Fax

Facsimile transmission presents a major implementation challenge in the new packet networks. Voice support is difficult enough, with its own stringent requirements for maintaining the quality of service and user experience of the PSTN, but fax transmission escalates the problem to a higher level. Simply speaking, for the new VoIP networks to succeed, it is mandatory to support the legacy facsimile equipment, which attaches to POTS service. The installed base of fax equipment is so large that the unspoken requirement is for complete and unqualified support for Group 3 fax at a minimum in any service deployment targeted for the business, small office, home office, and even residential offerings. A large percentage of homes with access to the Internet have at least simple PC-based fax capability, and as the number of telecommuters grows, this number is expected to increase.

What are the hurdles for supporting facsimile in a robust manner in a packet network? Let's revisit the PSTN for some of the basics. In POTS service, all calls are circuit switched and traverse digital TDM facilities between the local exchanges serving the calling and called fax terminals. These TDM facilities are extremely reliable and rarely, if ever, drop bits of digitized voiceband signals. The robustness of the PSTN network allows for reliable end-to-end message handshaking, modem training, setting of equalizer circuits, and nearly error-free fax image transmission. If there are line quality issues affecting the analog signals, they are mostly between the subscriber's premise, and their respective COs. The user experience has been for a fax call to go through on the first try, almost all the time.

In contrast to the simple transport of voiceband data on the PSTN, packet networks come with many qualifiers as to the achievable QoS regarding voice, as interpreted by humans. The user experience of the difference between toll-quality and the still nebulous carrier-quality voice may be insignificant for moderate packet loss, variable delay, and jitter. Voiceband data, on the other hand, is interpreted by machines, and they are far less tolerant than the human ear when things are not according to the highest quality. This is exactly the issue with fax support over packet networks. While the loss of a single packet during a human conversation may go unnoticed, the same lost packet during the handshake procedures of a fax call can result in a dropped call or lengthy recovery procedures with possible drop in speed as the outcome. All this is annoying and disturbing to users, especially if the affected call incurs long distance or international charges and must be repeated.

ITU-T Recommendation T.30 defines the procedures for the transmission of facsimile over the PSTN, which includes end-to-end capabilities negotiation between fax terminals and sending of image data encoded in a standard format. The major modulation schemes currently in use by the legacy equipment are shown in Table 6.1. Transmission of images for Group 3 fax is specified in ITU-T Recommendation T.4. The need for an expedient solution to support facsimile in packet networks has resulted in additional specifications that preserve a local nature of Group 3 signaling and transmission. Local signaling executes between a fax terminal and the network equipment to which it connects. This type of network equipment is a media gateway that provides analog line connection to a legacy fax device or analog telephone with an RJ11 connector. The calling and called fax terminals are thus faked into believing they are negotiating fax transmission with the other terminal over the circuits and trunks of the PSTN. The packet infrastructure on the network side of the gateways is then used to transport the image data and re-create fax signaling sequences at each gateway toward their local fax terminal.

There are currently two methods that accomplish this operation and both are standards specified by the ITU. Recommendation T.37 specifies store and forward, non-real time techniques for sending facsimile with legacy equipment connected via a gateway to a packet network. Recommendation T.38 specifies a real-time operation which does not use voiceband data transport, but instead uses packetized information to carry both the handshake sequences and the digitized image data itself between the terminals. We discuss both of those techniques in this chapter. T.38 is also the recommended protocol for networks implementing H.323 signaling, although implementations on the network side could be proprietary to optimize performance.

Both the real-time and non-real-time methods for facsimile support over packet networks have their own benefits and shortcomings, from both a technical and an economic perspective. Fax costs can be a significant part of the

TABLE 6.1 Major FAX Modulation Methods

MODULATION TYPE	FAX SPEEDS	QUICK NOTES
V.17	14400 12000 9600 7200	Half-duplex, synchronous. Uses V.21 modulation for handshaking. More reliable than V.29 at the same speeds.
V.29	9600 7200	Half-duplex, synchronous. Uses V.21 modulation for handshaking.
V.27ter	7200 4800 2400	Half-duplex, synchronous. Uses V21 handshaking, and Differential Phase Shift Keying for image transfer. It is a very robust modulation scheme. Also supports the lowest speed that is common to all fax modulation schemes.
V.34	Up to 33600 bps in increments of 2400 bps	Uses 1200 bps or 2400 full duplex, phase/amplitude modulation for handshake messages. Half-duplex phase/amplitude modulation for image data transfer. Uses line probing during startup sequence to probe line
V.21	300 bps secondary channels Channel 1 – Sender TX Channel 2 – Receiver TX	Conventional Group 3 fax. Used for all handshake messages between sending and receiving fax station to negotiate data rate, image resolution, compression scheme, etc. Not applicable and not used in V.34 fax.

POTS expenses for many corporations. Studies in this area have shown that a substantial portion of corporations' annual telecommunications budgets is allocated to long distance calls, of which about 40% represent fax calls. This is especially true in Asian countries. The availability of two methods to send faxes over packet networks has opened a new market in business segments, where previously there was no choice with POTS service. Both fax transmission techniques are expected to continue to enjoy success in the IP networks, and may even find their way into VoIP service offerings as the technologies mature and their acceptance in the commercial sector increases.

V.34 fax is very different in many respects than conventional Group 3 fax. One of our objectives in this chapter is to demonstrate the complexities of fax signaling over analog lines, and the issues associated with producing the look and feel of PSTN conditions with IP packet networks.

Fax transmission over IP with a hop on the PSTN can be a difficult proposition, because the hybrid nature of the end-to-end network precludes the use of a single protocol specification. Pure IP-based facsimile in the wide area is still a few years away, and will start materializing when the success of IP networks reaches the point of carrier interoperability across packet domains. The commercial acceptance of packet-mode fax machines thus hinges on the success of VoIP networks to support facsimile transport in a compatible and robust manner, offering the same user experience as the PSTN.

The T.38 specification is an example of how interworking between a IP-based packet domain and the PSTN can be accomplished to support real-time fax. For instance, assume a client on an H.323 LAN segment wants to fax a document to a remote fax terminal of a POTS subscriber. Since the media path between the originating endpoint device (the calling fax machine) and the gateway to the TDM network is IP-based, the challenge becomes how to best map between the requirements of the T.30 and T.38 specifications at the network boundary. This must be done in a manner that preserves the timing integrity of the end-to-end signaling, or the process will not be successful and the fax service will not be robust.

Let's look now at the details of the most common fax transmission methods. The call flow diagram in Figure 6.1 shows a typical error-free fax transmission between an auto-calling and an auto-answer terminal, such as two PCs, or a PC and a fax machine, or two fax machines. We use this diagram as a basis for explaining the basic fax operation and issues.

A fax call in conventional Group 3 facsimile is completed in five phases:

1. Phase A - Call establishment
2. Phase B - Attributes, capabilities, and control signaling
3. Phase C - Single-page fax transmission
4. Phase D - End-of-page signaling and multipage notification
5. Phase E - Call termination

After dialing the remote fax number, an auto-calling fax terminal plays a CNG tone, which is an 1100 Hz tone ON for 0.5 secs and OFF for 3 secs. The called terminal answers the phone and plays the CED (Called Station ID) tone, which is a 2100 Hz tone with phase reversals, for 4 secs. The called station also sends a DIS (Digital Identification Signal) carrying the station capabilities and optionally two additional signals, NSF (Non Standard Facilities) and CSI (Called Subscriber Identification). NSF is used to identify technical

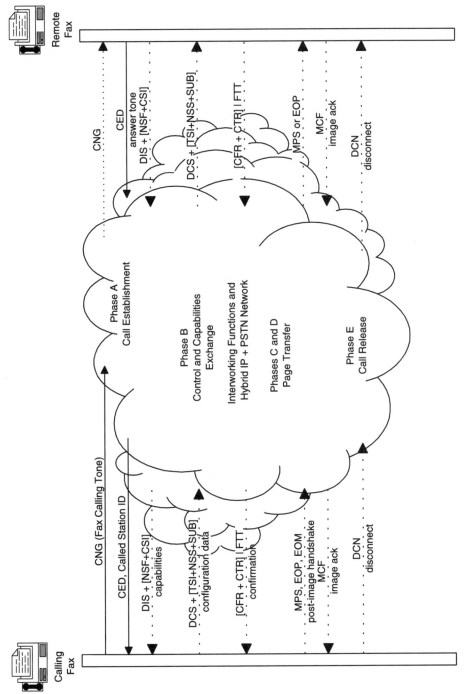

FIGURE 6.1 Conventional Group 3, T.30 Fax Transmission Call Flow

requirements for the station that are not explicitly covered by the ITU-T T series of recommendations. CSI provides the identity of the called subscriber in the form of a telephone number. This signaling exchange completes the call establishment—Phase A—of the process.

Attributes, capabilities, and control signaling exchange is performed using the 300 bps modulation mode of V.21. Messages are preceded by a preamble consisting of one second of HDLC flags to condition the line for each turnaround. Phase B begins with the calling terminal sending DCS (Digital Command Signal) to send configuration data, complete the digital setup, and respond to the DIS command. Other optional signals from the called station at that time are TSI, NSS, SUB, and PWD. For more detail on the meaning of these signals, please refer to the list mnemonics and abbreviations in Table 6.2. The TCF (Training Check Field) is sent by the sender, and the called station responds with CFR (Confirmation to Receive). At that time page transmission is ready to begin. The sender sends training flags to turn the line around and begins transmission, Phase C, in accordance to ITU-T Recommendation T.4.

At the end of each page the sender sends post-image handshakes (Phase D), which are either EOP (if that was the last page), EOM, or MPS (MultiPage Signal) if there are multiple pages to send. MPS results in re-entering Phase C. If the sending session wishes to return to Phase B at the end of a page, it sends an EOM (End of Message) command. An MPS signal must be acknowledged by an MCS command from the receiver. This process continues until the last page has been transmitted, at which time the sending station disconnects by sending a DCN command to the receiver. This terminates the fax call.

There are some immediate considerations if we are to implement a packet network that intends to carry voiceband traffic as digitized samples of analog signals. The first issue is whether connections between the fax station endpoints use compression. If not, and PCM G.711 media encoding is specified, the main consideration is to avoid packet loss. Packet loss will affect the modulation at the far end when PCM packets are played out, and could result in page retransmissions, or worse, dropped calls.

If compression and perceptual coding are used, then all bets are off if we attempt to simply packetize the digitized and compressed analog signal to the remote station. Perceptual coding removes the characteristics of the original waveform and it cannot be reproduced, as we have already explained. Even simple analog waveform compression can degrade the signal-to-noise ratio to the point where either the connection cannot be reliably established, or not established at all. Neither scenario is a winning situation. The ATM Forum VToA specification for packetized voice over native ATM mode (AAL2) specifies a channel speedup technique, whereby recognition of a fax tone (the

CED tone) would automatically result in speedup of the allocated bandwidth for the call up to G.711. This can be accomplished through signaling or automatic means. Once the channel speedup has been realized, this issue reverts to the previous one, that is, packet loss must be avoided and jitter minimized.

Implementations of the recognition for connection bandwidth speedup, echo cancellation, and silence suppression vary depending on the transport technology. The AAL2 specification defines exact procedures to ensure that the integrity of the end-to-end signaling is preserved. If the network topology includes a TDM hop on the PSTN, the design issues become more complicated.

Table 6.2 is a list of fax signals used in the T.30 protocol for Group 3 operation.

TABLE 6.2 T.30 Fax Signals

SIGNAL	NAME	COMMENTS
CIG	Calling subscriber identification	Sent by a terminal wishing to receive a fax to a remote terminal capable of transmitting.
CRP	Command repeat	Asks for the previous command to be re-sent.
CSI	Called subscriber identification	Sent by the called fax terminal immediately after the CED tone to identify itself by its telephone number.
DCN	Disconnect	Initiates Phase E—call termination.
DCS	Digital command signal	The transmitting terminal sends this signal after receiving DIS (below) to place the called terminal in a state ready to receive.
DIS	Digital identification signal	Identifies the capabilities of the called fax terminal.
DTC	Digital transmit command	Sent by a calling terminal that wishes to receive from the called end, after DIS.
FCD	Facsimile coded data	This message contains the actual fax image data.
FCF	Facsimile control field	The HDLC frame containing the signal information is divided into the FCF and FIF parts. Signals are sent as encodings of the FCF field in the HDLC frame.
FIF	Facsimile information field	This field provides optional clarification of the signal being sent.

TABLE 6.2 T.30 Fax Signals (Continued)

SIGNAL	NAME	COMMENTS
MCF	Message confirmation	This is a positive acknowledgement to the PPS signals (below) and indicates that additional messages can be sent.
NSC	Nonstandard facilities command	This is the response to the NSF command (below).
NSF	Nonstandard facilities	NSF indicates there are attributes to the operation of the fax station not specified by ITU recommendations. The attributes are coded in the FIF and the codings are not specified.
NSS	Nonstandard setup	See NSF.
PID	Procedure interrupt disconnect	This signal indicates the previous messages were received fine, but further transmissions are undesirable at this time and the calling station should enter Phase E—call termination.
PPR	Partial page request	Indicates the previous pages had frames received in error and should be retransmitted. The frames in error are coded in the FIF field of the HDLC frame.
PPS-EOM	Partial page signal—End of message	The PPS signals are used when optional Error Correction Mode is in effect, and are post-message commands for a single page.
PPS-EOP	Partial page signal—End of procedure	
PPS-MPS	Partial page signal—Multipage signal	
PPS-NULL	Partial page signal—null	
PWD	Password	Optional field to carry a password when polling mode is used and the calling terminal is the *receiver* of the fax.
RCP	Return to control for partial page	
RNR	Receiver not ready	

TABLE 6.2 T.30 Fax Signals (Continued)

SIGNAL	NAME	COMMENTS
SUB	Subaddress	This optional field carries a sub-address, in the form of a digit string, to help with routing toward the called terminal inside the terminal's domain.
TSI	Transmitting subscriber identification	Indicates that the FIF field in the HDLC frame of this signal encodes the calling terminal identification.
XID	Exchange identification procedure	Used during Phase A and indicates the called station has Group 3C attributes.

6.1 A LOOK AT A REAL-TIME TRACE OF THE T.30 PROTOCOL

The three traces shown in this section (Figures 6.2 through 6.4) were taken in real time during a fax call, with an HP-Telegra Max-Fax test instrument. The timing relationships between the T.30 protocol exchanges were captured on the trace and are analyzed in the following discussion to illustrate the protocols and timing relationships of the various signals.[1]

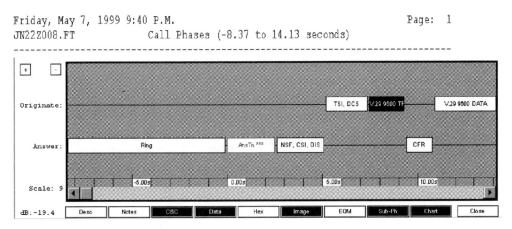

```
Friday, May 7, 1999 9:40 P.M.                                    Page:  1
JN22Z008.FT          Call Phases (-8.37 to 14.13 seconds)
------------------------------------------------------------------------
```

FIGURE 6.2 Real Time Fax Trace: Call Initiation, Answer, and Training (Courtesy HP-Telegra)

---

1.   The accompanying CD-ROM contains several traces from live fax transmissions for further examination of the properties of the fax signaling procedures described in this text.

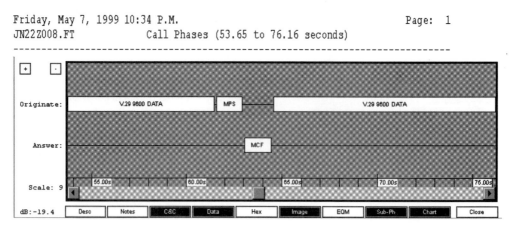

FIGURE 6.3 Real Time Fax Trace: Multiple Page Transmission (Courtesy HP-Telegra)

The first trace (Figure 6.2) shows the sequence of ringing and answering by the remote fax terminal. Starting about 1.66 seconds after answering the call, the terminal sends the CED tone for 2.6 to 4 seconds. The called fax terminal in this example is using the NSF signal to show it supports manufacturer-specific terminal parameters; however, the calling terminal does not reply with NSC, which means the contents of the NSF message were not recognized and are ignored.

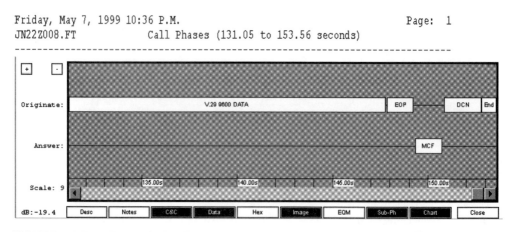

FIGURE 6.4 Real Time V.29 Fax Trace—End of Procedure (Courtesy HP-Telegra)

The CFR reply (ConFirmation to Receive) message confirms 1.5 seconds of zeros have been received, when in non-V.34 mode.[2] The sending terminal proceeds to send the encoded image data following the CFR reply. The speed and modulation scheme selected by the two terminals during this handshake sequence was V.29 and 9600 bps respectively.

The data of the first page (encoded in TIFF[3] format) is sent following the training sequence of all zeroes for 1.35 to 1.65 seconds (nominally set to 1.5 secs ± 15%). The remote fax terminal responds with CFR and the page is sent. In a multi-page fax MPS and MCF will be exchanged after the sending of the first page, and the second page is sent immediately afterward as shown in the trace of Figure 6.3.

In the last part of the trace (Figure 6.4), the sending terminal indicates with an EOP command that the last page has been sent, and after the receiving terminal confirms the data has been received with the MCF signal, the sending fax disconnects the call with the DCN command.

6.2 FAX OVER PACKET NETWORKS

The support of fax over packet networks has major business drivers. Fax is a major revenue earner for service providers and a major expenditure for corporations. More than half of the fax transmissions are long distance calls and therefore the desire to reduce costs is great. The number of installed fax machines continues to grow rapidly and is on track to reach the 70 million mark by the end of the year 2000, according to studies in the industry. The problem with the fax scenario we described in the previous section is that it is a POTS telephone call incurring toll charges, just like any voice call. The desire of the business sector to reduce the cost of fax has led to advances in packet technology to support facsimile transport.

We briefly mentioned the two ITU-T specifications for fax over packet networks, and we visit them in this section. Recommendation T.37 defines procedures for store-and-forward fax transmission over the Internet. The functionality provided through this specification is simple facsimile transmission with non-real-time requirements. Simply stated, the fax begins and ends with a local device emulating Group 3 facsimile operation, and the actual transmission of the image to the intended final destination fax machine occurs in a second step, a short time later. Recommendation T.38 on the other

---

2.   In V.34 mode, the CFR message acknowledges the receipt of DCS.   We discuss V.34 fax later in this chapter.

3.   Tag Image File Format. This file encoding format is explained later in this chapter.

hand, defines real-time procedures for fax support over IP networks, and this is the standard that has been accepted by H.323 for enterprise and wide area networks. Both standards address legitimate commercial needs with slightly different business drivers. We examine the major attributes of both, and some major requirements they impose on the underlying packet networks

6.2.1 Store-and-Forward Fax Over IP Networks—T.37

Recommendation T.37 defines two modes for non-real-time fax, *simple* and *full*. Simple mode supports plain transmission of data, but capabilities negotiation between terminals may not take place and is undefined in the specification. All fax terminals must support simple mode. Image data is sent in TIFF format, specified in RFC 2301, Profile S with Modified Huffman Compression. It supports Group 3 *standard* and *fine* image resolutions.

The fundamental element for T.37 fax operation is the Internet Fax Gateway, which emulates Group 3 operation toward the attached stations, and has a direct connection to a packet network, acting as a host or router.

In Figure 6–5, the Internet Fax Gateway provides the protocol mapping between the standard Group 3 fax terminal on one side and the IP network on the other. The protocol between the gateway and the fax terminal is T.30, thus ensuring complete backward compatibility with the legacy fax machine. On

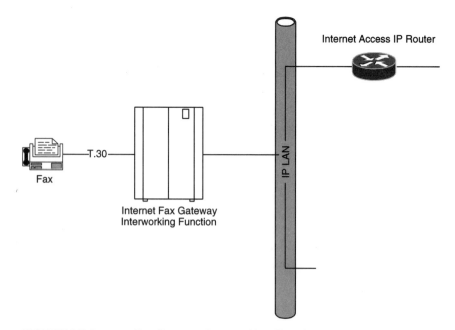

FIGURE 6.5 Internet Fax Gateway, Interworking Function

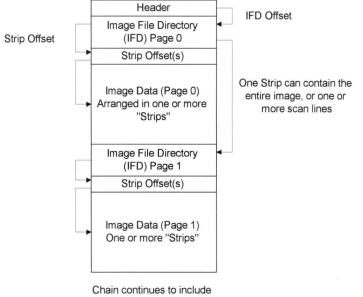

FIGURE 6.6 Basic TIFF image format

the network side, the gateway interfaces to the IP network and conforms to the requirements of RFC 3201, Profile S. It also conforms to RFC 2305 for errors in handling and delivery of the fax, information to trace the origin of the fax,[4] ensuring MIME[5] compliance at both ends of the IP fax gateways, sending notification to the originator of the fax regarding reception problems, and optionally using TIFF profiles for other fax types. The gateway must also implement the Simple Mail Transfer Protocol (SMTP). The Internet Fax Gateway functionality can be implemented inside the fax terminal, thus making it Internet-aware.

The TIFF specification defines the method for "…describing, storing, and interchanging raster image data," such as facsimile and scanned documents. It defines a core set of fields, shown in Figure 6.6, along with the method to arrange the image data in a file which includes all the document pages in chained fashion. The exact header field definition for the image encoding is specified in RFC 2301, "File Format for Internet Fax," L. McIntyre et. al., March 1998, and is beyond the scope of this text.

---

4. This is a legal requirement in some countries.

5. Multipurpose Internet Mail Extensions.

Images in both the T.37 simple and full operating modes are sent to the remote gateway as MIME-encoded email messages containing the rasterized image as the attachment. T.37 full mode adds the requirement to confirm that the fax was received properly, and negotiation of the capabilities of the fax terminals. Any Internet mail transport protocol can be used in full mode to carry the image data.

Delivery confirmations are returned to the sender as MIME-encoded Delivery Status Notifications (DSNs) for gateways, as described in RFC 1894. Senders and receivers require the use of Message Disposition Notifications (MDN), defined in RFC 2298.

6.3 REAL-TIME INTERNET FAX—T.38

Store-and-forward fax is a rather primitive approach to support non-real-time facsimile, with some fairly obvious limitations in functionality. Even so, the business side of the argument points to substantial interest for this type of service and it is experiencing continuing growth in the industry. Several service providers already offer Internet fax, sometimes in package deals with other services.

The alternative to non-real-time fax over IP networks is Recommendation T.38. The T.38 protocol gives the "look and feel" of real time facsimile by emulating the handshake activities of the T.30 protocol on the packet network side. Its basic idea is fax demodulation by a T.38 gateway at the source, packetization of all relevant handshake exchanges, sending of the IP packets across the network, and remodulation of the analog line by the receiving T.38 gateway from the information carried in the packet data. All this is accomplished with the elegant simplicity of just two types of messages (packets), T30_INDICATOR (indicator packets) and T_DATA (data packets), which are part of the Internet Fax Protocol (IFP) recommendation of the ITU.

Indicator packets carry information to the far end about the presence of a CNG/CED tone, modem modulation training, or preamble flags *each time* the line is turned around. Data packets carry the Phase C data and HDLC control frames. Packets may carry one or more HDLC control frames, or a complete image. Group 3 facsimile equipment (the legacy devices) attach to T.38-compliant gateways and execute the T.30 protocol in real time, without modifications or caveats. Adherence to the timing restrictions of T.30 is thus critical during the handshaking procedures between the terminals.

The IFP allows either TCP or UDP to be used as the transport protocol. When TCP is used, the IP payload is simply the TCP header and the concatenated indicator or data packet.

When UDP is used, the payload consists of a new layer header (UDPTL), followed by the concatenated indicator or data packet. The UDPTL header is a packet sequence number to account for packets arriving via different paths and out of order. The UDPTL payload also contains an optional Forward Error Correction (FEC) field to recover from bit errors. Also optionally, redundant messages can be included in a single UDPTL packet.

A simplified block diagram of the message flow under T.38 is shown in Figure 6.7. For exact details of the T.38 message types and exchanges, the reader is referred to ITU-T Recommendation T.38.

Flag sequences are required for every line turnaround and are transmitted as indicator (T30_INDICATOR) packets. Training is sent as an indicator packet, with the V-type modulation used by the sending terminal. This is used to adjust the speed of the terminal, for instance, to switch from sending image data with V.17 modulation to V.21 modulation for control sequences.

The same type of training is generated by the receiving gateway at the far end toward the sending fax terminal. The modulation training sequences have timing requirements which must be carefully adhered to in an end-to-end communication, in order for the presence of the IP network between the gateways to be completely transparent to the fax application.

Finally, the Training Check Field (TCF) can be used in one of two ways in T.38-compliant networks. For connection-oriented, TCP-based implementations, the TCF is generated by the far end gateway toward the receiving fax terminal. When UDP is used, the TCF needs to be sent across the packet network. The difference is in the decision logic of the speed selection, as shown in Table 6 of Recommendation T.38.

The call flow of Figure 6.7 shows the T.30 protocol being executed between the calling terminal and its local T.38 gateway. All signal types and their timing restrictions must be supported at that interface, regardless of what timing constraints may be challenging the gateway on the packet network side. The fact is, in the general case, communicating T.38 gateways can be located across several network segments, between one or more service providers. All the potential issues facing voice telephony, such as QoS at the packet level, can happen during a fax call.

It is also of interest that the T.38 idea of fax demodulation and remodulation is similar in concept to the method proposed in the ITU-T specification I.366.2 for ATM networks using AAL2 virtual circuits, although the proposed implementation would be very different.

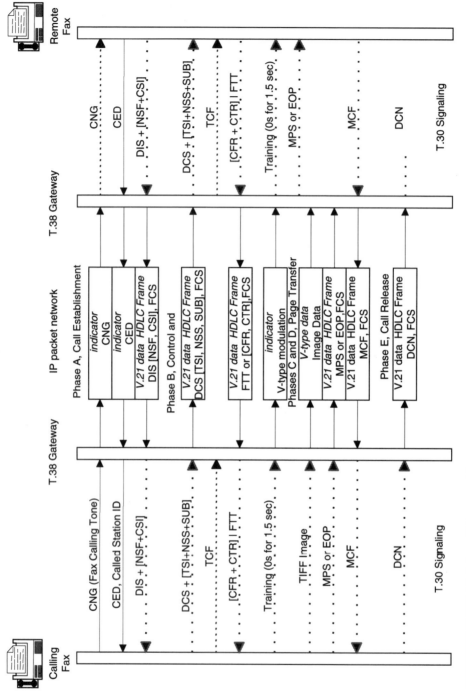

FIGURE 6.7 T.38 High Level Message Flow

298

6.4 BASICS OF V.34 FAX

The conventional Group 3 fax procedures we saw in the previous section are simple compared to the sophistication introduced by the V.34 protocol. This sophistication ensures the quality of the line supports data rates up to 33.6 Kbps and can sustain this quality for the duration of the call to avoid retransmissions, dropped calls, and lower than optimum speeds. In this section we look at a comparison of the procedures between Group 3 and V.34 fax. We begin with the basic error-free control sequences for speed negotiation, and proceed with primary channel quality characterization, control channel parameter negotiation, and, finally, image transmission. Traces from an actual V.34 fax captured using an HP-Telegra instrument are also shown to illustrate relative positions in the message exchanges and their relationship to the V.34 procedural diagrams from the ITU specification.

V.34 fax is clearly a solution for high-end applications and offers more than just higher speed of transmission. Aside from better matching of the line characteristics, it offers capabilities such as higher image resolution, gray scale and color, and 2400 bps speed resolution.

V.34 procedures implement very complex line probing techniques to characterize the quality of the link. In the PSTN, this process analyzes the combination of analog circuits and digital trunks along the path of a fax call. Trunks and circuits between telephone exchanges carry voiceband data in digital PCM form with very low Bit Error Rate (BER). Thus a digitized voiceband waveform's signal characteristics are preserved as it hops digital channels between exchange offices until it reaches the terminating exchange. Most of the line probing concentrates on characterization of the analog links between the terminals and their respective COs. On the other hand, the stochastic nature of packet loss in an IP network represents an additional potential problem in maintaining the integrity of a link for the duration of a call. In a wide area packet network, packet loss is a function not only of the BER of the physical links, but is also affected by traffic engineering issues between network elements. In general, statistical multiplexing, with link and node capacity over-subscription, is a dangerous thing to do if the network will be carrying digitized voiceband signals for general purpose modem and fax calls.

Methods proposed for transport of sensitive voiceband information in IP-based packet networks via waveform re-creation at the endpoints are being addressed in the industry as enhancements to the basic capabilities of RTP. There was significant work in progress in this area at the time this text went to print. ITU-T Recommendation I.366.2 also specifies detailed procedures to send faxes over ATM AAL2 connections. Both approaches deal with support for basic Group 3 fax, and leave V.34 for further study. This means V.34 fax over packet networks is at least a couple of years down the road, and maybe

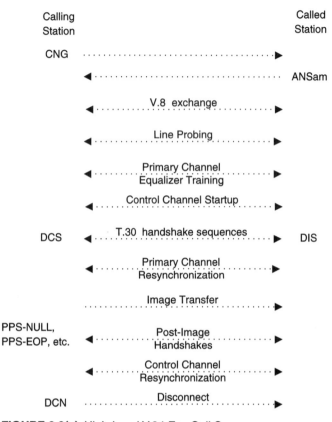

FIGURE 6.8(a) High-Level V.34 Fax Call Sequence

more. Let's take a look at the basics of V.34 and understand the complexities that make it a difficult candidate for support over VoIP networks.

Figure 6.8(a) shows the basic V.34 protocol and Figure 6.8(b) shows a high level visualization of the communications phases. V.34 uses the handshake procedures of recommendation V.8 to negotiate modulation methods and available speeds between the stations.

Line probing analyzes the physical channel across the audio spectrum and "learns" the line attributes for the best choice in speed selection. After equalizer training, the process continues with T.30 fax handshaking and image transmission per the recommendations of the T.6 specification of the ITU-T.

Figure 6.8(b) shows the fundamental phases of the V.34 fax protocol, and Table 6.3 presents a comparison between V.34 and Group 3 fax procedures.

Parameter negotiation for the fax call begins after the CNG tone or CI (Call Indication) has been sent by the calling station and recognized by the

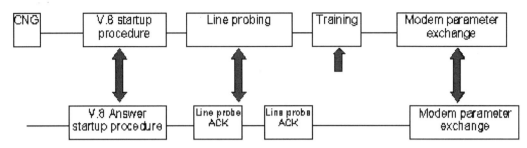

FIGURE 6.8(b) V.34 Fax Communications Phases

TABLE 6.3 Conventional Group 3 Fax/V.34 Fax Comparison

EXCHANGE TYPE	CONVENTIONAL GROUP 3 FAX	V.34 FAX
Handshake messages	300 bps FSK modulation. Half-duplex transmission.	1200 or 2400 bps QAM. Full-duplex transmission.
Data rate negotiation and line testing	DIS/DCS exchange. TCF to test the line. CFR or FTT handshake and possible fallback to lower speeds.	V.8 protocol to determine supported modulation methods and speeds. Line probing with tone pattern spanning the audio band (300–3400 Hz)
Data compression	Recommendation T.4, one-dimensional compression, or one- and two-dimensional compression for alternate lines.	Recommendation T.6, two-dimensional compression.
Image error handling	RTP/TN handshake message. Requests image retransmission. Optional Error Correction Mode protocol (ECM).	Error Correction Mode (ECM) protocol is mandatory.

remote station, which then responds with a special answer tone called ANSam.[6] Signal CI is optional and most likely your fax terminal will be sending the familiar CNG tone we all know from Group 3 fax. Call establish-

---

6.   Modified Answer Tone.

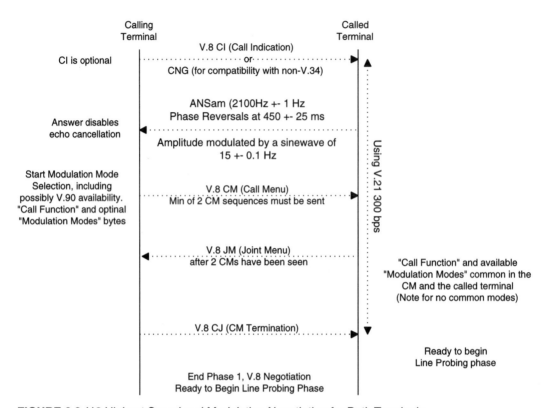

FIGURE 6.9 V.8 Highest Speed and Modulation Negotiation for Both Terminals

ment procedures continue after ANSam with the methods of the V.8 specification, to negotiate the speed availability and modulation methods.

After completion of the V.8 handshake, three additional steps are required before T.30 handshake exchanges can be initiated. These are line probing, equalizer training and control channel startup, as shown in Figure 6.8(a). The V.8 procedures of Figure 6.9 allow for fallback to modulation schemes other than V.34, for backward compatibility with older fax machines and data modems.

The ANSam tone is a modified version of the T.30 ANS signal and identifies the called device as V.34-capable. It is a 2100Hz ± 1 Hz signal with Phase Reversals at 450 ± 25 ms and is amplitude modulated by a sinewave of 15 ± 0.1 Hz. ANSam's amplitude ranges between 0.8 and 1.2 times the average signal amplitude, ± 0.01, and has duration of 2.6 to 4.0 seconds. All echo cancellers must recognize this signal and disable themselves for the duration of the fax transmission.

If the fax terminal is not V.34 compatible and does not recognize the ANSam, it does not transmit the Call Menu (CM) in the next step of the handshake, but instead follows T.30 Group 3 procedures for selection of another type of mutually available modulation scheme. The called terminal will then time-out within 2.6 to 4 seconds after not receiving CM in response to ANSam.

The Call Menu (CM) signal is a sequence of octets delimited by Start and Stop bits, which identify all the modulation modes available in the sending fax machine and capability for full-duplex operation. The menu coding is shown in Table 6.4 and it is sent using the same V.21 modulation scheme, asynchronously at 300 bps on the low channel, 500 ms after ANSam is detected and is repeated until after two identical Joint Menu (JM) sequences are received from the far end.

TABLE 6.4 CM Signal Coding for V.34 Fax

START	B0	B1	B2	B3	B4	B5	B6	B7	STOP	INFORMATION CATEGORY
1	1	1	1	1	1	1	1	1	1	Preamble
0	0	0	0	0	0	1	1	1	1	CM Sync Pattern
0	1	0	0	0	0	0	0	1	1	Call function – send fax
0	1	0	0	0	0	1	0	1	1	Call function – receive fax
0	1	0	1	0	0	0	x	V.34 hdx	1	Modulation 0 – V.34 fax
0	x	x	V.17	0	1	0	V.29	V.27	1	Modulation 1 – V.17, V.29, V.27
0	x	x	x	0	1	0	x	V.21	1	Modulation 2 – V.21
0	0	1	1	1	1	1	1	0	1	Frame End

The support of V.21 modulation on the menu lists is a moot point since this is the modulation used to send the CM and JM messages themselves. Note that if a V.34 terminal supports full-duplex mode, it *must* also support half-duplex mode.

The Joint Menu (JM) response from the called terminal is coded in the same manner as the CM message, and is shown in Table 6.5. It carries the modulation modes supported by the called terminal and is sent after two identical CM sequences have been received by the called terminal. The calling terminal will finally return a CJ (CM termination) signal, which acknowledges the JM from the receiving end.

TABLE 6.5 JM Signal Coding for V.34 Fax

START	B0	B1	B2	B3	B4	B5	B6	B7	STOP	INFORMATION CATEGORY
1	1	1	1	1	1	1	1	1	1	Preamble
0	0	0	0	0	0	1	1	1	1	JM Sync Pattern
0	1	0	0	0	0	x	0	x	1	Call function – matches CM
0	1	0	1	0	0	0	0	x	1	Modulation 0 – V.34 fax, hdx
0	0	0	x	0	1	0	x	x	1	Modulation 1 – one of V.17, V.29, V.27
0	0	0	0	0	1	0	0	x	1	Modulation 2 – V.21
0	0	1	1	1	1	1	1	0	1	Frame End

Note that bit 4 of each octet is the extension bit to distinguish the sequence encoding from the basic information category octets.

V.8 error conditions deal with non-reception of key signals. Here are some examples: If ANSam is not detected, the caller looks for normal DIS (plain Group 3 mode) and sends CI if the DIS signal indicates support for V.8. If the CM is not detected, ANSam is removed after four seconds and a normal DIS is sent. If the JM is not detected, the error recovery is not defined in V.8, and most likely the terminal will repeat the CM indefinitely, while looking for a JM or DIS, but it doesn't look like the call is going through. Finally, if the CJ is not detected, the JM will be repeated until a time-out occurs, and then a normal DIS is sent. The value of the selected time-out is not specified.

Once the modulation scheme has been selected and no errors have caused the call to be dropped, the next phase of the call setup process deals with Line Probing to determine which speed is optimal for the transmission of the page data.

The Line Probing phase uses tones and bit-encoded data, which are sent at 600 bps with binary DPSK. They are used by the originating and terminating modems to assess line characteristics and are referred to as INFO sequences. There are three such distinct sequences, one for each end of the transmission and one final one indicating the accepted symbol rate and related data. $INFO_{0a}$ is sent by the answering terminal. $INFO_{0c}$ and $INFO_h$ are sent by the calling terminal. INFO sequences 0c and 0a start with 4 fill bits of all 1s, followed by a sync pattern of 0110010. This is followed by 17 information bits, 16 CRC bits and 4 fill bits of all 1s.

The information bits carry the supported symbol rates, carrier frequency, ability to reduce transmit level below nominal, transmit clock source, and request for acknowledgment of INFO frame during error recovery. $INFO_h$ specifies the symbol rate requested by the receiving terminal, high or low carrier frequency selection, a possible power reduction request between 0 and 7 dB, length of training sequence requested, length of a pre-emphasis filter and choice between 4 or 16 point Constellation.[7] $INFO_h$ has the same start and end delimiters as the other two INFO sequences, but it contains 19 information bits.

The Line Probing sequences are shown in flow form in Figure 6.10(a).

After the INFO sequences have been exchanged, the calling station will send Tone B (1200 Hz), and wait for Tone A (2400 Hz). The calling station will send a phase reversal in Tone B for 10 ms, after the Tone A phase reversal is detected. At this point, the call modem can calculate round trip delay between the modems reliably. The line probing phase will continue with the exchange of the L1 and L2 signal sequence L1 is sent after Tone B, and L2 is sent after L1. Both L1 and L2 consist of 21 simultaneous tones across the audio spectrum from 150 up to 3750 Hz in increments of 150 Hz. The tones are sent for 6.67 ms. The calling station will send the composite L1 tone for 160 ms nominally, followed by the L2 tone for no more than 550 ms, plus the calculated round-trip delay. When the receiver detects the L1 and L2 signals, it sends Tone A, which prompts the sending modem to send Tone B. The receiver then responds with $INFO_{0h}$.

The L1 and L2 tones are identical, but L1 is transmitted at 6 dB above the nominal power level. They consist of cosines from 150 Hz to 3750 Hz, spaced 150 Hz apart. The signals are sent at a frequency of $150 \pm 0.01\%$. While the sender is sending L1 and L2, the receiver is characterizing the line and finally selects a data rate, which is communicated to the sender via $INFO_{0h}$.

The line probing procedure from a real fax trace is shown in Figure 6.10(b) and details of the procedure are shown in flow form in Figure 6.11 on page 308. The time duration of the L2 tone in the trace is about 150–170 ms. Tone phase reversals in the trace are denoted as Abar and Bbar. The HP-Telegra files in the accompanying CD-ROM contain additional captured V.34 fax traces for the interested reader.

---

7.   The interested reader can find all these details in the V.34 ITU-T specification, which is the ultimate implementation guide for V.34 fax.

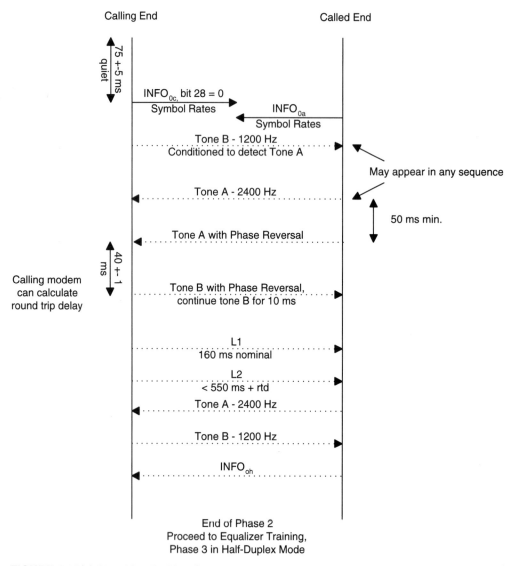

FIGURE 6.10(a) V.34 Line Probing Sequence

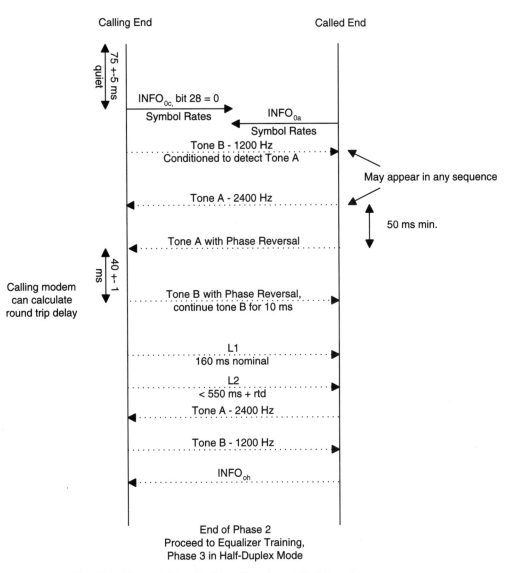

FIGURE 6.10(b) V.34 Phase 3 Line Probing (Courtesy HP-Telegra)

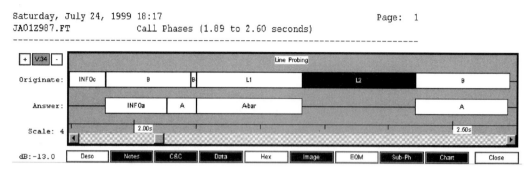

FIGURE 6.11 V.34 Duplex Procedure for Line Probing in Phase 2

At the end of the line probing phase, the symbol rate, carrier frequency, and power levels have been selected, and the stations will now proceed with equalizer training. Equalizer training introduces signals S1, $S1_{bar}$, PP, and TRN. Figure 6.12(a) on page 309 shows the basics of the training process, while Figure 6.12(b) on page 310 is another real-time trace from an actual fax call. It shows the relative occurrence and duration of the equalizer training signals.

Signal S is the preamble to equalizer training. The S_{bar} transition from S indicates the actual start of the equalizer training sequence. Signal PP is a 48-symbol sequence for the training of the equalizers, whereas signal TRN is used to further refine the receiving unit equalizer. The duration of the TRN signal is as requested by the called station with the $INFO_{0h}$ message exchange at the end of Line Probing (Figure 6.13 on page 311). During equalizer training all signals are sent using the symbol rate, carrier frequency, pre-emphasis filter, and power level selected with $INFO_{0h}$.

At the end of primary channel equalizer training, we reach the starting point of the T.30 control exchange. But the control channel needs to go through the startup phase shown in flow form in Figure 6.14 on page 311, which ends with both ends sending flags and getting ready to exchange handshake messages. Signal PPh is used for the control channel initialization and resynchronization. ALT is a sequence of scrambled alternating 1s and 0s, while the MPh signals carry the modulation parameter sequences. Signal E is a 20-bit sequence of scrambled 1s, and at the end of E both sides are sending flags.

The control channel is set up for the calling unit to transmit at 1200 Hz, and the answering unit to send at 2400 Hz with an 1800 Hz guard tone.

All the normal Group 3 fax control channel handshakes apply from this point on, except that control signals TCF and FTT are not used in V.34 fax. Both terminals send HDLC flags between handshake messages. After sending CFR (confirmation to receive), the called terminal will transmit HDLC

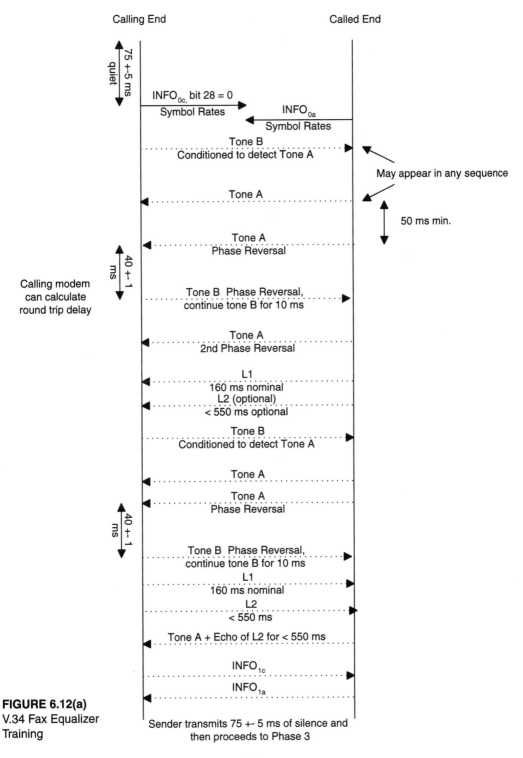

FIGURE 6.12(a)
V.34 Fax Equalizer
Training

The following text appears within the figure:

Calling End

Called End

75 +-5 ms quiet

INFO₀c, bit 28 = 0
Symbol Rates

INFO₀a
Symbol Rates

Tone B
Conditioned to detect Tone A

May appear in any sequence

Tone A

50 ms min.

Tone A
Phase Reversal

40 +- 1 ms

Calling modem
can calculate
round trip delay

Tone B Phase Reversal,
continue tone B for 10 ms

Tone A
2nd Phase Reversal

L1
160 ms nominal
L2 (optional)
< 550 ms optional

Tone B
Conditioned to detect Tone A

Tone A

Tone A
Phase Reversal

40 +- 1 ms

Tone B Phase Reversal,
continue tone B for 10 ms

L1
160 ms nominal

L2
< 550 ms

Tone A + Echo of L2 for < 550 ms

INFO₁c

INFO₁a

Sender transmits 75 +- 5 ms of silence and
then proceeds to Phase 3

309

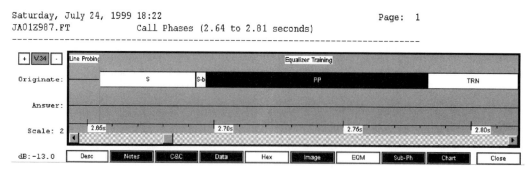

Saturday, July 24, 1999 18:22   Page: 1
JA01Z987.FT   Call Phases (2.64 to 2.81 seconds)

FIGURE 6-12(b) V.34 Phase 3, Primary Channel Equalizer Training (Courtesy HP-Telegra)

flags and the calling terminal will send a string of continuous 1s, until the calling terminal has sent a minimum of 40 1s on the line. When the 40 1s are detected, the called terminal will transmit silence for 70 ± 5 ms. After sending the 1s sequence, the sending terminal will stay silent for 70 ± 5 ms and transmit the primary channel resynchronization procedure shown in Figure 6.15 on page 312 and then send the fax data (finally!).

Signal B1 is a data frame of scrambled 1s sent using the selected modulation parameters. Signals S and S_{bar} are the same as in the equalizer training sequence we saw before. A real-time fax trace segment at the control channel startup process is shown in Figure 6.14.

After image data has been sent, the multipage sequence (MCF) handshake requires control channel resynchronization procedure. The details of the resynchronization procedure are shown in Figure 6.16 on page 312 shows the relative occurrence and duration of the signals from a real-time fax trace. Figure 6.17 on page 313 and Figure 6.18 on page 313.

Control channel resynchronization sequences continue for each line turnaround. It is possible that a receiving station may ask for a different control channel data rate, in which case it returns signal PPh instead of Sh, and the control channel is renegotiated before the next page is transmitted.

The line turnarounds continue until the entire document has been transmitted. The sender then sends PPS-EOP, the receiver responds with MCF, the sender replies with DCN, and the modems hang up.

6.5 GROUP 3 FAX ERROR CORRECTION MODE (ECM)

Error Correction Mode (ECM) is mandatory for V.34 fax, but is optional for the other V series recommendations for fax transmission. To understand ECM, we pick up the process with the selection of the frame size for page transmission during the T.30 handshake. Each page can be encoded and sent

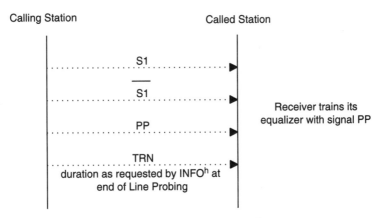

FIGURE 6.13 V.34 Phase 3 Equalizer Training Sequence

in up to 255 frames, at the selected frame size. The only options available are either 64 bytes or 256 bytes per frame. Frame size can be selected by the sender with a DCS (digital command signal) during the T.30 negotiation process. The receiver indicates its preference with DIS (digital information signal) or DTC (digital transmit command). The fine print of the T.30 specification alerts us that the receivers who wish a 64-byte frame size may be ignored by the sender, and thus the receiver must be able to accept 256 byte frames in any case.

Frames are encoded during call Phase C. Control signals are sent as HDLC frames having a FCF (facsimile control field) and an FIF (facsimile information field). The FCF identifies the control signal type from one terminal to the other. The FIF carries the information carried in the control signals.

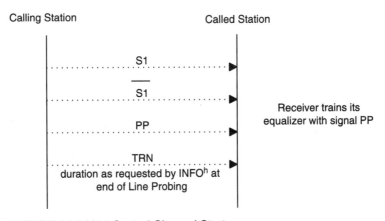

FIGURE 6.14 V.34 Control Channel Startup

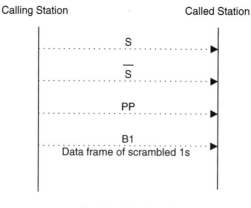

FIGURE 6.15 V.34 Primary Channel Resynchronization Procedure

When an error is detected during the TIFF page transmission, the receiver replies to the sender with a PPR (partial page request) signal in response to a PPS (partial page signal), indicating in the FIF field the frames that were received in error (Figure 6.19). The FIF is encoded as a bit field, whereby each bit is assigned to a frame number. All the frames with their respective bit set to 1 in FIF are requested for retransmission.

When the sender receives the PPR command, it sends the frames indicated in the received FIF and sends PPS again, before proceeding to send the next sequence of frames. If one or more frames are still received in error, the sequence restarts with the receiver sending a PPR with the FIF field pointing again to the bad frames. This can go on until all the frames are received correctly, or the fourth PPR is received by the transmitter. At that time, the transmitter may choose to fall back in speed or send a CTC signal

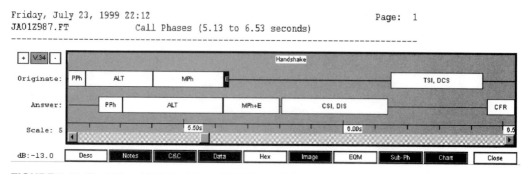

FIGURE 6.16 Real-Time V.34 Fax Trace, T.30 Control Channel Handshake (Courtesy HP-Telegra)

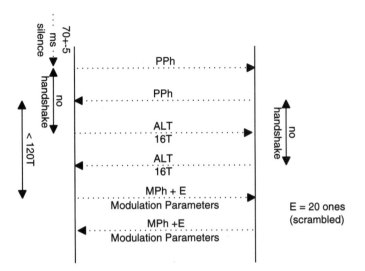

FIGURE 6.17 V.34 Multipage Procedure With Control Channel Resynchronization (Courtesy HP-Telegra)

(continue to correct) to the receiver, indicating that the errored frames will be sent promptly, or take both actions at the same time. When all frames have been received without errors, the receiver sends MCF (message confirmation) signal.

The T.30 protocol supports error recovery due to temporary inability of the receiving modem to accept image data, that is, basic flow control. The receiver indicates it's not ready by replying to an MPS signal from the trans-

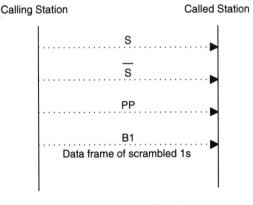

FIGURE 6.18 V.34 Control Channel Resynchronization Sequence

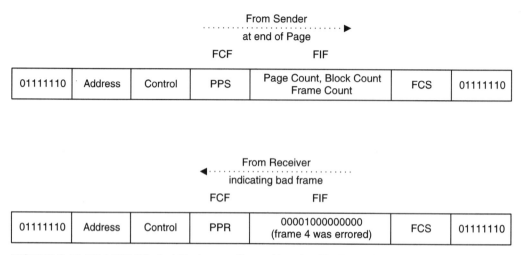

FIGURE 6.19 V.34 ECM Typical Exchange, Frame Received in Error, Request Retransmission

mitter with an RNR HDLC frame. The transmitter then sends an RR HDLC frame, and waits until it receives the normal MCF signal from the receiver. The receiver may choose to send RNR again, and the exchange repeats until either the MCF is finally received or a period of 60 ± 5 secs elapses, at the end of which the sender sends a disconnect DCN signal. The process is shown in Figure 6.20.

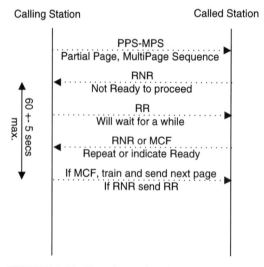

FIGURE 6.20 Flow Control in the T.30 Protocol

6.6 VOICEBAND DATA TRANSPORT REVISITED—AAL2

If voice over IP stopped with only voice over IP, things would be proceeding problem-free in the efforts of the service providers to bring integrated services and multimedia to the home and small office. Fax complicates matters, but there are approaches to solve the immediate problem of Group 3 fax support across packet networks. We saw one such approach already with the methods of T.38 in Figure 6.7. The reader must have reached the conclusion by now that, even at the highest level, fax signaling is a very sensitive and lengthy process compared to signaling to establish voice calls on IP networks, and is intended to achieve the maximum performance and quality for transmission over analog lines. Any impairment, whether natural or induced by traffic management parameters of the packet network, will degrade performance, and if not engineered properly, a network can be rendered unsuitable for support of reliable facsimile.

At this time there is no standard to cover V.34 fax transmission across packet networks. If you have a V.34 fax machine attached to the analog port of a packet media gateway, it will train in one of the Group 3 modes, using V.17, V.29, or V.27ter modulation.

The ITU is recommending fax relay, or in other words, demodulation and remodulation of facsimile for terminals across ATM networks using AAL2 service. The concept is not much different than the idea of T.38, but the implementation is quite different. Recommendation I.366.2 states "The basic function of facsimile demodulation is to detect facsimile traffic, demodulate the facsimile signals, and transmit the demodulated image data and associated control signals to the remote facsimile module… ." Sounds easy, and it is really not hard to see how this would work. At this time, there are not many instances of successful implementation of this specification and not much feedback on uncovered issues, so our brief description focuses simply on the merits of the specification.

There are five message types defined to accomplish modulation control signaling between calling and called station:

1. T-30_Preamble
2. Echo Protection Tone (EPT)
3. Training
4. Fax_Idle
5. T.30_Data

Modulation control and T.30 data (control sequences) packets are sent with protected payload[8] with a 10-bit CRC field, whereas image data packets are sent with unprotected payload.[9] The first four packet types signal to the far end the significant transitions in the handshake negotiation process. The last packet type transports demodulated V.21 handshakes, in the form of HDLC frames, including the flags.

The EPT signal is intended to disable echo cancellers and can be sent prior to high-speed modulation. It has a duration of 185–200 ms and offers a choice of two frequencies, at 1700 Hz or 1800 Hz. Modulation control is protected against packet loss by sending packets 3 times, at 20 ms intervals. This reduces the probability of losing a critical packet, assuming that any traffic congestion issues in intermediate routers can settle favorably within approximately 40–50 ms, the time between the first and the last packet. Otherwise, all three instances of the same packet can be lost during times of bad network congestion. The user and network engineer need to pay attention to the different time scales when comparing between a burst BER in a digital TDM facility on the PSTN and the time it takes to clear congestion issues in routers with many active calls through them.

The Training signal allows selection of V.17 long and short training. Fax_Idle is sent as soon the demodulating device has detected that the high-speed modulation with the local terminal is over. Finally, T.30_Data packets carry the T.30 sequences we have seen already, as completely encapsulated HDLC frames.

Image data is sent nominally at 20 ms intervals, which means the payload size of the packets varies with the selected speed.

This method of Group 3 fax support will be successful in ATM networks using AAL2, because it is as simple as the methods of T.38 and will be as robust as the technology itself allows. Still, the issue of robustness of fax support in any fax network is wide open, and our advice is to engineer the network parameters for the highest possible quality for facsimile. Since no one knows at the time the call is being placed that it will be a fax call, dynamic methods to groom the paths will be necessary, assuming there is available bandwidth in the narrowband links to the customer premise.

6.7 SUMMARY OF THE FAX DISCUSSION AND POSSIBLE ISSUES

Regardless of the physical medium that will bring us the next generation of integrated telephony service—cable, modem, or some form or another of DSL—the requirement for analog fax transmission is expected to survive for a long time. There is an inherent technological barrier in transporting complex waveforms using perceptual compression and coding and the problem is

8. Type 3 packets.
9. Type 1 packets.

only compounded by sending the digital samples over a topology that does not guarantee their delivery. The human ear is tolerant of waveform imperfections in the audible spectrum that result from coding, but fax machines are not. Significant effort is being expended in the standards bodies and R&D labs to find ways for facsimile to coexist with voice on the same physical medium over a packet-based infrastructure. But the requirements for each application are so different that, even if a solution is found to replicate voiceband waveforms reliably over IP networks, we will still not be done with the issues. One immediate performance benefit of fax over packet networks is the potential to avoid end-to-end emulation of analog links. This localizes the analog protocol exchanges strictly between the associated terminals and their corresponding gateways. The gateways simply forward the image data across the network in digital form, without fear of line quality degradation and other issues from the analog world. However, it is still unknown whether any savings from compression, voice activity detection, silence suppression, and perceptual coding will ever be realized in a manner that points to bits per second saved on a physical link as a result of using IP-based technology when support for robust facsimile is a requirement.

We conclude by observing that V.34 is also the technology used in V.90 modems. V.90 is a hybrid standard of analog signal modulation in the upstream direction, and digital transmission downstream. It is expected to be the final analog modem standard as digital services start rolling out on a wider and more affordable scale.

References

1. IETF RFC 2543 *SIP: Session Initiation Protocol.*

2. IETF RFC 2327 *SDP: Session Description Protocol.*

3. *A Comparison of SIP and H.323 for Internet Telephony,* Henning Schulzrinne and Jonathan Rosenberg.

4. *Signaling for Internet Telephony,* Henning Schulzrinne and Jonathan Rosenberg.

5. ITU-T Recommendation H.323 (1998), *Packet-based multimedia communication systems.*

6. ITU-T Recommendation H.245 (1998), *Control protocol for multimedia communication.*

7. ITU-T Recommendation H.225.0 (1998), *Call Signalling protocols and media stream packetization for packet-based multimedia communication systems.*

8. ITU-T Recommendation P.861, *Objective Quality Measurement of Telephone Band (300-3400 Hz) speech codecs.*

9. RFC 1483, Multiprotocol Encapsulation over ATM Adaptation Layer 5.

10. RFC 1889, *RTP: A Transport Protocol for Real-Time Applications.*

11. RFC 1890, *RTP Profile for Audio and Video Conferences with Minimal Control.*

12. RFC 1894, *An Extensible Message Format for Delivery Status Notifications.*

13. RFC 2205, *Resource reSerVation Protocol (RSVP) – Version 1 Functional Specification.*

14. RFC 2210, *The Use of RSVP with IETF Integrated Services.*

15. RFC 2301, *File Format for Internet Fax.*

16. RFC 2303, *Minimal PSTN address format in Internet Mail.*

17. RFC 2304, *Minimal FAX address format in Internet Mail.*

18. RFC 2305, *A Simple Mode of Facsimile Using Internet Mail.*

19. RFC 2508, *Compressing IP/UDP/RTP Headers for Low-Speed Serial Links.*

20. ETSI TIPHON TS 101 319, *Signalling for basic calls from an H.323 terminal to a terminal in a Switched-Circuit Network (SCN).*

21. ETSI TIPHON TS 101 329, *General Aspects of Quality of Service.*

22. *Delivering Voice over IP Networks*, Daniel Minoli, Emma Minoli, Wiley.

23. *Signaling in Telecommunication Networks*, John G. van Bosse, Wiley.

24. *Signaling System #7*, Travis Russell, McGraw-Hill.

25. *ISDN and Broadband ISDN*, William Stallings, Macmillan.

26. *ISDN and SS7*, Architectures for Digital Signaling Networks, Uyless Black, Prentice-Hall.

27. *Quality of Service, Delivering QoS on the Internet and in Corporate Networks*, Paul Ferguson and Goeff Huston, Wiley.

28. *Voice over IP Networks*, Marcus Goncalves, McGraw-Hill.

29. PacketCable™, *Network Based Signaling Protocol Specification.*

30. ITU-T Recommendation T.4 (1996), *Standardization of Group 3 facsimile terminals for document transmission.*

31. ITU-T Recommendation T.30 (1996), *Procedures for document transmission in the general switched telephone network.*

32. ITU-T Recommendation T.37 (1998), *Procedures for the transfer of facsimile data via store-and-forward on the Internet.*

33. ITU-T Recommendation T.38 (1998), *Procedures for real time Group 3 facsimile communication over IP networks.*

34. Bellcore (Telcordia) Notes on the Networks, SR-2275.

35. ITU-T Recommendation I.363.2, *B-ISDN ATM Adaptation Layer Type 2 Specification.*

36. ITU-T Recommendation I.366.2, *AAL Type 2 Type Specific Convergence Sublayer for Trunking.*

37. *ATM Trunking using AAL2 for Narrowband Services*, ATM Forum Document AF-VTOA-0113.000.

38. Dialogic Corporation white paper, *T.38 and the Future of Fax.*

The following Internet Drafts from the IETF are presented here for informational purposes only. The reader should check the current status of these references with the IETF before their contents are considered for system design.

39. INTERNET DRAFT, draft-huitema-sgcp-v1-1-00, *Simple Gateway Control Protocol (SGCP)* (abandoned draft).

40. INTERNET DRAFT, draft-huitema-mgcp-v0r1-01, *Media Gateway Control Protocol.*

41. INTERNET DRAFT, draft-ietf-mpls-arch-04, *Multiprotocol Label Switching Architecture.*

42. INTERNET DRAFT, draft-ietf-megaco-protocol-00, *MEGACO Protocol Proposal.*

Index

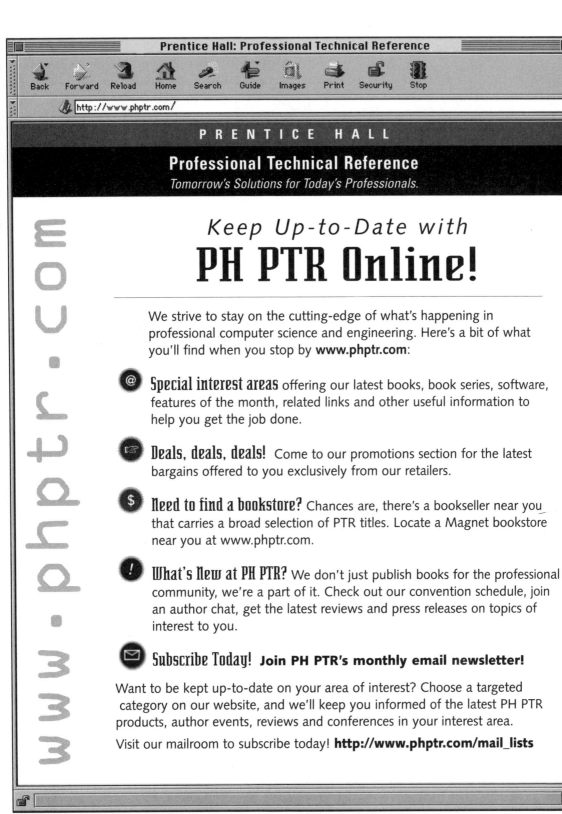

LICENSE AGREEMENT AND LIMITED WARRANTY

READ THE FOLLOWING TERMS AND CONDITIONS CAREFULLY BEFORE OPENING THIS SOFTWARE MEDIA PACKAGE. THIS LEGAL DOCUMENT IS AN AGREEMENT BETWEEN YOU AND PRENTICE-HALL, INC. (THE "COMPANY"). BY OPENING THIS SEALED SOFTWARE MEDIA PACKAGE, YOU ARE AGREEING TO BE BOUND BY THESE TERMS AND CONDITIONS. IF YOU DO NOT AGREE WITH THESE TERMS AND CONDITIONS, DO NOT OPEN THE SOFTWARE MEDIA PACKAGE. PROMPTLY RETURN THE UNOPENED SOFTWARE MEDIA PACKAGE AND ALL ACCOMPANYING ITEMS TO THE PLACE YOU OBTAINED THEM FOR A FULL REFUND OF ANY SUMS YOU HAVE PAID.

1. **GRANT OF LICENSE:** In consideration of your payment of the license fee, which is part of the price you paid for this product, and your agreement to abide by the terms and conditions of this Agreement, the Company grants to you a nonexclusive right to use and display the copy of the enclosed software program (hereinafter the "SOFTWARE") on a single computer (i.e., with a single CPU) at a single location so long as you comply with the terms of this Agreement. The Company reserves all rights not expressly granted to you under this Agreement.

2. **OWNERSHIP OF SOFTWARE:** You own only the magnetic or physical media (the enclosed software media) on which the SOFTWARE is recorded or fixed, but the Company retains all the rights, title, and ownership to the SOFTWARE recorded on the original software media copy(ies) and all subsequent copies of the SOFTWARE, regardless of the form or media on which the original or other copies may exist. This license is not a sale of the original SOFTWARE or any copy to you.

3. **COPY RESTRICTIONS:** This SOFTWARE and the accompanying printed materials and user manual (the "Documentation") are the subject of copyright. You may not copy the Documentation or the SOFTWARE, except that you may make a single copy of the SOFTWARE for backup or archival purposes only. You may be held legally responsible for any copying or copyright infringement which is caused or encouraged by your failure to abide by the terms of this restriction.

4. **USE RESTRICTIONS:** You may not network the SOFTWARE or otherwise use it on more than one computer or computer terminal at the same time. You may physically transfer the SOFTWARE from one computer to another provided that the SOFTWARE is used on only one computer at a time. You may not distribute copies of the SOFTWARE or Documentation to others. You may not reverse engineer, disassemble, decompile, modify, adapt, translate, or create derivative works based on the SOFTWARE or the Documentation without the prior written consent of the Company.

5. **TRANSFER RESTRICTIONS:** The enclosed SOFTWARE is licensed only to you and may not be transferred to any one else without the prior written consent of the Company. Any unauthorized transfer of the SOFTWARE shall result in the immediate termination of this Agreement.

6. **TERMINATION:** This license is effective until terminated. This license will terminate automatically without notice from the Company and become null and void if you fail to comply with any provisions or limitations of this license. Upon termination, you shall destroy the Documentation and all copies of the SOFTWARE. All provisions of this Agreement as to warranties, limitation of liability, remedies or damages, and our ownership rights shall survive termination.

7. **MISCELLANEOUS:** This Agreement shall be construed in accordance with the laws of the United States of America and the State of New York and shall benefit the Company, its affiliates, and assignees.

8. **LIMITED WARRANTY AND DISCLAIMER OF WARRANTY:** The Company warrants that the SOFTWARE, when properly used in accordance with the Documentation, will operate in substantial conformity with the description of the SOFTWARE set forth in the Documentation. The Company does not warrant that the SOFTWARE will meet your requirements or that the operation of the SOFTWARE will be uninterrupted or error-free. The Company warrants that the media on which the SOFTWARE is delivered shall be free from defects in materials and workmanship under normal use for a period of thirty (30) days from the date of your purchase. Your only remedy and the Company's only obligation under these limited warranties is, at the Company's option, return of the warranted item for a refund of any amounts paid by you or replacement of the item. Any replacement of SOFTWARE or media under the warranties shall not extend the original warranty period. The limited warranty set forth above shall not apply to any SOFTWARE which the Company determines in good faith has been subject to misuse, neglect, improper installation, repair, alteration, or dam-

age by you. EXCEPT FOR THE EXPRESSED WARRANTIES SET FORTH ABOVE, THE COMPANY DISCLAIMS ALL WARRANTIES, EXPRESS OR IMPLIED, INCLUDING WITHOUT LIMITATION, THE IMPLIED WARRANTIES OF MERCHANTABILITY AND FITNESS FOR A PARTICULAR PURPOSE. EXCEPT FOR THE EXPRESS WARRANTY SET FORTH ABOVE, THE COMPANY DOES NOT WARRANT, GUARANTEE, OR MAKE ANY REPRESENTATION REGARDING THE USE OR THE RESULTS OF THE USE OF THE SOFTWARE IN TERMS OF ITS CORRECTNESS, ACCURACY, RELIABILITY, CURRENTNESS, OR OTHERWISE.

IN NO EVENT, SHALL THE COMPANY OR ITS EMPLOYEES, AGENTS, SUPPLIERS, OR CONTRACTORS BE LIABLE FOR ANY INCIDENTAL, INDIRECT, SPECIAL, OR CONSEQUENTIAL DAMAGES ARISING OUT OF OR IN CONNECTION WITH THE LICENSE GRANTED UNDER THIS AGREEMENT, OR FOR LOSS OF USE, LOSS OF DATA, LOSS OF INCOME OR PROFIT, OR OTHER LOSSES, SUSTAINED AS A RESULT OF INJURY TO ANY PERSON, OR LOSS OF OR DAMAGE TO PROPERTY, OR CLAIMS OF THIRD PARTIES, EVEN IF THE COMPANY OR AN AUTHORIZED REPRESENTATIVE OF THE COMPANY HAS BEEN ADVISED OF THE POSSIBILITY OF SUCH DAMAGES. IN NO EVENT SHALL LIABILITY OF THE COMPANY FOR DAMAGES WITH RESPECT TO THE SOFTWARE EXCEED THE AMOUNTS ACTUALLY PAID BY YOU, IF ANY, FOR THE SOFTWARE.

SOME JURISDICTIONS DO NOT ALLOW THE LIMITATION OF IMPLIED WARRANTIES OR LIABILITY FOR INCIDENTAL, INDIRECT, SPECIAL, OR CONSEQUENTIAL DAMAGES, SO THE ABOVE LIMITATIONS MAY NOT ALWAYS APPLY. THE WARRANTIES IN THIS AGREEMENT GIVE YOU SPECIFIC LEGAL RIGHTS AND YOU MAY ALSO HAVE OTHER RIGHTS WHICH VARY IN ACCORDANCE WITH LOCAL LAW.

ACKNOWLEDGMENT

YOU ACKNOWLEDGE THAT YOU HAVE READ THIS AGREEMENT, UNDERSTAND IT, AND AGREE TO BE BOUND BY ITS TERMS AND CONDITIONS. YOU ALSO AGREE THAT THIS AGREEMENT IS THE COMPLETE AND EXCLUSIVE STATEMENT OF THE AGREEMENT BETWEEN YOU AND THE COMPANY AND SUPERSEDES ALL PROPOSALS OR PRIOR AGREEMENTS, ORAL, OR WRITTEN, AND ANY OTHER COMMUNICATIONS BETWEEN YOU AND THE COMPANY OR ANY REPRESENTATIVE OF THE COMPANY RELATING TO THE SUBJECT MATTER OF THIS AGREEMENT.

Should you have any questions concerning this Agreement or if you wish to contact the Company for any reason, please contact in writing at the address below.

Robin Short
Prentice Hall PTR
One Lake Street
Upper Saddle River, New Jersey 07458

Welcome to the IP Telephony Interactive Learning CD-ROM

The IP Telephony Interactive Learning CD-ROM is included with your purchase of *IP Telephony: The Integration of Robust VoIP Services*. This interactive, learning CD-ROM provides two off-line application programs (the actual interfaces) that are used by professionals today for VoIP protocol analysis and fax testing and analysis. Sample files let you work with several of the protocols contained in the book for voice, fax, and more! In addition, supplemental papers from HP Agilent Technologies and pertinent RFCs from the IETF have been provided to enhance your knowledge of VoIP and FoIP. The entire contents of the CD-ROM are outlined below:

1. The HP Agilent Technologies' Internet Advisor Off-Line is a state-of-the-art network analysis and troubleshooting tool. It includes sample "capture" files of H.323, MGCP, and SIP that can viewed and manipulated with the Off-Line Internet Advisor.
2. The HP Agilent Technologies' TelegraD/M fax test system is an industry leading tool for fax testing and analysis. The CD-ROM includes a number of sample files that let you analyze fax calls, generate fax calls, and review measurement results.
3. A number of HP Agilent Technologies' papers that will help you understand and implement VoIP and FoIP are available as PDF files.
4. IETF Working Group documents for Voice over IP.

This CD-ROM will supplement your understanding of Voice and Fax over IP with real-life sample files and papers that maximize your learning experience!

Technical Support

Prentice Hall does not offer technical support for this software. However, if there is a problem with the media, you may obtain a replacement copy by e-mailing us with your problem at: disc_exchange@prenhall.com